Anthropology of Food

To my parents
Clara Goddyn and Noël Pottier

Reality may lie in the world of ideas
but illusion demands that the body be fed

Raymond Firth, 1973

Anthropology of Food

The Social Dynamics of Food Security

JOHAN POTTIER

Polity Press

First published in 1999 by Polity Press in association with Blackwell Publishers Ltd.

Reprinted 2005, 2007

Polity Press
65 Bridge Street
Cambridge CB2 1UR, UK

Polity Press
350 Main Street
Malden, MA 02148, USA

A CIP catalogue record for this book is available from the British Library.

Library of Congress Cataloging-in-Publication Data

Pottier, Johan.
    Anthropology of food : the social dynamics of food security /
Johan Pottier.
       p.   cm.
    Includes bibliographical references and index.
    ISBN: 978-0-7456-1533-2
    ISBN: 978-0-7456-1534-9 (pbk)
    1. Food—Social aspects.   2. Food supply—Government policy
3. Food supply—Economic aspects.   4. Agriculture and state.
5. Economic anthropology.   6. Economic security.   7. Food relief—
Government policy.   8. Welfare economics.   I. Title.
GN407. P67   1999
306.13'49—dc21   98-52197
                                                              CIP

Typeset in 10½ on 12 pt Sabon
by Ace Filmsetting Ltd, Frome, Somerset
Printed and bound in Great Britain by Marston Book Services Limited, Oxford

This book is printed on acid-free paper.

For further information on Polity, visit our website: www.polity.co.uk

Contents

Contents

Preface

In *Babette's Feast*, the celebrated film based on Karen Blixen's novel, an ageing puritan community clings to the motto of its parson: 'Take no food for thought and raiment'. Enter Babette, a French maid who settles in the village and learns the language and ways of rural Denmark. When Babette's only remaining link with France, a lottery ticket annually renewed, brings her fortune, she spends the lot on a real French dinner, which she, a former chef at the Parisian Café Anglais, prepares in honour of the now deceased parson. The banquet of turtle soup, *blinis demidoff*, *cailles en sarcophage*, and lavish amounts of Clos Vougeot and Veuve Clicquot 1860, is an earthly joy that makes it difficult for the villagers to uphold the parson's motto. As the forbidden delights from Paris produce their healing effects, celebrants reminisce, bury their quarrels and reclaim the peace they all long for.

The culinary delights in this book are of a different nature, being ethnographic gems from food-focused anthropological research, but their impact, I hope, will have a similarly restoring and reclaiming effect. The book is not about exotic foods or bizarre preparations; its focus rather is on the current state of the official debate on world food security, and how this debate has become divorced from the everyday realities food-insecure people face. Officials responsible for food security planning now accept that the problem of food insecurity is multi-faceted, yet continue with a professional approach and language that have little affinity to the complex social worlds food-insecure people inhabit. Official debate, as the 1996 World Food Summit in Rome reminded us, now assumes a uniform language for problem identification and solving; a language which speaks of 'enabling policy environments' and 'poverty alleviation', but shies away from discussion of the power imbalances that underpin and perpetuate existing forms of social inequality and injustice. What are these forms and their under-pinnings? How do they evolve? How do food-insecure people perceive them? Can they ever be redressed through policy intervention? These are some of the questions with which this book is concerned. Much is made in policy circles of the commitment to understand and respect the viewpoints of food-insecure people. The chapters in this book are devoted to these perceptions. Treating food-insecure people as a distinct category, we are concerned with their varied perceptions of the value of land (chapter 3), of aspects of farm labour organization (chapter 4), of the way markets operate (chapter 5), of relief-from-hunger strategies (chapter 7), and of the shape and impact of agrarian development policies (chapters 6 and 8). The task is to contrast these perceptions with the frameworks and theories that policy-makers adopt (chapter 2), and to reflect on the future direction of empirical research and policy-making (chapter 9). The social dynamics of food security, as lived and perceived by those who suffer insecurity, must be reclaimed if the policy debate on food security is to emerge out of its present impasse.

As much of the book deals with everyday lives and concerns, with 'cultural' complexities in a fast-changing world, I have found it useful to start off with thoughts on how social anthropology is conducting its own search for a meaningful contribution to the contemporary world (chapter 1). While anthropology never was a stranger to the food security debate and, indeed, can look back on a formidable record of unique insights delivered over more than half a century, current theoretical advances promise to preserve and enhance the discipline's relevance.

In writing this book I have incurred many debts. Top of the list are the SOAS students whose critical comments and enthusiasm for the 'Anthropology of Food' course have enriched my own thinking. I extend my gratitude to all the colleagues who have encouraged me along the way, sometimes through insightful reflections on draft chapters of the book, sometimes by facilitating my participation in their 'Food' seminars. I particularly wish to thank James Fairhead, Henry Bernstein, Andrew Turton and Richard Tapper (all at SOAS, University of London), Melissa Leach (IDS, University of Sussex), John Borton (ODI, London), Preben Kaarsholm (Roskilde University, Denmark), Michael and Susan Whyte (University of Copenhagen, Denmark), Joachim Voss (IDRC, Canada), Villia Jefremovas (Carlton University, Ottawa, Canada), Abdul Aziz Saleh (Andalas University, Sumatra, Indonesia) and Manuela Palmeirim (University of Braga, Portugal). A special thank you also goes to the African colleagues involved in the 'Food Systems

Under Stress' research project, particularly to Patrick Orone (Makerere University, Uganda) and Claude Mararike (University of Zimbabwe), and to the project's sponsors: the International Development Research Centre (IDRC), Canada, and the Ford Foundation, Nairobi, Kenya.

For the writing space they offered when I needed peace and quiet, I acknowledge the kind hospitality of Inês, Emma and Paul Nicholson-Ferreira (Stoke Newington, London), and of Frank Genus at Ital Rest, Treasure Beach, Jamaica. For technical support with computers and printers, I am grateful to Stella Cardus and Peter Barker (Desktop Display, Brighton). And last but not least, for their understanding, patience, generous support and willingness to be on stand-by when I missed my turn in the kitchen (yes, it happened), I give thanks to Agnès, Sam, Tim and Fifi.

1

In Search of Relevance
Anthropology in the Contemporary World

Anthropology's voracious appetite for self-questioning is unrivalled. Virtuous to some, unpleasant to others, anthropology always finds more questions than answers. And when there are answers, there will be further questions; about authorship, about who the anthropologist is and how she is positioned to claim what she believes to be true.

I would like to think that by writing a little something about myself first, I can get the question of my own 'positioning' out of the way. Wishful thinking, I know; the question of how authors are positioned never fully dissipates. Still, let me start by reflecting on certainty and doubt in research I have carried out in Rwanda, where the banana grove features as a focal point in debate on how farming can be 'rationalized'. The grove has its supporters; they call it *la vache des pauvres*, the paupers' cow. They value the grove as a space for intercropping and raising valuable regular income. Agronomists see it differently, are sceptical: the only valuable practices are those that can be systematized, enforced. It is their voice that counts. In the mid-1980s, agricultural experts and government officials in Rwanda proposed drastically to reduce areas for banana production. They banned plantations from ecological zones deemed unsuitable.

In an attempt to explain why agricultural extensionists and political authorities so dreaded the popular banana grove, Augustin Nkundabashaka and I once turned to the richly detailed literature on Ryangombe (Pottier and Nkundabashaka 1992). In this cult, the banana grove features as a space of danger and intrigue; sometimes integrating the sexes, sometimes dividing them. Being a dark, shady burial ground, the anomalous banana grove is also associated with ancestral spirits, madness and ignorance. We deduced that those wanting to 'rationalize' peasant farming regarded the grove as a physical-cum-conceptual space too awkward to appear in the plans of any official serious about good farming practice.

This cultural gloss on policy retains explanatory value, yet there have been moments of doubt. How could we be sure that the official attack on banana (beer) production stemmed from subconscious fear? There was no clear answer, for the policy was rarely implemented. Did this confirm our explanation or were we instead merely confronted with a 'rational' policy discourse of which donors would approve? And who were we anyway – Burundian sociologist–pastor trained in France and working in Rwanda; Belgian anthropologist trained and working in the UK – to make a statement on the psychology of agronomists and politicians for whom Western-style farming was dogma? Such occasional doubt, fed by the rising tide of postmodern angst in the social sciences generally, was a source of some discomfort. And yet we *knew* our explanation had value, we *knew* we would defend it if challenged. Our subversive reading of the landscape was not, we maintained, in any way inferior to that of elites empowered to speak on behalf of peasant farmers.

This episode of mild doubt ended when Rwanda slid into chaos in the summer of 1994. Three weeks after the war and genocide ended and Rwanda's new government was sworn in, I returned there for another reading of the landscape. This time the stakes were high. My brief, awesomely simple, was to answer the question: will Rwanda plunge into famine? Five weeks later, after researching a variety of agro-ecological locations, I arrived at a resolute 'no'. Against the tide of incessant warning by 'disaster experts' – that Rwanda's rural population had lost entire crops and eaten virtually all seeds – I remained confident that no such thing had happened. Conversations with farmers – about cropping calendars, displacement in the face of war, the movement of troops, and seed – and visits to markets that were just starting up again had established that Rwanda's seed patrimonium was not depleted in the manner claimed (Pottier 1994b, 1996). The point is this: compared with the first attempt at reading Rwanda's landscape, which left me with some doubt regarding its full validity, the post-war reading of a seemingly ravaged landscape and economy gave me no reason for doubt whatsoever. Going against popular-expert opinion, my 'no famine' verdict later proved consistent with unfolding realities.

On reflection, anthropology's propensity to challenge orthodox interpretation, in this case that the massive destruction of human life equalled an ecological disaster, had proved right and relevant. The experience strengthened my resolve to write the present book. Could I state with the same confidence, I wondered, that anthropology's long-standing interest in food and food-related issues was, and remained, relevant to the contemporary world? Many questions in this book are down-to-earth. What is it that anthropologists and other social scientists know 'for certain' about the social and economic factors critical to food production and food access? What do they know about land, for instance (about its accessibility, the effects of commoditization, its relevance to livelihood), and what have they learned about on-farm labour organization (about its changing character, the level of specialization, remuneration, its role in the construction of gender and other identities, and so on)? And what has anthropology said regarding the multiple interconnections between food production, markets for commodities and labour, food aid and famine prevention, and the nature of development and agrarian policies? To what extent are these food domains autonomous, to what extent constitutive of one another? Many questions in this book focus on policy: How are policy directives made and absorbed? Are they merely accepted or rejected, or locally transformed? And how is farmer knowledge valued and worked into new policies? Answers to the latter question indicate that anthropologists are indeed 'studying up', an activity exceedingly relevant to the contemporary world (Ahmed and Shore 1995: 33).

While it is not the first time such questions have been addressed (cf. McMillan 1991; Scoones and Thompson 1994), it remains attractive to bring them together into a single text. This is so not only because anthropology is under pressure to prove its relevance and prepare for the future (Ahmed and Shore 1995; Moore 1996), but also because many expert practitioners continue to work in a highly fragmented world. When I first thought about writing this book, which was before Rwanda and the Great Lakes region imploded, I had been much moved by the testimony of a Kenyan woman farmer whose expertise had been overlooked in the questionnaire on agriculture to which she responded. Jon Moris (1991) recalls the incident:

> We had completed the formal questionnaire when the respondent, an old woman, asked if she could now please tell us some facts. She was, she claimed, the person most knowledgeable about growing yams in the community. . . . These plants, she insisted, were very important for poor women like herself who only had a little land. Now she was old and would soon die: could we please convey [her] observations to the Agricultural Department so that other women might be helped?

The reply disappointed.

[A]gricultural officials had no place in their programmes for yams. It was not, they explained, a priority crop. There was no-one to receive the old woman's tape-recorded empirical observations, garnered over a lifetime spent growing yams. The extension system was entirely oriented towards receiving messages from its research scientists: there was at that time no means of conveying new observations upward into the formal system. (Moris 1991: 55)

By exposing the limitations of the survey and the injustice done to her, this Kenyan farmer confirmed the need to critique the world of aid and policy and to consider how lofty development goals and scientific principles might themselves contribute to food insecurity.

Anthropology in a Globalizing World

Taking stock of how anthropology informs the social, economic and political dimensions of food (in)security can be a way of reflecting on its preparedness for engagement in a fast-changing world. Giddens's recent comment on the future of anthropology aptly conveys what the old Kenyan farmer left unsaid. For Giddens, '[a]nthropology must be ready to contest unjust systems of domination, along the way seeking to decide what "injustice" actually is, and be prepared to bring potentially controversial issues to light' (Giddens 1995: 277). Only then will anthropology 'contribute to the collective effort that the social sciences as a whole need to make to confront a social world which has changed almost out of recognition in a few short years' (1995: 277). As 'domination' and 'injustice' are regular themes in the anthropological literature on food and agriculture, there will be ample opportunity to give these terms substance – and context.

Equally, we must ask what the present world situation *actually* is. No social scientist today, no matter what her specific interests, can shun this wider issue. For Norman Long, the present world situation is one in which a multiplicity of complex and changing interconnections prevail. They are 'based on financial commitments, commodity flows, producer and consumer associations, technology and knowledge disseminations, and political negotiations and struggles that are transnational in character' (Long 1996: 49–50). This interconnected world comes complete with new 'types of authority and regulatory practices', forms quite different from those that marked nation-states before the Cold War ended (Long 1996: 50). These new forms of regulation and authority include *inter alia*, structural adjustment programmes imposed by the World Bank (WB) and the International Monetary Fund (IMF), the high external-input farming approach promoted by the Sasakawa and Global 2000 foundations, measures to protect regional markets such as those created by the EU and ASEAN, a string of UN world summits (on environment, food, population), and the renaissance programme of the New Pan-Africanism which seeks to combine the exploitation of untapped mineral resources with the revival of political democracy. As a new geopolitical space, large parts of Central and Southern Africa are now governed by post-adjustment, anti-aid leaders who work hand in glove with giant mining corporations like American Mineral Fields, Barrick Gold and Tenke, to name but a few.

However, within this multiplicity of global interconnections, 'world' forces are beginning to reveal themselves as more complex, more fragmented and less hegemonic than initially thought. And conversely, 'local' responses are turning out to be more diverse, more dynamic, not as fragile as assumed during the heyday of modernization theory. In the Cold War years, analysts talked mostly of centre–periphery relations of domination that would beat local communities everywhere into uniform submission. Homogenization was on their lips. Today, the neat global–local dichotomy has become suspect. 'The centre' is no longer viewed as 'a monolithic entity sustained by grand narratives of progress, but as a set of situated and interrelated knowledges and practices, all of which are simultaneously local and global' (Moore 1996: 9). Anthropology's new-found quest is to grasp the interdynamic of globalizing and localizing processes. Not only are the effects of central planning and intervention highly specific, but they also in turn impact on what goes on at so-called global levels.

The globalizing world of hi-tech farming and agribusiness is an appropriate illustration. True, globalizing processes have produced broad, recurring patterns in farming technology and organization on the ground (for example more women worldwide are now engaged as part-time workers in agriculture and in food processing industries), but equally true, none of these transformations have been uncorruptedly imposed. The challenge is to appreciate how the different actors involved (e.g. peasant smallholders, commercial farmers, transnational companies, policy-makers, banks and various agrarian organizations) struggle to negotiate outcomes (Long 1996: 46). The new argument is that technology is 'forever being reworked to fit the production strategies, resource availabilities and social desires of the farm household' (Long 1996: 48). Differently put, the outcome of technology transfer (as it used to be called) is that globalization and localization fuse to create new patterns of agricultural development.

The growing consensus that globalization encompasses a multiplicity of interactive discourses and practices undermines the view that global markets would be out to destroy heterogeneity. The argument used to be that harmonious relations, embedded in timeless gift-giving economies, were being replaced by homogenizing, impersonal relations; one (presumed) bounded world making way for another (presumed) bounded world. But the envisaged gift-to-commodity sequence and accompanying progression from the personal to the impersonal are not borne out in those areas where 'real markets' have been studied (see chapter 5), nor have rural labour relations become fully proletarianized (see chapter 4). One of the objectives of the present book is to scrutinize the empirical evidence on which it can be claimed that the spread of commodity markets does not inevitably result in homogenization and cultural impoverishment.

The homogenization paradigm has also come under attack outside the debate on agrarian change. In refugee studies, for example, it is now increasingly realized that conventional refugee images, especially that of 'the refugee', work to obscure the actual (and varied) circumstances refugees experience (see e.g. Malkki 1995: 13). Malkki's critique can be extended, as we shall see in chapter 6, to the homogenizing image of the universally enslaved, hybrid-crop-producing peasant farmer. Have such farmers lost their culture and confidence to become dehumanized, as Vandana Shiva (1992) claims, or have they absorbed and integrated new consumption opportunities in a spectacular demonstration of Miller's thesis that 'none of us [is] a model of real consumption and all of us [are] creative variants of social processes based around the possession and use of commodities' (Miller 1995: 144)? In passing, I note that homogenizing images may well appeal to policymakers because they remind us of the ambiguous myth of the human 'community' in which 'diversity is only formal and does not belie the existence of a common mould' (Barthes 1992/1957: 100; cited in Malkki 1995: 12–13). This notion of a human essence pervades much policy thinking. It is manifest, for instance, in the persistent claim that farmers everywhere are rational beings whose chief ambition is to maximize output.

Within anthropology, current reflections on the world we live in aim radically to alter conventional ways of viewing change. They invite us to appreciate not only the empirical diversity of what happens when policy is implemented, which is what much of this book is about, but also the fact that globalizing and localizing forces are dynamically interrelated. This means we must go beyond the notion of externally induced impact and need to consider how so-called 'local cultures' reshape the so-called 'external' structures. We need to ask to what extent state and market are 'endowed with diverse and localized sets of meaning and practices' (Long 1996: 52).

While the need to focus research on the interdynamic of globalizing and localizing processes, including the reshaping of 'external' structures, will here be spelled out mostly as a set of questions for future research (see especially chapter 9), the ethnographic repertoire of studies on food security, a topic that is vast and varied, certainly supports the thesis that changing local conditions

> are not dictated by some supranational hegemonic power or simply driven by international capitalist interests. Changing global conditions – whether economic, political, cultural or environmental – are, as it were, 'relocalized' [and reworked] within national, regional or local frameworks of knowledge and organization . . . These processes entail the emergence of new identities, alliances and struggles for space and power within specific populations. (Long 1996: 43)

The concept of 'relocalization' stands central to the themes broached in this book.

Social Anthropology, Food Security and Relevance

Exploring anthropology's rich repertoire of empirical and analytical contributions to the study of agrarian change and food security is one way in which anthropologists may respond to the growing awareness that what threatens the discipline is not a crisis of *representation*, but a problem of *relevance* (Ahmed and Shore 1995: 15). Akbar Ahmed and Cris Shore explain:

> Social anthropology as we know it is in danger of becoming marginalized and redundant unless it adapts to the changing world which now threatens to undermine its cherished theories, methods and practices. This means, above all, *re-evaluating its conventional objects of study and developing new domains and methods of enquiry* that are commensurate with the new subjects and social forces that are emerging in the contemporary world. It also means engaging with contentious issues and problems of wider public concern, and communicating with a wider audience than the restricted community of academics that has hitherto been its arena. (Ahmed and Shore 1995: 15–16; emphasis added)

I share the conviction: nihilism must not be allowed to push anthropology into the abyss; the discipline's 'future as a generalizing social science is more promising than its critics and detractors have led themselves to think' (Ahmed and Shore 1995: 40; see also Giddens 1995: 275). While postmodernism must be valued for the healthy scepticism it encourages regarding 'the claims and methods of science (or any philosophy which purports to offer truth)', anthropology must also 'resist the temptation of defining itself as an interpretive quest in search of meaning, whose interpretations, like those of the novelist, are mere "fictions"' (Ahmed and Shore 1995: 32). The two readings of the Rwandan landscape with which this chapter opened will have brought home, I hope, why anthropology must not reconstitute itself as the maker of fiction. Whereas my thoughts on the deeper meaning of the banana grove may have edged me towards the world of the novelist, my subsequent post-war reading of that same complex landscape was informed by dialogical research, the very stuff of which anthropology is made. In Rwanda in 1994, I undertook a conventional, some might say holistic, job in which a multitude of questions, answers and observations were combined to give me the certainty that the 'impression' I was forming was more truthful than that of the experts who cried famine.

It is not too late for anthropology, far from it in fact, since the discipline has never ceased to provide innovative perspectives. Regarding food and food policy in the 1990s, for example, anthropology has been at the forefront of debate, as when the (so-called) international community discovered how 'the household' needed to come into stronger focus in discussions of food security (International Food Policy Research Institute (IFPRI) Report, June 1992). The discipline also injected new life into the debate on 'free market' policy and 'real' markets (see chapter 5) and of late has offered new insights into the problem of biodiversity (Guyer and Richards 1996). In short, in the world of food, agriculture and food policy, anthropology has found a way of coping with intellectual uncertainty. A broad look at its contribution to themes that inform the food security debate, which is what this book offers, is a useful platform from which to contemplate the discipline's future role.

Being optimistic about anthropology's future does not mean, however, that we can ignore dilemmas. Awkward questions must be addressed. I take very seriously, for instance, Escobar's contention that development anthropology exists within a Western-centred system of knowledge and power which it actually recycles (Escobar 1991: 3). This places the development anthropologist 'at the service of power' (1991: 2). Escobar's critique may well apply equally to those who situate themselves within the anthropology of development.

This said, I do not wish to be part of a discipline that does not attempt to inform and influence those whose decisions make a difference to the world. As an academic both in and out of development, I agree with Gardner and Lewis that '[if] both anthropology and development are facing crisis in the 1990s, both too contain the possibilities for positive engagement and change. Anthropology can contribute to more positive forms of development thought and practice, both by working *in* development and also by providing a critical account *of* development' (Gardner and Lewis 1996: 25). The awkward vantage-point, the being betwixt and between, is reminiscent of Raymond Firth's calling anthropology the 'uncomfortable discipline' (Firth 1981). Uncomfortable anthropology may be and remain, irrelevant it must not become.

During previous crises, too, it has been the interest in food, agriculture and diet which has enabled anthropologists to prove or rediscover their relevance in a changing world. This happened very clearly in the USA in the 1970s, a time of deep scepticism about the value of academia and its (dubious) service to government. At that point, the discipline's earlier (1940s) interest in 'food habits' was revived to become part of a 'search for new involvements and for new concepts, methods, models, and definitions to problems' (Montgomery and Bennett 1979: 133). This active search renewed anthropology's interest in interdisciplinarity and in policy questions.

As anthropology moves into the twenty-first century, again affected by crisis, its students may once more want to turn to food and agriculture for inspiration in the search for new involvement and intellectual orientation. Unlike the intellectual crisis in the USA in the 1970s, however, anthropology's current crisis comes at a time when the discipline's interest in food, agriculture, food security, and health is peaking. This is evident from the publication of a recent reader on food and culture (Counihan and van Esterik 1997) and an edited volume on food, health and identity in Britain (Caplan 1997). This makes present and past contributions to understanding food and food-related topics an ideal test case for gauging the role anthropology might play in tomorrow's world.

In this book, then, we ask whether anthropology's contribution to the study of food and agriculture is such (or can become such) that the discipline is (becomes) fit to provide guidance in a fast-changing world. This includes establishing whether anthropology's contribution, based mostly on intensive, single-site studies, can respond to the challenge that it must trace 'cultural formation[s] across and within multiple sites of activity' (Marcus 1995: 96). The challenge is double-edged. Not only must anthropology expand the conventional locus of its research and become multi-sited, but it must also ensure that ethnographic output becomes available in accessible form. All too often still, planners receive 'rambling ethnography with a few comments about what they should not do' (Robertson 1984: 301). I agree. Making relevant ethnography more accessible, however, as I hope to do through this book, also includes challenging those areas where development planning is 'dominated by values ... whose dogmatic narrowness is poorly understood and very seldom challenged' (Robertson 1984: 302). Anthropology must both clarify and challenge.

Challenges are especially appropriate where international agricultural research practices remain governed by a scientific elite which proclaims allegiance to participatory research. This elite's approach often encourages the perception that farmer knowledge is a set of easy-to-access abstract principles, and overlooks the all-important question of how people relate to their knowledge (Fairhead 1990: 23); nor indeed does it show how researchers and farmers interact. Modern science has only just begun to recognize that the social and natural world is 'bubbling with change, disorder and process', and that consequently it has to relinquish the positivist myth that reality, knowledge and environment are ordered, stable and governed by scientific certainties (Drinkwater 1994: 33–4, quoting Toffler in Prigogine and Stengers 1985: p. xv). Environment, as Ingold writes, is never 'fully created. It is, as it were, "work in progress"' (Ingold 1992: 51). Likewise, knowledge is constituted by the myriad dynamic ways through which people categorize, code, process and impute meaning to their experiences (Arce and Long 1992: 211).

Another area where challenge is appropriate relates to the context in which text is produced. The Kenyan woman farmer whose expertise on yams was ignored because it was not a priority crop in policy circles made this point very clearly, albeit implicitly: Western analysts are driven by selective visibility. And here development workers and academics alike must be on full alert. Sarah White (1992) demonstrates this for Bangladesh, a country textually represented mostly by authors who are or were development practitioners from the West. Their influence on textual representations is particularly evident in writings on women. Academics too, even 'pure' ones, need to ask uncomfortable questions about how they themselves are positioned.

In search of relevance, and ready to question the positioning of any social scientist or policy-maker, we begin this book with a look at the most recent World Food Summit (Rome 1996), in which world leaders and food experts offered advice and worked towards a new definition of food security. The opening question is simple enough: how does expert opinion compare with the perceptions and strategies of vulnerable groups and individuals?

2

Food Security
in Policy and Practice

This chapter focuses on the definition of food security as adopted at the World Food Summit in Rome, November 1996, and asks how this much expanded definition compares with themes and concerns in empirical research. The question is this: to what extent do high-level policy formulations of food security reflect the complex real-life experiences and perceptions of the food-insecure (and *which* food-insecure?) people they intend to serve? This fundamental question underlies all subsequent chapters.

Defining Food Security

What food security is and how it can be improved are themes 'widely-debated and much-confused' (von Braun et al. 1992: 5). Part of the problem is that the concept is concerned with interconnected domains; with questions of agriculture, society, environment, employment and income, marketing, health and nutrition, and public policy.

Since the concept was launched at the first World Food Conference in 1974, food security has 'evolved, developed, multiplied and diversified' (Maxwell 1996: 155). In its initial conception, food security was a global supply problem; what the world needed was more secure flows of basic foodstuffs at stable prices. Defined in global terms, food security equalled the 'availability at all times of adequate world food supplies of basic foodstuffs ... to sustain a steady expansion of food consumption ... and to offset fluctuations in production and prices' United Nations (UN 1975). The focus on supply and price stability reflected two concerns: the underperformance of agriculture in 'Green Revolution' areas, especially in South and South-East Asia, and the uncertainties caused by large-scale cereal exports to the Soviet Union. Both forces were a drain on efforts to achieve supply stability (Clay 1997: 8).

It is useful to remember that the humanitarian crises which erupted at the time of, or just before, the first World Food Conference – drought in the Sahel, floods in Bangladesh and north-east India – were in policy circles perceived as one-off events brought on suddenly by natural forces. It was not until the early 1980s, with the stimulus of Amartya Sen's seminal work on hunger and markets (Sen 1981), that a new perspective on food security emerged; the focus shifted from supply to demand. Sen's emphasis on *accessing* food led to a new definition. Food security, the Food and Agriculture Organization (FAO) argued in 1983, meant ensuring 'that all people at all times [had] both physical and economic access to the basic food that they [needed]' (FAO 1983).

Poverty and Hunger, the 1986 World Bank report, continued in that vein: the challenge was to guarantee 'access of all people at all times to enough food for an active, healthy life' (World Bank 1986). The European Union (EU), too, took this broad approach, but emphasized the importance of household food security. For the EU, food security was 'the ability to acquire enough food to satisfy minimal nutritional requirements at both national and household levels' (Tuinenburg 1987: 499).

The EU concept of food security differed from food self-sufficiency, which meant that a country or household produced enough for its own consumption. A high degree of food self-sufficiency, the EU claimed, was 'not necessarily a precondition of food security' (Tuinenburg 1987: 499). This latter point remains contested, though, since commodity markets are notoriously volatile. Maxwell (1990) recognizes this. Whilst supporting the EU distinction between self-sufficiency and security, Maxwell acknowledges that well-functioning markets must not be assumed: 'growth in non-food agriculture, including cash crops for export, can have a greater impact on incomes and, provided that food marketing systems function well, *sometimes a large assumption*, simultaneously improve command over food' (Maxwell 1990: 7; emphasis added).

The 'large assumption' carried a double warning: 'cash cropping may undermine the food security of the poorest groups if it is associated with rapid increases in social inequality [Maxwell and Fernando 1989: 1683–6]. [In addition,] under certain circumstances food prices may rise, even where marketing is inefficient' (Maxwell 1990: 7). Despite this double warning, many policy experts believed firmly that cash cropping and (what they call) deregulated markets were intrinsically sound. Their belief in the neo-liberal paradigm appears to have sprung from the realization that policy-makers dealing with food security face a particular dilemma. On the one hand, and this is the argument against the neo-liberal paradigm, they know that higher incomes as a result of cash cropping do not necessarily lead to nutritional benefits for the small-scale producers involved (DeWalt and Barkin 1991; Longhurst 1988: 29; Sharpe 1990). The vast majority of sub-Saharan women involved in cash cropping, for example, work 'for their husbands' (Whitehead 1990b). On the other hand, and hence the dilemma, cash may mean survival: its lack is a fundamental reason why individuals, households and groups may fail to cope with prolonged food shortages (Fleuret 1986).

How can planners get the balance right? Can they both stimulate the cash economy and make it safe? To gain insight into the debate, we need a detailed understanding of local-level conditions. We need to ask: Who receives the income from cash cropping? What is the cash spent on? Who is responsible for feeding households? Who decides on food distribution? (Command over food within households is an extremely difficult research topic.) We must ask too: How much land and labour does cash cropping claim? How exactly do markets operate? Apart from these last two questions, which are tackled in later chapters, these issues will be introduced here.

That answers to the above questions are complex, possibly confused, is clear from the Rome 1996 declaration on world food security and action. Dropping the customary focus on 'basic foodstuffs' and going for the widest possible approach, the declaration reads:

> food security, at the individual, household, national, regional and global levels ... exists when all people, at all times, have physical and economic access to sufficient, safe and nutritious food to meet their dietary needs and food preferences for an active and healthy life. ... [The definition recognizes that poverty is a major cause of food insecurity and that] poverty eradication is essential to improve access to food. (FAO 1996: 3)

The Rome Declaration reflects postmodern uncertainties. These are acknowledged especially in the awareness that 'the relationships between household food security in terms of access to basic foodstuffs or the constituent elements of a balanced diet and actual nutrition and health status [are] complex rather than simple and direct' (Clay 1997: 26). The nutritional status of vulnerable groups, Rome delegates agreed, is determined by pathways more complex than previously assumed.

The intricate linkages between food intake and health are outside the scope of this book. The focus rather is on perceptions of livelihood and economic security, as held by policy-makers and food-insecure people. Perceptions will be explored particularly regarding those 'big areas' that will continue to be central to any enquiry into the food question: agrarian transformation; food and labour markets; food aid and famine responses; agricultural research and intervention. If policy-makers are serious about responding to the 'diverse nature of the problem as experienced by poor people themselves' (ODI 1997: 2), then they will need to focus on how poor people – as a *diverse* category – experience not only agrarian change, but also the presence of aid programmes and markets.

Attempts to address context specificity were another indication that Rome delegates were moving towards the postmodern (cf. Maxwell 1996). Edward Clay captured the spirit of Rome: 'Food security now involves food preferences which are socially and culturally determined. The potentially high degree of context specificity implies that the concept has both lost its simplicity and is not itself a goal [any longer] but an intermediating set of actions that contribute to an active and healthy life' (Clay 1997: 10). The promise that more attention will be paid to socially and culturally determined 'food preferences' deserves comment, however, since there are echoes here of earlier, now settled, debates in anthropology. First of all, policy-makers and the people they plan *for* (only occasionally *with*) may hold very different views on what constitutes a household. Despite good intentions, the dominant policy approach is likely to remain that of the bounded nuclear household; an approach which belies the diversity and complexity of commensal and domestic arrangements, and of members' contractual experiences. Anthropologists have for some time now emphasized that a unitary concept of household is untenable (Guyer and Peters 1987: 205), but the critique has not deterred policy-makers (see Solway 1994, discussed in chapter 7).

Social and cultural perspectives on food security may well receive the same treatment: that is, doubts about the utility and necessity of understanding complex approaches are likely to be raised. Notwithstanding the good intentions expressed in Rome, policy-makers will undoubtedly ask how far they should go – and can go – in taking cultural views seriously. Surely, they will argue, they must not take note of that which is (to them) blatantly irrational? And how many perspectives should they consider anyway? Local understandings of 'hunger', the term possibly closest to the concept of food insecurity, may well contain viewpoints that do not interest the official whose job it is to improve food security. Consider these examples from Congo-Zaire. Among the Ntomba of Lake Tumba, 'hunger' denotes the absence of rice from the diet (Pagézy 1985), while 'prolonged hunger' among the Aluund denotes social breakdown and moral decline (De Boeck 1994). It is easy to advocate respect for food *preferences* (for example, 'the Ntomba eat rice'), much harder to appreciate *perspectives* and build them into policy (as when hunger is equated with social and moral decline). Cultural perspectives, moreover, are contestable.

That policy-makers may opt for a minimalist approach to culture is manifest in the recent 'self-targeting of commodities' version of food aid. Allegedly reflecting the aid community's 'much greater sensitivity to differential consumption patterns of relatively poor households' (Clay 1997: 37), self-targeting is based on the principle that certain foods are culturally classified as inferior. These foods, policy-makers infer, must be more acceptable to lower-income consumers. The logic goes that where a food-based intervention either subsidizes or supplies such a commodity, the relatively poor will disproportionately access the programme. But, in real life, the delivery of such self-targeting foods does not always achieve the hoped-for response:

> There is evidence from Cape Verde and Egypt that some subsidised maize and wheat have been used for animal feed. There is also some evidence from East and southern Africa that yellow maize may be disposed of in this way... In the case of rice (Mozambique, Cape Verde) and non-cereals (vegetable oil in Bangladesh, milk products in China), these are more likely than other commodities to be regressive in the distribution of benefits. (Clay 1997: 38)

On top of these concerns, we also need to ask how 'the poor' perceive such self-targeting. How do they, as a *differentiated* group, view the offer of foods culturally labelled inferior? Does self-targeting enable the poor (and *which poor?*) to access what they really want or is the strategy perceived as a social control mechanism which stigmatizes and reinforces social hierarchy? Perceptions must be looked into. Also, there is the cultural problem that feeding self-targeted foods to animals does not necessarily imply rejection (cf. Wolde Mariam 1986, 1990).

There is a second reason why the allegedly improved responsiveness to cultural issues may be little more than a token gesture. The Rome concern with food preferences, as opposed to social and cultural (and therefore contestable) perspectives, recalls the tendency in ITK, the debate on Indigenous Technical Knowledge, to focus only on concepts and knowledge useful to Western science. Conventional ITK focused on agricultural practices and knowledge that could be *extracted and used* in policy (Fairhead 1992b); what did not fit was discarded. The Rome 1996 concern with food preferences may end up mimicking conventional ITK: 'preferences' could become mostly *bits* of information (ethnographic at best, exotic more likely) extracted from, and then mistaken for, the totality of complex, cultural approaches to food production and food use. Sensitivity to cultural *perspectives* on food requires more than the simplistic 'people X enjoy food Y'.

In exploring key debates in food and livelihood security we are interested in the contrast between agency approaches and views held by food-insecure groups and individuals. This book highlights such contrasts as they are found in the domains of agriculture (chapters 3, 4, 8), food marketing (chapter 5, 6), and famine management (chapter 7). The aim is not to provide a comprehensive overview of livelihood strategies, nor is it to cover food cultures from around the world, but rather to establish what gaps may exist between perceptions policy-makers hold and the 'lived' realities of people who experience food stress. If the Rome declaration is a serious commitment to understanding the problem of hunger as poor people experience it, then policy-makers will need to develop not an appreciation of easy-to-sample 'food preferences', but an understanding of local perceptions as socially constructed, contested and negotiated.

Has Rome 1996 made policy-makers more eager to access local perspectives and realities? Several conference interventions suggest rather the opposite; there was hesitancy, reluctance too. While delegates appreciated that hunger is multifaceted and rooted in poverty, proposed solutions were mostly technical and global. The International Rice Research Institute (IRRI), for instance, turned the spotlight on the problem of overfertilization in irrigated agriculture and called for better implementation of the Integrated Pest Management scheme. Land, when discussed, was approached in terms of higher yields and the fight against erosion, while land shortages were portrayed as affecting *nations*, not communities or households or individuals. Thus it was said that India and Bangladesh had insufficient land (*NRC Handelsblad*, 9 November 1996), but no reference was made to the in-country factors that structure and skew distribution and access. Land had no political context. In fact, despite the Declaration's emphasis on the need to remove 'constraints on access to food', the whole Plan of Action shies away from any frank discussion of existing political and institutional obstacles to food security. The Declaration brings us a long list of good intentions phrased in apolitical language; it is a text all heads of state and government can agree to, because it is empty of hard facts regarding the incidence and structural causes of poverty. The level is that of rhetoric rather than action. Take, for example, the first 'commitment' the heads of state and government pledge to honour: 'We will ensure an enabling political, social, and economic environment designed to create the best conditions for the eradication of poverty and for durable peace, based on full and equal participation of women and men, which is most conducive to achieving sustainable food security for all' (FAO 1996: 5).

Vagueness and simplicity, as if the will to reform required no more than the flick of a mental yes-button, permeate the pages of the Declaration. Its language is internationally recognizable and inoffensive, typical of the Western-dominated way of discussing and deciding, also known as 'AgreeCulture' (Mooney 1996: 48), but there is no serious contextualization of the social and political issues that will need confronting. One journalist summarized what the Rome Summit had concluded:

> Food security for all can be guaranteed provided that action is taken now. The political and institutional causes of underdevelopment and poverty must be removed, there is a need to invest in technology to make agriculture sustainable, and the problem of population growth needs to be tackled as agreed during the [Cairo] Conference on Population in 1994. (based on FAO statement, *De Morgen*, 9 November 1996; my translation)

That, roughly, was indeed the plan, with a commitment to sustainable 'food trade and overall trade policies' (FAO 1996: 2) thrown in for good measure. Like many other buzz-words in use, 'sustainability' was not defined.

Other 'solutions' were equally grand: curb meat consumption and grow more grain for humans (Lester Brown, Worldwatch Institute); liberalize trade (USA); provide soft loans to enable 'African farmers' to invest in artificial fertilizers (IFPRI, FAO, WB). IFPRI's Director General confirmed that the initiative, which had already started in Malawi, Mali and Ghana, would not involve the application of more pesticides, nor would local peasant farmers be coerced by the authorities (*De Volkskrant*, 14 November 1996). No coercion! ... Coercion, which exists at so many levels and in so many guises, is a fascinating topic in anthropological hands (see Dzingirai 1992, discussed in chapter 9; Schoepf and Walu 1991, discussed below). It is a topic in which we ask: what *actually* happens?

The Rome emphasis on technical solutions also carried the clear message that 'conflict, terrorism, corruption and environmental degradation contribute significantly to food insecurity' (FAO 1996). Of course, these four factors must be stressed, yet they are all too easily and conveniently located *inside* the 'Third World'; the implication being that both the blame for food insecurity and the responsibility for finding a solution are domestic issues beyond the control of the so-called international community. Locating problems and solutions firmly inside the 'Third World' – which is a representation, not a place

(Koptiuch 1997) – implies that externally led policy interventions as we know them can continue with impunity, that the international community need not question its own role in the creation and maintenance of conflict, terrorism and poverty. The 1996 Declaration was indeed remarkably silent on how structural adjustment programmes (SAPs) and trade liberalization have contributed to hardship worldwide – a point attending NGOs were quick to pick up.

Since Rome produced mostly global-technical solutions, along with a reminder that the Cairo agreements on population control needed implementing, it was small wonder that some participating countries felt their sovereignty was being interfered with (*NRC Handelsblad*, 9 November 1996). Perhaps Rome too, like the 1995 Beijing Conference on Women, was akin to 'global theatre', a staged occasion of North–South solidarity whereby the South was once again reconstituted through Northern discursive mechanisms (Spivak 1996: 2). Despite the acknowledgement of many uncertainties, the 'global' talk in Rome was still that of a confident elite.

So we ask: how does this global-elite talk compare with the general drift of ground-level observations on how food-insecure people think and organize? (I am not fooling myself, academic researchers too are an elite that needs situating, but I do regard them as being comparatively close to the people among whom they research.) Our ethnographic exploration into *perceptions* relating to food and livelihood security, and how these are shaped by precepts and experiences, begins with a deceptively simple question: given the policy-makers' central concern with access to food, how is food *actually accessed* in everyday life?

Food Sharing and Consumption: Problems of Observation and Measurement

How does one find out what someone has eaten? That someone has been denied food? That someone has snacked? Or that someone has eaten elsewhere? As has long been recognized, these vitally important questions are extremely difficult to answer (cf. Richards and Widdowson 1937).

Methodological uncertainty still haunts the debate. One reason is that complexity and secrecy are characteristic of consumption arrangements. To anthropologists this is hardly surprising, since households are never neatly bounded, but rather consist of interacting individuals who are also members of other social groupings. For instance, on food sharing practices among the Mende of the Gola Forest, Sierra Leone, Melissa Leach writes:

The group which eats from a single cooking pot varies from day to day. Guests appear and must be shown hospitality; temporarily recruited farm workers must be fed. Women often 'reorganise' cooking arrangements to suit their own economic and social interests, and men are expected to allow them this autonomy. Indeed few . . . women could state to whom they regularly dished out food, saying rather that 'I give to whom I please'. Women cook for visiting members of their own families, and reciprocate for goods and services (e.g. childcare) by sending cooked food to friends and kin in other parts of the village. (Leach 1991: 46)

Found throughout Africa, these food transfers may turn extra secretive when poverty deepens and the ideal of household self-sufficiency becomes difficult to uphold. Megan Vaughan observed this in matrilineal Chewa society in Malawi, where groups of sisters who eat communally, sometimes with other maternal relatives, cook food separately before sharing it at the point of eating (Vaughan 1983: 277–8).

The complexity and fluidity of consumption organization can be such that the term 'household' ceases to be useful. Margo Russell writes on Swaziland:

As to who cooks, who provides, who prepares, it is difficult to generalize when the resident domestic group undergoes dramatic changes in size and membership from one day to the next with the coming and going of people who, although members of the homestead, also keep house elsewhere, nearer work. The arrangements are *ad hoc*, practical. (Russell 1993: 758–9)

Given the complex nature of food-sharing arrangements, it is small wonder that nutritionists face uncertainty when attempting to collect 'hard information' on food intake. Not only is observing intake next to impossible, and '24-hour recall' a poor substitute, there is also the problem of quantification. Questions as basic as 'can food requirements be measured?' and 'what are the minimal requirements?' remain without satisfactory answers. One problem is that measuring involves a unique encounter, the visit by 'experts', which distorts behaviour (Pacey and Payne 1985: 135). Studying nutritional status also requires an understanding of energy intake and expenditure. And here again nutritionists admit to being ill equipped, since there are no clear 'signs or symptoms . . . to establish the threshold between adequacy and inadequacy' (Payne 1990: 14).

Payne, however, is sceptical about the social science theory, commonly stated as fact, 'that the cause of much malnutrition in women and small children is unfair distribution of food within households' (Payne 1990: 19). His unease with the maldistribution theory derives from the experience of how difficult it is to establish whether discrimination occurs. For Payne, discrimination can 'only be detected on the basis of concurrent measurements of both intakes and expenditures of energy at the individual level, with, in addition, some assessment of outcome in terms of the nutritional status' (Payne 1990: 19). Very few studies provide that kind of data.

One notable and influential exception is a comparative study of findings from Malawi and Bangladesh by Wheeler and Abdullah (1988), who conclude in favour of a 'functionally balanced' distribution of foodstuffs and nutrients. Making particular use of Chimwaza's (1982) data on a Chewa community (Malawi), Wheeler and Abdullah argue that differential allocations do not persist throughout the year or, more accurately, that if they do persist they do not do so to the same degree. When the male intakes Chimwaza calculated are considered over an entire year, the results show that Chewa men do have a higher intake than women, but this, Wheeler and Abdullah argue, is just half the picture. Within this broad structure of unequal access, they claim, there are ways through which the distribution of food is 'functionally' adjusted. First, the data indicate that women 'received an equitable share of total energy when body size was taken into account. [Second,] when food was in short supply, the male–female and male–child differences in energy intake lessened, and were related to work load. When the women worked harder relative to the men . . . they approached an equal food intake' (Wheeler and Abdullah 1988: 443–4).

From this, Wheeler and Abdullah deduce that

> while the framework of food allocation did follow the 'cultural' ideology in that men are served separately, and first, and that men had the greatest overall amounts of prestigious food, the end result was 'functionally' logical, in that the shares of men, women and teenagers were roughly in line with their needs, and that women's work patterns, as well as men's, influenced allocation. . . . [When] food supplies were lowest, so was the relative advantage of the men in regard to food intake. (1988: 444)

This thought-provoking challenge to the 'resource control' perspective, which holds that inequalities of power between spouses skew intra-household allocations away from women (Whitehead 1981: 109), has excited policy-makers and analysts who, in the words of Payne, now agree that

> in respect of *regular and predictable seasonal food shortages*, discrimination is, if anything, in favour of children: even in favour of girl children. Again, if anything, men show greater seasonal changes in weight status than women (Rosetta 1986) – partly because the latter seem to

have more effective means of metabolic compensation. (Payne 1990: 19; emphasis added. See also Payne and Lipton 1994: 103)

The argument against intra-household discrimination, then, may be acceptable in the context of 'regular and predictable' seasonal short-ages, but two comments are in order. First, relevant and reliable ethnographic data are scant; Wheeler and Abdullah review just two situations. The Malawi data, moreover, derive from a highly specific situation, Chewa culture, which gives women access to a rather varied range of resources and options on which to draw (Vaughan 1983; also Englund, 1999). Positive seasonal adjustments in Chewa women and children may well therefore originate in the specific arrangements facilitated by matriliny. Secondly, hunger is increasingly endemic. That households and individuals modify their patterns of food use to adjust to seasonal changes in food entitlement (Payne 1990: 20) may be true, but we must ask whether such adjustments are sustained in a world where poverty is spreading and where the rights and obligations of women and men have become more ambiguous. Some of the case materials that follow will caution against over-optimism, as does Vaughan's research on the 1947 famine in southern Malawi (Vaughan 1987). As a counter to overdeterministic approaches to discrimination, the 'functional' perspective Wheeler and Abdullah advocate has virtue, but, as a possible incentive to policy complacency, the perspective had better not be taken at face value.

A further reason for caution is that indirect ways of monitoring nutritional status may reveal serious imbalances. Thus, in the context of South Asia, Bina Agarwal (1994a, 1994b) argues that gender bias against women is revealed through indicators such as mortality, hospital admission, household health expenditure, and especially female-adverse sex ratios. While Agarwal admits that the evidence on skewed intra-household food allocations is not fully conclusive, she presents 'considerable evidence of intra-household gender inequalities in the sharing of benefits from [household] resources', especially regarding access to basic necessities such as health care (Agarwal 1994a: footnote 62). Such discriminations are regionally patterned; they are more common in the north of India, and also in the case of intra-household food allocations. Barbara Harriss writes that '[d]iscrimination in energy and protein intakes through the allocation of food within the household seems to be greater in the north than in the south. In the north it is least "fair" for very young and very old females, and probably for adult women with special needs associated with pregnancy and lactation' (Harriss 1990: 405).

Intra-regional differences also exist, as can be seen in India's matri-lineal–matrilocal north-east where women are clearly not socialized into total submission to husbands. Here, women do not always eat 'last and least while feeding the best food to their sons and husbands' (Agarwal 1994a: 433). Agarwal, though, is not optimistic about the direction of change, since these mainly matrilineal and bilateral communities (for example Garos) are increasingly influenced by inheritance practices that discriminate against women. This raises the issue of how development policies and legislation impact on the structuring of gender relations – a theme to which we shall return regularly.

Having remarked on the paucity of detailed, reliable studies in food energy intake and measurement, a comment on the quality of empirical social science research is also appropriate. As Harriss (1990: 353) observes, reinforcing a point made earlier by Gita Sen (1982), there is still a lot to be done before research on intra-household relations in South Asia will match the quality of similar study in West Africa. At the beginning of the 1990s, researchers in South Asia had yet to embark on a full exploration of how households could be arenas of unequal material exchange. The comment applies to South-East Asia as well, from where Ben White (1989: 22) also urges researchers to take a leaf from African ethnography.

Food Security in the Postmodern World: Is a Culturally Sensitive Approach Still Possible?

The earlier discussion of 'self-targeting' in food aid raised several important questions. How do 'the poor' perceive the gift of foods culturally labelled inferior? Are 'they' agreed on what constitutes cultural acceptability? And whose cultural labels are we dealing with? As such questions, the latter two especially, must be asked and answered by those who assume policy responsibilities, we do well to pause and reflect on how anthropologists today handle 'culture'.

My approach in this book is to let ethnographies of the experience of everyday life guide us to major theoretical positions. To convey the current anthropological approach to culture, within a situation of food insecurity, I turn to the story of a young woman trader in Kinshasa, Congo-Zaire, at the beginning of the 1990s.

Case Study 2.1: Food Security and Gender in Kinshasa, Congo-Zaire

In the early 1990s, Kinshasa's women traders – whether poor or middle-class, whether married or not, whether their husbands were employed or not – all said they needed to trade and earn substantial 'additional income' to secure for their families even the most modest of living standards (Schoepf and Walu 1991). The need for this additional income resulted from the structural adjustment programme to which Zaire had agreed. Despite their much-enlarged contributions, however, women traders testified to the precariousness of their economic strategies, the excessive length of the working day, and the severe difficulties in controlling resources and incomes. Difficulties mostly took the form of struggles with husbands.

A revealing testimony involved 'Ma Cousine', the cousin of a trader whom Walu and Schoepf interviewed. Her story, in the trader's words, was as follows:

> Ma Cousine accumulated some capital after her children were grown and wanted to create some security for herself so she bought a plot with an unfinished house. She did not consult her husband because she knew he would refuse, since he often took her money to spend on other women. When her husband found out about the house, he threatened her: 'either you give me the deed or I'll throw you out. You can go live in that house and support yourself.'
>
> He brought her father to Kinshasa from the village and told him: 'My wife cannot make decisions without my authorization. Do I know how much she makes from her trade? Perhaps she got the money from adultery?' Her father had received bridewealth which he would have to return if his daughter's husband repudiated her. The son-in-law had always come to his aid when he had a money problem. Besides, he saw how well off his daughter was, living in a big house, with fine clothes, servants, and a car. She should be grateful to her husband, instead of causing problems! He added the weight of his counsel: 'Daughter, he is your husband; he paid bridewealth for you. . . . You must follow your husband's wishes. He decides. If he says no, that is the way it is.' (Schoepf and Walu 1991: 145–6).

But the husband's sisters viewed the situation differently:

> Women need somewhere to go when husbands replace them with a young wife. Or when husbands die and their families grab everything! Her father was out of his element (*dépaysé*) in the city. He did not see his daughter's contribution to her household, which for some years had been larger than that by her husband. (Schoepf and Walu 1991: 146)

The sisters were struck too by the father's failure to invoke the *old* rural norm according to which each person is entitled to the proceeds of their labour. This norm, upset by colonial legislators who colluded with local (male) chiefs and judges, lives on in the collective memory. The father, moreover, ignored the *new* but increasingly common practice whereby successful women traders build homes in

their fathers' villages to have a place to go to when widowed or divorced. What seemed clear-cut to the husband and the father was less
so when put into the context of the social dynamics that had evolved
historically.

Conscious of how ephemeral a woman's prosperity is, the husband's
sisters urged him to pardon his wife and allow her to keep the house.
When he refused, Ma Cousine capitulated; she did not want to be held
at fault for breaking up her marriage and risk a curse should her father
and uncles be ordered to return the bridewealth. The threat of moral
sanction 'helped' Ma Cousine reconsider her position. She ceded the
deed, her husband sold the house – and kept the money to himself
(Schoepf and Walu 1991: 146).

What does this tell us about culture? First and foremost, the story
shows that negotiation and contestation are part of the fabric of everyday life. Ma Cousine did not win, but she and her husband's sisters
fought hard for what they believed would be a fairer world. Equally
important, arguments about 'correct' behaviour were not won or lost
on the basis of pure economic reasoning. The arguments through which
Ma Cousine's position, and that of women generally, was attacked,
revealed how economic reasoning intersects with moral reasoning; or
to be more precise, with a dominant morality favouring men and emerg-
ing out of the colonial encounter.

Culture, then, is about change and struggle. Sometimes, seemingly
well-established norms can come in 'for review' when material conditions change. Take, for instance, the well-known cultural 'fact' that
cassava in most of sub-Saharan Africa is the undisputed property of
women. This 'fact' may appear solid, yet in rural Zambia in the late
1980s, as economic uncertainty and poverty began to bite, women
feared that men would challenge their right to the crop on the logic
that cassava had become 'household wealth' (Gatter 1993: 163). This
redefinition of cassava, prompted by government putting a price on it,
amounted to a redefinition of norms and expectations (see also Carney
1988, discussed in chapter 3).

In contrast to classical economy and demography, which treat culture as a set of discrete rules or beliefs, anthropology has moved towards a more flexible position. This has come about in two stages.
Initially, while culture was still regarded as an organized system of
shared meanings, anthropologists highlighted how these meanings were
'often more pervasive than explicit, a set of basic assumptions and
images that generate[d] rules and beliefs but [was] not reducible to
them' (Levine and Scrimshaw 1983: 667–9). Today's definition of culture goes much further. As anthropology has zoomed in on culture's

pervasive fuzziness, its present preoccupation is with understanding diversity and contestation. Karsten Pærregaard (1997) outlines how

> our notion of culture has shifted from that of a distinct lifestyle prac-
> tised by a territorially bounded group of people to a compound design
> of different forms of lives lived by people in separate worlds. [This]
> raises questions concerning not only our use of the concepts of place,
> community, and identity, but also our understanding of people's own
> use of them. (Pærregaard 1997: 39)

When applied anthropology gained popularity in Britain in the 1970s, it too treated culture as comfortably bounded, with discrete rules and beliefs, and easy to access. The opinion was that 'cultural factors' could be accessed through well-designed surveys and built up as an inventory of cultural resources (Cochrane 1979: 12–14, 46, 91). What mattered here was that 'cultural integrity' (*the* culture) should be understood and respected to prevent opposition to externally designed projects. The approach today is very different. Having dropped the bounded approach, anthropologists now allow 'culture' to be a plurality of malleable forms of coded behaviour and experience which, although patterned, are open to contestation. Culture has become amorphous live material, essentially political in scope, something administrators and policy-makers find difficult to handle (see chapter 8).

Social Dynamics of Food and Livelihood Security: Basic Themes in Empirical Research

Policy-oriented academic research recognizes the pre-eminence of certain broad principles. It is widely accepted, for instance, that food domains are interconnected; that the impact of policy intervention varies between locations and over time, and also within locations; that such interventions may produce negative effects; that entitlements to resource use are structured; and that responsibilities in food provisioning continue to be shouldered mainly by women.

Drawing on recent ethnographic research, the rest of this chapter outlines some of these generally recognized, broad principles, but questions the extent to which generalizations can be made.

The Interconnectedness of Food Domains

What people eat, what they grow, how they trade, who they turn to in need, are linked issues. In everyday life, agriculture, trade and food distribution constitute domains that are patterned, interlocking and mutually constitutive. Each domain is also susceptible to external influences.

The interconnectedness of the food domains, however, along with the social norms and actions that underpin them, is so far poorly reflected in policy design and implementation. Projects and programmes, writes Kathleen DeWalt, 'often fail to appreciate the complex nature of the relationships between agricultural production, income, and food consumption and nutritional status. These relationships are social, cultural, and economic, as well as biological and ecological' (DeWalt 1991: 126). DeWalt's chief concern is that 'few strategies for agricultural development anticipate the effects of technological change on patterns of consumption, specifically food consumption, and ultimately nutritional status' (DeWalt 1991: 126).

The need to appreciate how farming decisions, marketing strategies, income-generating activities and structures of authority interrelate is appropriately demonstrated in Erica Wheeler's essay on labelling, in which she critiques the most common objective in nutrition programmes, which is to 'feed the child and teach the mother' (Wheeler 1986: 135). The policy-makers' assumption here is that 'if women only knew what to do, they would be able to deploy existing resources (time, labour, fuel, water, cash and food) to feed their families better' (1986: 135). This kind of prognosis uses the model of a household where access to a healthy diet is constrained by women's ignorance and lack of skill, and where the 'vulnerable' young child suffers without exception. Such an approach separates mothers and their children as a target-group from the full range of structural factors that regulate household food supply and internal distribution. Wheeler examines several variations of the 'feed the child and teach the mother' approach, yet remarks how each one of them fails to address the key determinants in food access: employment and wage rates, food prices, land tenure, market structures, etc. The outcome, Wheeler argues, 'is that women are blamed for the end result of processes over which they have no control' (1986: 135).

Policy-makers still treat the main food domains as separate, and continue to accord agriculture the highest priority; consideration of yields comes before consideration of nutritional benefits (McMillan 1991). This lack of coordination between food-related departments is rooted in what Chambers calls 'normal professionalism', the tendency to specialize and plan without regard for what others do (Chambers 1986). One of the objectives of this book is to show that rather than separate the food domains, planners must integrate them in a framework which simultaneously addresses food production *and* marketing *and* consumption, and which establishes how these domains are mediated through various sets of discourses in which economic, social and moral arguments are mixed. (This is not to suggest that policy decisions will ever be politically neutral.)

In view of the interconnectedness of food domains, recent writings on food security propose a focus on livelihood and economic security, rather than on food *per se*. It is relations – economic, social, political, religious, all interwoven – that determine who will eat and live well, and who will not. Current farming practices often exemplify why there is more to 'food security' than food. Whatever its scale, good farming requires income and, therefore, good interaction with local and distant markets for goods and labour. This is well captured in Paul Webber's (1996) discussion of how farming households in Kusasi, north-east Ghana, undertake a range of micro-enterprises (petty trading, craft production, beer brewing, casual labouring, etc.) to supplement farm incomes and ensure the farm's survival. Nonetheless, 'only in a minority of instances do they generate sufficient income to invest in the farm system in order to raise productivity' (Webber 1996: 449). As poverty deepens, the significance of these manifold interconnected activities can only augment.

If this book has separate chapters on inseparable domains, the justification is heuristic: separation serves to highlight intersecting nodes. In the chapter on farm labour, for instance, it will become clear that farmers' production decisions incorporate their views not only on production itself, but also on marketing, consumption, political patronage and aid, cosmology, and social relations in general. It is this web of relations and perceptions that has prompted anthropologists to view agriculture as an idiom for social expression (see Richards 1989; Gatter 1993: 181).

Political Economy and Culture: Global Trends, Local Realities

The impact of 'global forces' differs according to location. (This simple but crucial insight precedes the debate, introduced in chapter 1, that 'global' and 'local' interpenetrate.) In exploring the impact issue, we look first at the impact of colonial and post-colonial policy interventions in agriculture, then at the impact of broad cultural conventions. The aim, a modest one, is to show through selected ethnographic studies that centrally designed policies and regional cultural conventions are never experienced in the same way and with the same intensity in all places, nor by all people sharing the same habitat. In addition, we will establish how, when policy interventions ignore local contexts, and especially the local imbalances in power and resource uses, they will themselves obstruct the course of social development.

How the impact of centrally planned intervention is mitigated by specific variables has been documented in a number of empirical studies. Among them is work by Jill Belsky on Kerinci district, Sumatra, Indonesia (Belsky 1993), which focuses not only on the area's history of differential impact, but also on the consequences for development opportunity today. Demonstrating how successive cash-cropping regimes have impacted across areas and social groups, and over time, Belsky emphasizes that the colonial past and the localized engagements with history determine whether today's food-insecure people can in fact benefit from programmes that are technically sound. Here is a close-up on two villages Belsky studied.

Case Study 2.2: Two villages in Kerinci, Sumatra (Indonesia)

Belsky's argument is that what food-insecure people grow in their upland farms – food crops, tree crops, etc. – depends not only on national and international factors, notably colonial and post-colonial economic policies and world markets, but also on how these factors combine with site-specific variables, particularly access to land.

The two villages being compared, Sungai Ning and Koto Lebuh Tinggi, differ in terms of their population make-up and infrastructure. Situated near an important market centre, Sungai Ning is divided between long-time residents and a group of Javanese migrants who arrived in the 1950s and 1960s. The migrants and their descendants work only the degraded upland slopes, where coffee used to be monocropped in the 1930s. When they settled on the slopes of Sungai Ning, the migrants continued with the crops (cassava) and farming techniques they knew. Cassava production, however, combined with population increase, furthered the process of soil fertility depletion that had set in when coffee was monocropped (Belsky 1993: 136). Coffee monocropping had been popular in Sungai Ning because of the village's 'favourable' location near an administrative centre. As they remain economically and politically weak, Sungai Ning's upland farmers are unable to purchase lowland rice fields, nor can they sharecrop. Without access to irrigated rice, their households are seriously food insecure (Belsky 1993: 133).

Koto Lebuh Tinggi, a less centrally located and therefore (officially) 'less favourable' village, shares some characteristics with the first site, but its upland farmers are more prosperous. This relative prosperity is explained in terms of the area's isolation which, throughout the twentieth century, has meant less policy interference, more autonomy and better-managed soils. What saved Koto Lebuh Tinggi's uplands was the area's 'poor' response to the coffee boom. Coffee was cultivated, but rarely monocropped (Belsky 1993: 136).

The contrast in their histories explains not only why differential rates of food insecurity exist in the two villages, but also why today they respond differently to new policy initiatives, even when technically sound. The absence of in-migration, the low population density, the more isolated location and continued intercropping give Koto Lebuh Tinggi farmers today – *including those who are less food secure* – the livelihood security they need to take advantage of the agro-forestry schemes on offer. Unlike the food/rice-insecure of Sungai Ning, upland farmers in Koto Lebuh Tinggi are more cash-secure and able to invest. Upland farmers in Sungai Ning, on the other hand, produce low-value crops with stable yields which, although doing well on the degraded soils, do not favour capital accumulation. The initiatives in agro-forestry are beyond their reach.

In short, despite their similar physical environs, upland farmers in the two locations contrast sharply in how they have responded and continue to respond to policy initiatives. It is the more isolated, more autonomous upland farmers of Koto Lebuh Tinggi who take advantage – and control – of the externally planned initiatives that aim to reduce food insecurity.

The importance of local history as a critical factor in explaining varied responses to policy is also demonstrated in Martin Greeley's study of how a Scheduled 'Tribal' population in India experienced the delivery of 'green aid' (Greeley 1991). The project in question again aimed to make agriculture more sustainable through a series of technically sound interventions but, again, it failed to mobilize the food-insecure people it particularly wanted to reach. The reason, again, was that the project's designers had ignored the structure and significance of local power relations. Targeted households could not participate because of the determining force of centuries of oppression through inequality in land ownership and use rights (Greeley 1991: 41). As with Sungai Ning in Kerinci, the socially disadvantaged 'target' population found the temporary risk of a switch from annuals to perennials too high: heightened food insecurity, even short-term, was not something they could realistically face. Among the Scheduled 'Tribes', the food-insecure perceived that their 'subjective' strategy for food self-sufficiency was a better bet than the largely theoretical prospect of selling perennials and buying in food. As the grain banks required to tide them over did not materialize, the project went ahead for the sole benefit of secure groups, i.e. those who owned valley bottom land and could afford the risks.

There are lessons here for those who want to better understand how farmers experience food security: resource-poor farmers do not separate food security management from environmental management, for they must continuously balance immediate and longer-term needs (cf. Davies and Leach 1991: 43; Hansen 1991). These farmers' integrated perspectives, which reflect livelihood concerns, clash with the approach taken by 'green aid' technocrats who believe that *if only* they could sort out the environment, food security would follow. The approach parallels the faulty 'if only mothers would know' approach in nutrition education (Wheeler 1986). International, even national planners rarely share the more integrated livelihood perspectives of the farmers they claim to serve.

How well-intended 'green aid' objectives may clash with realities on the ground is also well demonstrated in Paul Doughty's analysis of the impact of PL 480 food aid to Peru (Doughty 1986), a country 'rediscovered' by the USA in 1975. A decade after the PL 480 imports began, aiming to support amongst other things the 'greening' of an Andean region, Peru's agricultural production had slumped. The availability of an urban-class diet in the form of wheat foods (noodles, bread) and rice had contributed to a change in cuisine, and hence to a decline in the demand for Andean tubers and other crops (Doughty 1986: 57). This decline contrasted starkly with the conviction of US citizens and government officials that 'assistance provided by PL 480 and similar programs [was] a temporary step on the path towards achieving adequate levels of food production' (Doughty 1986: 49). As with the examples from Sumatra and India, the intervention addressed a worthy environmental goal, but paid little or no attention to how beneficiaries would or could respond.

Just as we need to be careful not to assume that centralized policy regimes impact uniformly (and always for the better), so we need to take care not to overstate the presumed uniform impact of regional cultural conventions. While certain cultural influences have spread over vast regions to determine how social groups and individuals use resources, their impact nonetheless is once again mediated by more specific factors such as locality, class and age. Part of the dynamic is that even well-established norms may come to be challenged when poverty demands it.

In the literature on food and livelihood security, the broadest regional cultural influence considers typologies of 'ideal-typical' household forms. It is customary to suggest a contrast between the more corporate forms of householding, which are centred around the conjugal bond and found in 'a belt of "patriarchy–patriliny–patrilocality" stretching from northern Africa to Bangladesh, across the Middle East and across the northern plains of India', and household systems where the cohesiveness of the conjugal unit is much weaker (Kabeer 1994: 116). The latter are found in the Caribbean, parts of Latin America and in sub-Saharan Africa. This region of weak conjugal cohesion,

Kabeer suggests, contrasts with the patriarchal belt where 'male farming systems' are organized around cultural rules that 'focus on male responsibility for the protection and provisioning of women and children'. Within this belt, 'the practice of female seclusion, patrilineal inheritance and patrilocal residence interlock to produce corporately organized, patriarchal household forms' (Kabeer 1994: 116). The situation, Kabeer argues, differs sharply from sub-Saharan Africa, the region of Boserup's (so-called) female farming systems (Boserup 1970), for which

> the empirical literature suggests the prevalence of non-coterminous units of production, reproduction, consumption or residence and the significance of lineage, rather than conjugal, ties. Here women and men are assigned responsibilities for separate aspects of household provisioning and assigned separate resources to enable them to discharge their obligations. . . . In general, women and men tend to cooperate in producing the obligatory component of collective subsistence needs and to use their residual time to pursue their own-account initiatives. (Kabeer 1994: 116)

While this broad regional contrast has some explanatory value and appeal, one must be careful not to read too much into it. The chief weakness in the contrast is that it is based on a dichotomy, 'female' versus 'male' farming, which is flimsy. The terms are markedly ambiguous. As Whitehead points out, the idea of a 'female' farming system 'does not specify whether women work in agriculture as farmers in their own right, or on farms that belong to others, and notably, of course, on farms that belong to men' (Whitehead 1990b: 437). In view of these ambiguities, it would be misleading to use the broad regional contrast at face value. And yet, the contrast *is* being used as a guiding principle. An example is the assertion that 'in most of sub-Saharan Africa women's responsibilities for a higher proportion of food production, processing and allocation decisions [prevent the high level of] gender discrimination [found in the Indo-Gangetic plain]' (Clay 1997: 26).

Even when this broad focus on sub-Saharan Africa is broken down, as happens when a contrast is made between areas where women have separate farms and accounts (found especially in West Africa) and areas where women's access to resources is more strongly controlled by husbands and senior men (especially in East and Southern Africa), it is still necessary to consider situations on a case-by-case basis. For not only do we find in these sub-regions 'cultural pockets' (for example, matrilineal cultures) that make us want to question the validity of the contrast, we must also consider the possibility that recent decades of economic recession and generalized poverty have produced similarities on both sides of the broad divide. The outcome is that conditions in West Africa, presumed to be more conducive to household food security, can end up looking very similar to those found in the patriarchal belt which stretches from North Africa to Bangladesh. One of Kabeer's own compare-and-contrast exercises suggests quite clearly that a dichotomy based on gender segregation versus no-segregation is limited indeed. The contrast between Bangladesh, where purdah restricts women's work outside the home, and The Gambia where over 70 per cent of women are estimated to be in the labour force and working for their own accounts, may at first appear very significant – but not for long. The initial contrast is as follows. Gambian women have extra-household options, farm along gender-segregated lines and have adequate food intake. There is little evidence of female disadvantage in nutrition and, as noted in at least one study, there is 'greater female advantage in nutritional indicators among children as well as adults (Svedberg, 1988). Estimates from The Gambia [also] show higher female life expectancy than male (35:32 years) [*New Internationalist* 1985], unlike the pattern in Bangladesh and South Asia' (Kabeer 1994: 123). For women in Bangladesh, in contrast, 'there are widespread findings of female disadvantage in basic well-being', as reviewed by Mahmud and Mahmud (1985). Living within the 'belt of patriarchy–patriliny–patrilocality', which restricts their autonomy, Bangladeshi women are nutritionally disadvantaged in almost all age groups, but this is 'particularly marked among women and children from landless households and women who are pregnant and/or lactating' (Kabeer 1994: 122).

    The contrast fades, however, when it is recollected that Gambian women provide around 60 per cent of total energy expended in 'visible' farming activities (Haswell 1981), and that their less visible but routine domestic and child-care activities are 'relentlessly performed even during periods of high energy expenditure in the production of the staple food crop' (Haswell 1981: 17; see also Kabeer 1994: 124). Thus, when workloads and well-being indicators other than nutrition are taken into account, the contrast between Bangladesh and the Gambia virtually disappears. Kabeer appreciates this:

> [the] demands on Gambian women's time and energy show up in forms of female disadvantage which resemble those observed in Bangladesh. In both cases, this disadvantage is concentrated in women's child-bearing years. While Gambian women have a higher life expectancy overall than men, there is marked excess female mortality among women in the reproductive years (15–50). . . . In both countries, maternal mortality rates are extremely high. (Kabeer 1994: 125)

Such marked similarities give us reason to doubt the ultimate relevance of an analytic framework built around the concept of gender segregation in crop production and field work. Moreover, as Kabeer so well demonstrates in relation to the food question in Bangladesh, desperation drives poor women to defy established protocol (Kabeer 1990; see also chapter 4 below).

To conclude, the concept of ideal-type household forms has some explanatory value, not least because it draws attention to the critical importance of appropriability, control and autonomy (Kabeer 1994: 117), yet we need to accept too that real lives are complex and that broad generalizations are severely limited. Specifically, I would advise caution regarding the theory that gender-separate farming is always in the best interest of women's economic security and that of their households. The equation deserves detailed scrutiny, also with an eye for variations 'from door to door' (which may be greater than between 'cultures'), as I will highlight shortly by presenting some of Fairhead's research findings on Bwisha, Congo-Zaire (Fairhead 1990).

Negotiating Responsibility: Gender, Patriarchy and Food Provisioning

While responsibility for food provisioning is a matter of ongoing discussion within households, there are clear signs that women are taking on more and greater responsibilities. Landmarks here are the imposition of (European) war-effort food production quotas (see e.g. Fairhead and Leach 1996: 247–8), and more recently programmes for structural adjustment. But before we jump to grand conclusions – for example that all women everywhere suffer the same fate under SAPs, or that all women in West Africa have comparative advantage – it is instructive to ask exactly how responsibilities and rights are negotiated in 'real' settings. Doing so will also help us better appreciate why the category 'women' needs breaking down.

The following illustrations, from the Gola forest in Sierra Leone (Leach 1991, 1994) and Bwisha in Congo-Zaire (Fairhead 1990), provide the full flavour of how men and women negotiate tasks and expectations as part of an ongoing process. The value of these two ethnographies lies in their demonstrating how *expectations* surrounding food provisioning have in recent times become more ambiguous. Previously embedded in the work routines of large production units, expectations have only recently become more publicly articulated and confronted.

How do such discussions unfold? How do women (and *which women?*) negotiate and strategize to keep households food secure?

Case Study 2.3: Gola Forest Women, Sierra Leone

When food security was still achieved within large, corporate descent groups, contributions to (what we now call) household food security were made through tasks essential to cultivation, not in terms of actual food provisioning. Men initiated the cultivation cycle by clearing land, and allocated farms to wives and junior kinsmen. Once tree crop cultivation became popular, which stimulated the transition to smaller (household) units of production and consumption, many husbands opted out of food farming and 'promised' to purchase rice to compensate for the loss of their labour. Unlike land clearing, however, which is open to public inspection, periodic rice purchases are more private. This has opened the door for new tensions within households.

Already by the late 1960s, it was clear that male contributions were unreliable, sometimes non-existent. Women increasingly needed to get by through reliance on their personal sources and networks. There was still, however, as there is today, agreement between spouses about who should provide what:

> Mende have clear ideas about how certain provisioning responsibilities should be divided. A married man should ensure that his wife/wives and children are provided with staple food, by meeting farm-household production expenses and, as is common today, purchasing supplementary rice. He should provide clothing, by purchasing at least one 'double lappa' of cloth for each wife each year. A husband also expects to take responsibility for long-term investments such as house construction. Wives are expected to provide the sauce, purchasing ingredients such as salt and extra vegetables. They meet expenses associated with their private farming and trading activities . . . and they meet additional expenses associated with their own children. (Leach 1994: 189–90)

While powerful incentives continue to ensure that men mostly meet their obligations, certain responsibilities have nonetheless become ambiguous. The range includes 'relatively new expenditures for which there is little precedent, such as clinic medicines, kerosene and imported consumer goods' (Leach 1994: 190).

Ambiguity is also fostered by the recent shift to buying in small quantities. The result of economic uncertainty and poverty, this shift clouds men's understanding of their own responsibilities. Often hampered by limited cash, men increasingly resort to purchases by cup instead of sack (for rice) or by pint instead of kerosene tin (for oil). In doing so, they may redefine the purchases they make as 'small things', items more appropriate for women to buy (Leach 1994: 190–1). To add to the problem, only a minority of men still work the upland farms where women's intercrops grow best; the supply of sauce ingredients has thus become less certain (Leach 1994: 95).

In today's uncertain times, food shortfalls are increasingly made up from resources that women control. As was borne out also in the case of Ma Cousine in Kinshasa, Gola women must now secure *additional income* to ensure adequate supplies of food and other necessities. One standard way for raising this additional income is by selling intercrops (various leaves and vegetables) in the village. Women also use networks of kin and friends, and join savings groups and credit schemes, to meet pressing consumption needs. Women may thus 'build up the number of favours owed to them, "investing" in the network, by repeatedly giving to or doing things for other women, so that they are well placed to call in their debts when they need a particular item' (Leach 1994: 198). Young wives not in polygynous households often receive little and are therefore most concerned to retain ties with their natal kin for security. Women may also resort to 'covert' strategies. These include the discrete appropriation of coffee and cocoa from the farms of husbands and male kin, on which women labour for no or little reward, and receiving small but repeated gifts from lovers (Leach 1994: 198).

To remain in control of supplies and achieve basic food security, Gola women must activate a full range of strategies. Older women with grown-up children are best placed to make the most of the opportunities networks provide.

The Gola ethnography points to a real-life contradiction which warrants further reflection. The contradiction is this: while the discrete appropriations of coffee and cocoa confirm that women involved in shared production have difficulty obtaining their fair share of benefits, it is hard to be optimistic about the process of gender segregation which has developed within *food crop* production in Gola.

What is the hypothesis? Gender segregation in production and accounting, it has been suggested, enhances women's ability to control the proceeds of their labour, which in turn enhances the possibility of achieving household food security (Kabeer 1994: 118). Research which backs the thesis includes Whitehead's pioneering work among the Kusasi of north-east Ghana – where there are 'household' fields as well as 'independent' fields for men and women (Whitehead 1981), and where household heads *have the obligation to ensure that granaries are filled* – and research by Jones (1985, 1986) among the Massa in Cameroon, which 'suggests that segregation occurred by field rather than by crop. [Here too,] *both men and women were expected to contribute* to household supplies of red sorghum, the main staple' (Kabeer 1994: 119, emphasis added).

These ethnographies from West Africa show that benefits accrue to gender-segregated production and accounting; there is no quarrel with that. But the two studies also draw attention to the existence of expectations and obligations that are *actually* fulfilled. In other words, both studies suggest that the focus of enquiry must go beyond the rather technical issue of whether men and women share or segregate their crops and fields. Put differently, it is feasible that *what matters is not so much whether segregation occurs, but whether men and women are willing and still able to honour existing expectations.* It is exactly on the issue of 'willingness and ability' that uncertainties and ambiguities are now increasingly in evidence. Gender-shared work, moreover, as Fairhead's Bwisha case material shows, is not inherently bad for women's economic security. Whether it is bad, and how bad, depends on the quality of the 'conjugal contract' (cf. Whitehead 1981), and these contracts are dynamic. It seems prudent therefore to add a proviso to Kabeer's hypothesis: gender-segregated production arrangements in agriculture can boost the household food supply *provided that men and women continue to honour expectations that remain clear-cut.* The question today is whether such expectations survive.

The final case study, then, adds further context to the question of whether gender segregation in production (and/or trade) enhances household food security. The emphasis this time is on how women and men negotiate cooperation. Far from being a technical issue, negotiations reflect the importance of, amongst other things, poverty and bridewealth.

Case Study 2.4: Farming in Bwisha, Eastern Congo-Zaire

When in the late 1970s Bwisha men and women began to grow surplus food for their own accounts, social analysts began to view households as 'battlefields' where spouses quarrelled because of money (e.g. Schoepf and Schoepf 1988: 118). Beans, the supreme cash crop, were at the centre of these quarrels. Bean production had speeded up agricultural intensification and encouraged a more individuated approach to agriculture. The situation seemed clear-cut: men sought lump-sum profits; women sought to keep their households food-secure.

This dichotomy based on gender detracted, however, from the important distinction Bwisha people made between 'cooperating' and 'non-cooperating' households: couples who could still 'hear and listen to each other' in a relationship of mutual trust and respect, and those who could no longer do so (Fairhead 1990: 199). The distinction lives on. Cooperation, as Fairhead uses the term, does not mean that women and men pool and share resources indiscriminately, or that there is a common household budget. What 'cooperation' refers to is that generalized but hard-to-define way in which conflicting interests are resolved to a couple's mutual benefit (Fairhead 1990: 199). Such cooperation is more difficult to maintain when a household is or becomes poor.

How gender roles are created and recreated, and whether gender segregation necessarily means better household food security, can be inferred from arrangements for intercropping. Let us look at how these are negotiated for the coffee-(bush)bean association, which in the lowlands works well ecologically and financially (Fairhead1990: 229–32). The 'catch' in these arrangements is a social one: the issue arises whether men, who control coffee, and women, who control beans, can agree to work together. (Fairhead observes likewise for banana–bean intercropping arrangements, where men and women again have separate interests.) Since women from non-cooperating households rarely benefit from their husbands' coffee, many are antagonistic towards the association. Crop association – which leads to fuller 'separate purses' for both spouses – is achieved only where there is a degree of harmony, where spouses 'understand each other'. (This does not mean that non-cooperating husbands who know about the ecological advantages of intercropping with beans would not try to promote it by coercion. They do. And women do find refusal difficult indeed.) The general point, though, is this: gender-shared work patterns do not necessarily imply that women must lose out. It is the 'how well they get on' factor which determines how much each of the spouses stands to benefit or lose. And 'how well they get on' depends on the status of their conjugal contract. The implication is that we need to look beyond the technicality of the gender-shared /gender-segregated framework and ask questions about the ever-evolving nature of a given marital relationship and of the *sources of power* that determine it.

For Bwisha, we must therefore ask questions about land and bridewealth; two sources of power at the heart of every bargaining exercise. Non-cooperating husbands in Bwisha are mostly young, recently married and poor; they have either not yet inherited any land or never will. Moreover, being poor, they are unlikely to have married with bridewealth, which means that their control of the labour of their wives is reduced. Because of this reduced leverage, such men are particularly keen (that is, sufficiently desperate) to grow food as a cash crop they control; they do not cooperate with their wives to achieve a smooth food supply for household consumption, but will instead grow focused crops, mainly beans, for their own financial benefit (Fairhead 1990: 246). When this kind of sex segregation occurs, both parties forgo the ecological and financial benefits that accrue from intercropping.

In sum, the segregated–shared dichotomy is too simplistic for the Bwisha scene. As the practice of intercropping coffee and beans shows, sharing is financially profitable to women *provided their conjugal contract is based on trust and cooperation*. Where trust and cooperation are absent, and because they do not own land, women cannot profit (apart from discrete gleaning) and their households will suffer more hunger.

Having questioned the usefulness of one broad framework, I must now point to a generalization which does hold. Even when there is understanding between spouses, women in Bwisha must use new strategies to optimize their control of the household food supply, as nowadays 'the market eats too much'. Times may be getting harder, as in the Gola Forest, but this has not resulted in men taking on any extra responsibilities for household food provisioning. Men do recognize some personal responsibility, but only when 'the hunger bites hard'. Not surprisingly, women and men now argue about how hard times 'really' have become.

Conclusion

The 1996 World Food Summit acknowledged uncertainty regarding the variables that determine nutritional status and health, but reconfirmed that food insecurity ultimately derives from poverty. Summit delegates also promised to pay more attention to how food-insecure people – a category in need of deconstruction – perceive their insecurity.

These good intentions, however, have emerged within a policy environment which is not well equipped to respond to social complexities. This environment has a strong tendency to simplify matters, for example through the use of catch-all terms and phrases, and technical solutions. This is likely to continue, as the solutions proposed in Rome indicate. And yet, as this chapter shows, ordinary people's lives are mostly far from simple, but complex and ever-evolving. Regarding food provisioning, all of the ethnographies reviewed indicate that responsibilities are not fixed, that they are instead negotiated and renegotiated as political and economic circumstances change.

In this respect, the Bwisha and Gola ethnographies suggest that future discussions of gender responsibilities in food provisioning will benefit from a clearer focus on male economic uncertainty and impoverishment (cf. also Kabeer 1990; Kandiyoti 1990; Pottier 1994a). The situation is potentially explosive. Many young married men, for example, now experience how their economic weakness results in more economic independence for their wives, a situation they find threatening. Consequently, they strive to hang on to the patriarchal values and forms of authority derived in part from their past economic power. Kandiyoti's analysis of the impact of modern farming in Turkey corroborates the concern by warning that any decrease in patriarchal control is likely to be superseded by novel forms of exploitation (Kandiyoti 1990: 187, 189).

Women's adjustments are sometimes subtle and hardly visible, as when the layout of fields is slowly altered, while under different circumstances they may be forced to break with conventions (Kabeer 1990; Mbilinyi 1990). (These adaptive responses are discussed in chapters 4 and 5 below.) But, and this is important, despite all the investments women make (for example, investing in personal and lineage networks; investing in trade), they/we rarely manage to increase their own economic security and that of their households. Moreover, women who have secured space for own-account farming and trading are not necessarily getting the best deal; they still face the prospect that they must play 'the market' well, which is exceedingly difficult in terms of time management (see Gerke 1992, disscussed in chapter 4 below). The pitfalls of the market, along with the obstacles raised by men who cling to the privileges of patriarchy, make it very clear that the benefits women gain from gender-segregated activity do not automatically translate into better economic and food security. How difficult it is for women to *openly* challenge the strategies of the men who have authority over them was seen clearly in the story of Ma Cousine (see also Kabeer 1990, discussed in Chapter 4).

Ambiguities over roles and expectations are on the increase. Understanding these ambiguities – why they arise, how they are resolved – should be key to all future research on household food security. Discussing technical aspects of food security and trade is unrealistic when the debate remains divorced from an understanding of the actual logic on which gender roles are continuously negotiated.

Despite admitting to uncertainties, delegates at the 1996 Food Summit in Rome steered well clear of these complicated but crucial processes. Perhaps this reflects what an IFPRI briefing paper prepared for the Beijing Conference on Women concluded, namely that the positive impact of women's contribution to household (and national) food security, along with women's struggles to absorb shocks to household welfare, still goes formally unrecognized (Brown et al. 1995). The authors urged policy-makers to act to reduce asymmetries between men and women in access to agricultural and other resources. Such asymmetries, however, as this chapter has made clear, exist in fluid social worlds that can only be grasped through detailed empirical research. These fluid worlds, in which smallholders must value land and organize labour, are explored further in the next two chapters.

Also in need of recognition and correction is the asymmetry which exists within agricultural policies and research. This asymmetry favours elite crops over the crops poor people grow and consume, for example, wheat over sorghum in India (Harriss 1988: 164) or vegetables and animal feed (sorghum) over local beans and maize in Mexico (DeWalt and Barkin 1991: 36–8). A basic reorientation in agricultural research priorities is therefore required. Østergaard (1992) puts the challenge thus: 'Incorporating nutritional concerns explicitly into rural programmes would greatly increase the benefits of agricultural planning and could neutralize its possible negative effects' (Østergaard 1992: 115).

Likewise, DeWalt and Barkin argue that: 'Government and donor agency policies need to be redirected to focus on the kinds of commodities that are produced and, more importantly, on the kinds of producers who will produce them. More availability will not mean much to rural and urban poor who cannot afford to purchase the food' (DeWalt and Barkin 1991: 37).

In theory, it's simple and easy to implement; in practice, it's a good deal more difficult. Major obstacles exist in the powerful international grain lobby, which has no interest in solving nutrition problems (see chapters 6–8), and, at more local levels, in power struggles within households and beyond.

3

Land and Livelihood
Land Ownership, Access, Reform and Research Responsibilities

In the food security projects reviewed in chapter 2, it was their inability to access irrigated land that excluded resource-poor, politically weak farmers. For the 'green aid' project in India, exclusion was a question of *local politics* – and something could have been done *locally*, through grain banks, to ensure poor people's participation. Land was also mentioned at the 1996 World Food Summit, where countries like India and Bangladesh were said not to have enough land. The Rome reference to land, however, implied that local politics was not much of an issue. Conference delegates pinned their hopes on *technical solutions*: improved agriculture and population control.

The subordination of substantive issues (access to land; the value of human life) to technical considerations (improved seed; population control techniques) is typical of the institutional language of development. This language works as a powerful representational field and differs from locally situated languages that express everyday experience. The Rome reference to land, couched in aggregate neutral terms, suggests there is truth in the claim that institutional languages of development are 'in crisis when ethnographized' (Arce 1999).

It is legitimate, therefore, to ask how important land is, still is, in people's quest for food security. More precisely, we ask how land is viewed and talked about in situated languages. Do ownership and access still matter to the food-insecure or are there acceptable alternatives? Does variation exist, spatially and socially? My asking these questions, my interest in the diversity of the experience of modernity (not just regarding land, but also, in later chapters, regarding labour, food markets, food aid and agricultural intervention) reflects the now well-established view that non-Western worlds must not be regarded as passively subjected to the imperial gaze of Western developers (Kandiyoti 1999; Long and Long 1992). What analysts must do instead, as Kandiyoti makes clear, is to pursue the idea of 'a splintering of hegemony, with seemingly contradictory features of both greater homogeneity and interconnectedness and counter-trends of fragmentation and particularism' (Kandiyoti 1999).

While the awareness that paradox is inherent in modernizing encounters has yet to inform mainstream research on food security, anthropologists have for some time now shown that modernization projects do not produce homogenous results. The upland farmers in the two Kerinci villages discussed in the previous chapter exemplify this. But new evidence is also coming to light. For instance, as the ethnography of collective farming in the former Soviet Union now shows, the USSR's modernity project – collectivization – never impacted with a high degree of uniformity. The grand project did not result in a dramatic undercutting of 'local' social relations, but rather strengthened and sometimes created 'various forms of parochialism and ethnic consciousness' (Kandiyoti 1999). Pre-Soviet forms of organization, moreover, colonized Soviet institutions, thus forcing the conquering Soviet system to adjust internally.

In this chapter and the next, we ask what impact the 'global' forces of commercialization and 'modern' agriculture have had on communities that allegedly used to achieve food sufficiency. (I say 'allegedly', because the achievement is sometimes merely assumed; the product of an imagined, mythical and 'merrie' pre-colonial past, as Watts (1983: 78–9) has argued for Africa.) Free-market style or communist, 'modern' agriculture *has* impacted on land ownership, access and use, but the question is: to what extent? Taking land as its focus, this chapter asks about the nature of contemporary transactions in land. Are resource-poor farmers losing land because of commercialized agriculture? Are they also losing rights of access to land they do not own? Is this happening everywhere or are there regional differences, instances, for example, where the power of territorial kinship groups has prevented land alienation? What is the gender dimension to access and ownership? How are local responses to (possible) alienation structured? And how effective are national programmes for land reform in re-establishing lost rights?

The extent to which (so-called) local communities have themselves impacted upon (so-called) global forces that affect them is outside the scope of this and the next chapter, but the issue will be addressed in the discussion on agricultural research and intervention (chapter 8). The section which now follows presents an overview of 'global' forces and considers their impact on the ability of smallholders to control and access land.

Colonialism, Commercialization and New Technology: Broad Trends

The broad politico-economic regimes that affect the lives of small-holder farmers are rooted in colonialism. For Africa, the roots lie in the European colonists' need to make the conquest of the continent pay for itself. To finance the conquest, four types of political economy emerged as solutions. First analysed by Samir Amin (1976), the typology remains useful for explaining why certain land allocations and production practices exist. Jonathan Barker (1989) summarizes the four dominant solutions as: the production of taxable export crops by peasant farmers (especially in West Africa and Uganda); settler agriculture (throughout Africa, but especially in Kenya and Rhodesia, now Zimbabwe); plantations run by transnational firms; and the creation of labour reserves (Barker 1989: 81–4). This broad framework, however, is today, as it was in the past, no more than a crude approximation of reality, since most colonies and post-colonial states have attempted to combine solutions. The result, as Sara Berry acknowledges in her longitudinal review of four contrasting rural economies (Berry 1993), was that the impact of agricultural commercialization became diverse. Variation existed both in the pace of production increases for sale and in the terms on which Africans participated (Berry 1993: 100).

Nonetheless, it is widely agreed that the overall impact of commercialization has been to make farmers less secure, less self-sufficient in food and farm inputs, more dependent on external assistance. Despite a myriad local adjustments to the colonial 'solutions' imposed on Africa, food security in many households has turned problematic. For many analysts, the pre-colonial past appears to have been much more secure, since farming practices were regulated through institutionalized means that could be controlled locally. Practices included the use of drought-resistant crops and various intercropping techniques, established use-rights in land, and the regulatory role of religion (Barker 1989: 63; Raikes 1988: 92). Rarely owned in the Western sense of having exclusive rights in exchange for cash, land was an economic resource to which people had use-rights, along with the 'obligation to use [it] wisely for the good of the community on behalf of the ancestors who were often perceived as its spiritual guardians' (Davison 1988: 10–11).

Colonialism and commercialization made practices of land occupancy more exclusive, disinvested women of their rights, altered the deployment of household labour, and caused inter-generational and gender conflicts. Before commoditization, women's control of and access to land was much better defined and respected than it is today, as was women's control of the crops they grew (Davison 1988: 13). Today, instances where African women control land are not so frequent, though they are found in West Africa and, provided certain conditions prevail, in the 'matrilineal belts', for instance, of Central Africa (Poewe 1979), parts of India (Agarwal 1994a) and Minangkabau, Sumatra, where women inherit ancestral rice land directly from their mothers (Kahn 1980: 53). The broader issue here is that colonial states have played 'a role not just in regulating people's lives but in defining gender ideologies, conceptions of "femininity" and "masculinity", [thus] determining ideas about what sorts of persons women and men should be' (Moore 1988: 129). Creating societal agreement about the kinds of people there ought to be is indeed one of the chief projects of the modern, post-Enlightenment state (Nagengast 1994: 109). In Africa, as elsewhere, colonial state bureaucracies introduced policies and legislation that disadvantaged women (Agarwal 1994a; Whitehead 1990b: 443).

Taxation *in cash* was a major instrument for dislocation. The transformation of grain-based tax systems into cash payments resulted in labour migration and export crop production and, at the communal level, undermined the authority structure. Pottier and Fairhead (1991) document this process for highland Bwisha, Congo-Zaire, where land in the 1920s was controlled by the heads of residential clans. Economically and ritually powerful, these heads solicited ancestral favours to ensure good crop and human fertility. Several decades later, the authority system crumbled. Heads saw their religious power undermined by missionary zeal (Catholic, Protestant and Islamic), while their economic authority waned because of the availability of alternatives to food farming – wage work in local plantations and, later, opportunities for migrant labour in Uganda. Under pressure, clan centredness, which had sustained large landholdings, gave way to a structure of nuclear-type families, each with small landholdings that would ever fragment. The next phase in this secularization process came when the state claimed ownership of all land and alienated it to plantations. (Such state intervention occurred throughout most of sub-Saharan Africa, mainly around independence.)

The collapse of, or threat to, religious practices that once ensured fairly egalitarian access to sustainably managed natural resources has been observed also for other parts of the world. Van der Ploeg (1990) and Salas (1994) highlight this for Andean potato farmers. Before 'improved' farming techniques became available, Andean farmers intercropped to maintain good soil fertility, had advanced drainage systems, and practised terracing to prevent leaching and nutrient losses. They also used social networks to exchange genetic stock from which new cultivars were selected (van der Ploeg 1990: 186–7). This dynamic technical approach is/was interwoven with a spiritual devotion to Mamapacha (Nature). Andean farming knowledge and practice are premised on the notion that humans and nature were interdependent. As Salas explains,

> Nature (*Mamapacha*) is not a dominating force nor is she dominated by the community of humans. There is an interdependency of both, descending from the cosmological order, so that the relationship between nature and society is not only of equality, but also assumes religious character. Nothing is just profane or just utilitarian in the Andean culture. (Salas 1994: 61)

Importantly, agricultural practices and knowledge were localized and socially constructed. Embedded in local livelihoods and cosmologies, Andean knowledge about farming was thus 'as diverse as the ecological conditions which [varied] from village to village, from hill to hill' (Salas 1994: 62). It makes sense, therefore, to speak of knowledges (plural!). For both van der Ploeg and Salas, the threat posed by the 'scientific potato', the chief catalyst in commoditization, is such that it has led to serious displacement of local practices and irreversible loss of diversity, flexibility and security (see chapter 6 for details).

Stephen Lansing's study of terrace ecosystems in Bali also reveals the centrality of belief and ritual in land access and management (Lansing 1987, 1991). Given the crucial importance of timing in rice fields, Lansing shows for the district of Ganyar how the *nyungsung* rice ritual optimizes the availability of rainfall and sunshine for the first rice crop. The ceremony ensures that the harvest falls inside the dry season and that pest populations are minimized (Lansing 1987: 329–30). Timing the first rice crop to perfection – a crop which has good taste and is life-sustaining – also ensures optimal conditions for the second, short-maturing rice crop. At the highest level, coordination is achieved through the main annual festival at Pura Ulun Danu Batur, Bali's supreme water temple. As in the Andes, in Bali too social analysts claim that the balanced approach to farming is threatened by the presence of commercial markets for hi-tech agriculture and by the availability of alternative knowledge/authority regimes. As it undermines both farming ways and authority structures, the process is not dissimilar to what happened in Africa once cash crop production got under way.

We must be careful, however, not to regard these colonial processes as always having had a negative impact on local authority structures. Sometimes, just like Kandiyoti (1998) shows for the Soviet East, new economic opportunities had the opposite effect of strengthening 'local' authority, economically and ritually. Labour migration in the Mambwe region of northern Zambia, for instance, resulted in the emergence of village-based agricultural work-parties that boosted the authority of local chiefs and headmen (Pottier 1988: 165; Watson 1958: 108). Similarly, chiefs in the adjacent Bemba-speaking area worked with colonial administrators and missionaries, and later with social and natural scientists, to produce a concept of Bemba ethnicity bound up with both a mode of production and a chiefly system (Moore and Vaughan 1994: 19). In Rwanda as well, in the early decades of the twentieth century, colonial administrators consolidated their grip on the colony by boosting the political, economic and ritual authority of an influential ruling house, the *nyiginya* (Tutsi) dynasty, engaged in military conquest. Such examples caution that the extent to which local political and economic systems were eroded in colonial Africa must not be exaggerated. While the commercialization of agriculture, along with migration, may have eroded the economic power base of numerous large production groupings, there is evidence too of countervailing tendencies whereby Europeans established or reinforced 'local' authority over land. (This explains the problematic nature of the term 'local'.)

This mixed picture of 'global' change and bottom-up manoeuvring is one reason why Sara Berry (1993) is optimistic that group and individual claims to land in Africa have stayed open to interpretation. The commercialization of land transactions in modern times, Berry shows in her review, did not erode the pre-colonial processes of political manoeuvring and negotiation. On the contrary, struggles over land, as over the interpretation of 'custom', have intensified and are not necessarily a source of insecurity, at least not at the level of group claims. This is so, Berry suggests, because contradictory pressures have slowed down the process of land alienation. The chief contradiction is between rising land values and exclusive forms of land control, on the one hand, and, on the other, the largesse of politicians whose stay in power depends on their mustering popular support. The need to build up a political following mitigates against exclusive land rights. 'Because of these contradictory pressures, claims over land have tended to multiply over time' (Berry 1993: 104).

The often made assumption that rights in land consolidate in the face of commercialization, as happened in South and South-East Asia, has not materialized in Africa on a significant scale. Parker Shipton writes along the same lines. Contestation is ongoing: 'custom and tradition about land and other things ... [are] inventable, manipulable, renegotiable, and selectively invoked to serve personal ends' (Shipton 1994: 351). A valued illustration of how 'contradictory pressures' have prevented land alienation is David Parkin's classic study of Kaloleni, a Giriama community near the Kenya coast (Parkin 1972). Kaloleni's successful entrepreneurs invested heavily 'in tradition' (for example in funerals and weddings) to enlist the support of elders who could testify on their behalf in any disputes over rights to land and palm trees. The deference entrepreneurs paid to elders was not a dying remnant from the past, but an integral part of the new situation.

This is not to suggest that land alienation in Africa does not exist or that every contestation is resolved for the common good. Some recent contestations have been very violent indeed, particularly when linked to the creation and maintenance of racial or ethnic difference. Shipton reminds us that intersettled land has been the reason for ethnic cleansing pogroms. 'Often, as lately among Moors and Fulani or Toucouleur in Mauritania, or between Kalenjin and Kikuyu (and others) in Kenya, these disputes involve land long ago lent or granted – the oral histories usually clash on this point – and now, under changed conditions, wanted back' (Shipton 1994: 364). One of Central Africa's most striking outbreaks of violence against those who were granted land 'long ago' was the killing in 1993 of several thousand Banyarwanda – Hutu and Tutsi – who lived in Kivu, eastern Congo-Zaire. They died at the hands of militias controlled by so-called 'autochthonous' groups whose erstwhile leaders had granted the land rights under colonial rule (Pottier 1998).

South Africa is another poignant example of how 'race and ethnicity, like land tenure, are about arbitrary cognitive classification and exaggerated difference' (Shipton 1994: 363), as are Zimbabwe, Kenya, New Zealand and the USA. Independence rarely changed anything. Thus, in Kenya, where an African bureaucratic elite replaced most of the large-scale colonial farmers, '[the] nineteenth and early twentieth century processes that tended to put the lighter skins in control of the darker soils, and vice versa, have been only partly reversed by spontaneous squatting and voluntary, state-run resettlement programmes. . . . Still less have these processes been alleviated in Zimbabwe' (Shipton 1994: 363–4). Zimbabwe's lingering problem surfaced dramatically in early 1998, when seventeen years of unfulfilled government promises regarding land reform and resettlement, coupled with corruption accusations and rising food prices, brought riots to the streets of Harare.

Despite these violent clashes over land, Berry's generalization that a principle of 'contradictory pressures' operates *within* groups does appear to hold. The result is that landlessness remains a less than common phenomenon in sub-Saharan Africa; a situation which contrasts starkly with those parts of Asia where commerce, commoditization and class formation took root several centuries ago.

Commercialization under feudal-type conditions (South and South-East Asia), communism (East Asia) and the emergence of 'improved' agricultural technologies (everywhere) are prevalent forces in agrarian change in Asia, and have affected people's rights in land. Empirical research, however, is concentrated mostly in South and South-East Asia where landlessness was well established by the beginning of the twent-ieth century. Later on, with the arrival of the so-called 'Green Revol-ution' (GR) in the 1960s, the incidence of landlessness grew again. In East Asia in contrast, and China especially, landlessness has not emerged as a serious issue.

Processes of class differentiation in South and South-East Asia are regularly traced back to the late eighteenth century. For instance, in their historical study of a village in north-central Java, Hüsken and White (1989) insist that to view Java as homogeneous until the advent of the GR is to ignore the three-tiered hierarchy already in place some 200 years ago. On the basis of the study, Hüsken and White refute the long-held view that the commercial and technological innovations in rice production of the 1960s and 1970s would have provoked *new forms* of social differentiation (cf. Geertz 1963; Palmer 1976). According to Palmer, commerce and technology had engendered schisms 'between (a) farmers, on the one hand, and landless laborers and very small owner-cultivators on the other, and (b) between those landless laborers who are offered . . . limited work at any time and those who are unable to share in job opportunities' (Palmer 1976: 24; quoted in Hüsken and White 1989: 237). While Palmer's observation has value in that it reflects an acceleration of ongoing social processes, it would be erroneous, say Hüsken and White, to regard the schisms as new forms of differentiation. It was not the GR that introduced rural capit-alism to Java and ended 'involution' (1989: 236).

The roots of social differentiation in rural Thailand can also be traced to times long gone, to before 1782, when a distinction between com-moners and serfs on the one hand, and ruling nobles on the other, already existed (Hirsch 1990). Again, the GR did not 'provoke' this social differentiation, but built upon it and multiplied the divisions. It is necessary therefore, Hirsch argues, to move away from the notion that class formation has left contemporary rural society 'polarized'. The notion is too simplistic, because contemporary local classifications go beyond the question of land ownership to take account of employ-ment and income levels (Hirsch 1990: 27; also Anan 1984: 409–11). The change suggests that off-farm, income-generating activities may act as worthy alternatives to working the land; a possibility consid-ered in the next section.

The contention that class difference and landlessness have been in existence for centuries must not detract, however, from the fact that landlessness accelerated in the wake of GR-related indebtedness; selling off land being a common way out for indebted peasants who had no other means of raising cash. Sometimes, though, the 'sale' remained within the family – only to result in new debts for the younger generation. Hirsch recalls situations in which adult children bought land from parents who could not afford to let them inherit. To raise money towards the purchase, these children often had to borrow themselves, so the cycle of indebtedness continued (Hirsch 1990: 97).

Inter-class land transfers, whereby absentee landowners increase the amounts of land they already control, are also a modern feature of the Philippines, where the extent of the problem of landlessness was starkly exposed in a census in 1970. The census showed that 'over 60 per cent of all rice farmers were tenants nationally and over 80 per cent in the Central Luzon ricebowl adjacent to Manila' (Fegan 1989: 130). The land reforms which President Marcos had launched in the 1960s, only to halt them abruptly, had done little to alleviate the plight of landless sharecroppers. While the reforms enabled some tenant grain farmers to purchase land rights, their number was offset by the many non-grain smallholders who lost their land in the same decade (Fegan 1989: 133–4). Big landowners, on the other hand, never suffered any serious losses as they found ways around the reform laws.

In India too, with some exceptions (for example Kerala State, see below), small farmers have rarely benefited from land reform. Aiming broadly to eradicate absentee ownership and improve the conditions of small tenants, India's 1947 reform programme imposed ceilings on land ownership and attempted to fix fair rents (Sen 1982: 32). But very little changed in reality. Absentee landlords again found loopholes to avoid being affected, sometimes retaining their land by having it looked after by relatives or friends. This happened especially in the advanced GR regions. The reforms did remove some large absentee landowners, but benefited mostly the richer farmers and larger tenants who expanded their holdings and shook off excessive rents (Sen 1982: 32). Small tenant farmers, on the other hand, usually lost out. After investing unsuccessfully in costly, 'improved' farming methods, small tenants were regularly pushed out of agriculture and into the casual labour market (see chapter 4).

The problem that smallholders in South and South-East Asia struggle with and may lose their land as a result of – the high cost of GR technology – remains relatively unknown in China, possibly Vietnam too, where landlessness has not developed to the same degree. Despite the changes in food production strategy introduced after Mao, land in China continues to be collectively owned and is only distributed to households for use (Croll 1983b: 469; also Bramall 1995). This does not mean that there are no production problems, but they have more to do with the deployment of labour than with access to land.

In Vietnam, food production is still governed by efficient cooperation on smallholdings rather than by the extensive recruitment of landless wage workers. The country's recent decollectivization drive and transition to a free-market economy ('Doi Moi'), however, mark the return to more skewed patterns of natural resource distribution, even though the decollectivized land, previously cultivated on a cooperative basis, was initially redistributed equitably according to household size (Le Thi Nham Tuyet 1985: 213; Statistical Publishing House 1995: 182). Pre-colonial, 'traditional' village life in Vietnam was never overly egalitarian or harmonious; a point which even James Scott (1976) insisted on when outlining the importance of a village subsistence ethic with strong moral arrangements (see Salemink 1998 on the debate between Scott and Popkin, 1979). Today, disparities in food-production trends are re-emerging by region and within regions; class and ethnicity are two factors in this. The withdrawal of services previously guaranteed through the cooperative system, especially the distribution of seeds and fertilizers, implies that households now need to organize on a more individual basis if they are to access these inputs. Access, moreover, depends on the smooth operation of markets, something no longer guaranteed for Vietnam's remoter regions.

Green Revolution Technologies: The Need for a Political Framework

Before we look at detailed, situated studies of land distribution and access, let us be clear about the main technical features of the GR. It can be said, but at the risk of oversimplification, that the 'typical' pre-GR farm ensured its own production and reproduction. Seed used to be carried over from one harvest to the next, fertilizer was derived from cattle manure, disease and pests were controlled by cropping strategies. Irrigation, if practised, was on a small scale and with the help of water tanks and canals (Sen 1982: 33). The Green Revolution ended these self-reliant practices. The promise of higher yields through 'improved' seed strains (HYVs) meant that seed now had to be renewed through purchase, at the heart of which lay a transnational trade in genetic materials. Thus, in the Punjab village Murray Leaf studied, the wheat strains that replaced the local *desi* wheat were 'based on the combination of genetic material of Mexican dwarf varieties with local taller varieties' (Leaf 1983: 232). Further costs related to pest control and the acquisition of pump-sets and tubewells. Sophisticated and expensive, these inputs imposed an unprecedented dependence on formal institutions, for example new information networks (research and extension, farmers' associations), credit institutions (cooperatives, banks), new market outlets (cooperatives, marketing boards) and water-users' associations (White 1985: 123). The institutionalization of inputs and credit led to a restructuring of gender relations, as women often lost access to resources and property rights. The role of advanced technology in the restructuring of gender relations is detailed in the next chapter.

Aware of the high cost of GR technology, many governments at first attempted to restrict access to the better-resourced, politically more influential farmers. Indian officials, for example, argued that it was more difficult for small farmers to profit from the new technology. In reality, though, and depending on the crop grown, smallholders often became keen participants. Thus, in India's wheat-growing zone many farmers adopted at least some of the new inputs (HYV seeds, fertilizer, irrigation) as 'improved' strains were fairly hardy and responded well to even small doses of fertilizer.

Empirically informed social analysts know that the adoption of 'improved' technology needs to be placed firmly within a political framework. Hart, Turton and White are explicit on this point and insist we take 'account of the power structures within which technological change and commercialization occur' (Hart et al. 1989: 2). They take issue with perspectives that explain agrarian differentiation solely in terms of technological peculiarities (e.g. Bray 1983, 1986; Hayami and Kikuchi 1982).[1] One reason for insisting on an explicit political framework is that government interest in 'improved' farming technology often originates in political uncertainty. Take Suharto's 'New Order' regime in Indonesia, for example, which turned to hi-tech agriculture to strengthen the political agenda. Raking in substantial international grants and loans, and benefiting hugely from the OPEC windfall of 1974, Suharto commanded a partnership with farmers, large-scale and small, whereby farmers received costly inputs. Subsidization was stepped up after the disastrous 1972–3 harvests (Hüsken and White 1989: 252), but at the expense of dropping the land reform laws initiated by former President Sukarno. From then on, 'any efforts to protest against illegal attempts to expropriate land [were] in general ruthlessly suppressed' (1989: 249). Paradoxically though, this ruthless political oppression did not mean that food production levels could be allowed to drop. Suharto's 'New Order' regime recognized the importance of basic food availability and reasonable prices *for its own survival*.[2] Not surprisingly, the national rice campaign was carried through irrespective of the damage it

inflicted on non-rice-based production systems (see e.g. Persoon 1992).
Secure staple food for all is a powerful political tool in streamlining
populations.

The modernization of paddy rice production and land use followed
a similar path in Thailand, where the official interest in hi-tech farming again set in after political unrest and insurgency threatened the
political order. As Anan shows for the northern Thai village of Ban
San Pong, problems of tenancy and landlessness were rife there in the
1960s, then aggravated under the 'growing contradictions in intensive
commercial production that turned many bankrupt small landowners
into tenants' (Anan 1989: 99). The ensuing conflict, which led to an
increased sense of urgency regarding social gaps (Hirsch 1990: 22),
made Thai leaders realize that better-yielding, high-input agriculture
could become an effective weapon in quelling political unrest. State-
led rural development programmes thus 'concentrated on potential
trouble spots for the government, mainly in the north-east under the
United States-backed Accelerated Rural Development scheme' (Hirsch
1990: 21).

Unlike in Indonesia, however, where a totalitarian state ensured basic
food security for the great majority of its population, GR farming in
Thailand did not ease smallholders' economic insecurity. Unsubsidized
and putting a premium on borrowing, modern farming became congruent with small farmers 'going under' and losing their land. Institutional credit hindered more than it helped. The pattern was similar to
that in India, where a vast number of poor rice-growers got 'the push'
when opportunities for semi-permanent male labour dried up. This
stagnation made many poor but landholding farmers so acutely indebted to landholders that they ended up forfeiting their lands (Harriss
1977).

To understand how wider political and economic forces have contributed to agrarian change, it is necessary to adopt a framework that
focuses simultaneously on global occurrences (for example the availability of international capital, scientific agricultural research) and the
local variables with which they interact (for example political systems
of patronage, debt levels). Within such an integrated framework,
straightforward transitions, for example towards full land alienation
or full polarization, mostly turn out to be too simplistic to reflect
realities on the ground accurately. Benjamin White (1989) makes the
point in his excellent summary of contemporary analyses of agrarian
change in South-East Asia. Two contrasting approaches are common,
he argues, both justifiable but only when applied together. The first
argues that peasant farmers live in a strictly polarized, capitalist world,
where they invariably lose their land and livelihood. The second takes
a stance against polarization and asks 'why so many millions of house-

holds manage to hang on to tiny farms and resist the process of polarization . . .' (White 1989: 29). White resolves the dilemma, much like
Kandiyoti and Berry do for the former USSR and Africa respectively,
by pointing out that the two approaches reflect opposed yet coexisting
tendencies; they are not mutually exclusive. When considered simultaneously, the two bring to light 'the sheer complexity of the forms which
differentiation takes' (White 1989: 29).

More specifically, White (1989) objects to the reductionist suggestion that polarization in South-East Asia's wet-rice economies would
have emerged because 'impersonal market relations' replaced 'traditional moral principles' (Hayami and Kikuchi 1982: 60). Hayami and
Kikuchi accept that multi-stranded personalized relations persist, but
regard them as dying a slow death. White, in contrast, shows that
polarizing tendencies and personalized (moral) relations can and do
coexist. The latter are not remnants of a 'traditional' past, but essential to differentiation (White 1989: 24; see also Arce and Long 1999;
Parkin 1972). White's argument applies to rural India too (see Harriss
1977, discussed in chapter 4), and echoes what Berry argued for land
in Africa: strict polarization in terms of exclusive ownership on the
basis of cash has not emerged, because there are contradictory tendencies at work.

To appreciate the sheer complexity involved in agrarian change, we
now turn to two historically situated empirical studies, one from Asia
and one from Africa. Although they are not exhaustive in terms of the
range of variables they cover, the two reveal important complexities
and dynamics. They also invite us to consider how researchers choose
their units of study, and how the choice may influence findings on the
consequences of reduced access to land. Both ethnographies – the first
one upbeat, the second raising concern – challenge existing interpretations of land scarcity.

Land and Livelihood: The Importance of Situated Studies

Reductionism in the study of agrarian change can only be countered
through detailed empirical research which does not force data into
preconceived frameworks. To illustrate this with reference to the 'polarization' debate, I turn to Jens Lerche's study of Pariawan village,
Jaunpur district, in east Uttar Pradesh (UP). Lerche subscribes to the
view that culture is structured yet dynamic, that change is not a unilinear
process but the outcome of contestation and negotiation (Lerche 1995:
489). The appropriateness of the approach is confirmed in the social
history of Pariawan, which shows that while landlessness has been an
unstoppable process for the not-so-secure, its occurrence has not led

to outright polarization and destitution. In Pariawan, many who lost land have used initiative to diversify the sources of livelihood on which they draw, often by moving into off-farm employment. The outcome has enhanced their livelihood security.

The second case study is more of a cautionary tale. Returning to Leach's Gola Forest ethnography, we consider the significance of land from the perspective of women who lose access. Their story, one of concern, is an invitation to fine-tune the thesis that access to land in Africa remains fairly democratic as it is still open to interpretation (Berry 1993; Shipton 1994).

Case Study 3.1: Land and Livelihood in Pariawan, UP, India

Until India's independence, Pariawan was dominated by the landed Thakur caste whose members held all political power and all superior land. The land was tilled partly by landless, 'untouchable' Chamar labourers, who were considered the property of the landed class, and partly by tenants from the low but touchable Yadav. Thakurs treated Chamars as *niji*, literally 'our own'; a relation said to be forever. As part of their duties Chamar women would clean courtyards daily, a chore known as *tatwari*, and act as midwives. Chamar women also formed the core of the Thakurs' agricultural workforce; they were beaten frequently, and sexual abuse, which male Thakurs considered legitimate, was common (Lerche 1995: 493). Thakurs usually made a small piece of land, one-third of an acre or less, available as payment, plus food during work periods and, at harvest time, a bigger share in the harvest than non-bonded labourers would receive.

As in most other parts of India, land reform in Pariawan proved successful only for some, especially the larger (Yadav) tenants, while small tenant farmers did not benefit at all. On the contrary, the latter lost their access to land when the new Yadav landowners turned out to prefer to do much of the (now modernized) agricultural work themselves. Employment for Chamars fell by half. Cut off from the 'traditional' payment of a tiny plot of land, many Chamars became practically landless (Lerche 1995: 492). For Chamars who remained in a dependent situation, change for the better came in 1972 when they took matters into their own hands and, through a spirited strike, managed to move 'the balance of power . . . towards a less unfavourable position' (Lerche 1995: 495). The strike, the first in village history, ended the degrading *tatwari* work and, on a collective level, strengthened the Chamars' bargaining position *vis-à-vis* the political elite.

Although most Chamar households had lost access to land, they did not become paralysed in a social world split in two. Free from their bonded relations, most Chamars diversified and entered better-paid employment, 'ranging from government jobs to coolie jobs in the towns' (Lerche 1995: 493). As a class, Chamars began to have 'households' in government service, 'households' in agricultural labour, and 'households' in non-agricultural labour. Individual household members also diversified, so much so that 'around 40 per cent of the households [in Pariawan became] engaged in government service, factory work or business activities' in addition to agricultural labour (Lerche 1995: 492). Some financial dependence on Thakurs continued for the poorest Chamars, but the majority enjoyed better terms and more freedom of choice in deciding who to approach for financial assistance.

The success with which Chamars in Pariawan reacted to landlessness fits well with research on the longer-term impact of the Green Revolution (Gerke 1992; White 1992), and with research in areas where agricultural work opportunities increased as a result of double or treble cropping (Harriss 1977; Leaf 1983). Landlessness does not invariably mean destitution.

But, and here we ask questions about the unit of study, analysts interested in food security need also look *inside* the household to gauge what the loss of land means to those responsible for food provisioning. And those responsible, as seen in chapter 2, are often women who are having to cope with uncertain male contributions. When the labour market for Pariawan women is looked at in detail, it emerges that the benefits from off-farm opportunities have not spread equally to women. The predicament of the low-caste, Chamar woman is lamentable indeed. Her labouring days are excessively long, she makes money only when agricultural work is available, and her wage is less than a man's. At harvest time, 'women and children [receive] one-and-a-half to two *sers* (*c*.1 kg.) of the crop for each day they cut. . . . Men receive anywhere from two to five *sers* per day' (Sharma 1985: 77).

Leach's ethnography on Sierra Leone's Gola Forest, undertaken before the warfare which subsequently engulfed the region, also provides information which shows that loss of land may trouble women more than it does men. The Gola study is particularly interesting as it raises specific concern whilst confirming Berry's (optimistic) conclusion that claims to land have proliferated over time (Berry 1993: 119). This proliferation, Leach shows, carries a significant cost for women food providers.

Case Study 3.2: Land Use and Contestation in the Gola Forest, Sierra Leone

Before tree cash cropping took off, farming in Gola was organized around a large residential grouping, called *mawee*, which comprised between forty and fifty adult members who contributed their labour to the making of a collective 'big farm' in return for guaranteed subsistence. This farm was located in the uplands, where rice, the staple, would be intercropped with crops women controlled (Leach 1994: 82).

The situation changed in the 1950s and 1960s when young men, and, to a lesser extent, women, acquired greater social and economic independence; they stopped making 'big farms' (Leach 1994: 85). With many men moving out of food farming, the farms moved to swampy lowlands, where they became smaller. The shift was accompanied by a narrative which praised and justified the new locus as ideal for women's activity (Leach 1994: 93). The drawback, however, was that intercrops could not grow in the wet swamp soils. This impaired women's strategies for obtaining sauce ingredients and hunger foods (Leach 1994: 95). Women whose husbands continued to farm the uplands were lucky; their supply of intercrops remained secure. Such women sometimes helped out friends, other women, whose access to the uplands had lapsed.

Leach's concern is that these resource-use arrangements between women may end, because of increased population pressure and *new claims on land*. The pressure has already resulted in conflict regarding the position of strangers (migrants), and worse may come. Leach foresees that women's mutual help arrangements will collapse as 'people with weaker claims and/or lesser political influence . . . lose out in the competition for access to increasingly scarce and valuable sites, and in ensuing disputes over resource use' (1994: 97). Recent cases in which strangers' swamp use was revoked in favour of influential lineage members support the hypothesis of collapse.

In sum, while contestations over land and land use continue in Gola, it is doubtful that they will improve food security at the household level. Recent developments in land use and land claims rather suggest that the politically weak, a category containing most women and their dependants, stand to lose from such contestations. This illustrates how vitally important access to land continues to be from a food security perspective, and calls for a historically informed discussion of women's relationship to land.

The value of the two case studies must also be looked at from the angle of research methodology. Importantly, both studies focus on mundane issues – income, sauce ingredients – which, once understood in their full context, cast a different light on broadly based theory. In looking at income patterns, the first study questions whether landlessness must mean destitution; in looking at sauce ingredients, the second questions whether continuous contestations over land rights are beneficial when considered from the point of view of women and food security. The second study especially shows that 'big issues' in research must concentrate also on small màtters; what makes them big are their local meanings.

Women, Power and Access to Land

How women's access to land and property is structured has preoccupied anthropologists for some time. Major contributions have come from Esther Boserup (1970) and Jack Goody (1976), both of whom have revealed important 'links between women's status, the sexual division of labour, forms of marriage and inheritance, and the economic relations of production' (Moore 1988: 45). Boserup and Goody subscribed to a broad contrast between African and Eurasian inheritance systems, the latter characterized by 'diverging inheritance' (meaning that children of both sexes inherit) and 'dowry' (meaning that daughters receive parental property on getting married). Both types prevail in Eurasia, but are unusual in sub-Saharan Africa (Goody 1976: 6). One implication is that most sub-Saharan women gain access to land not in their own right, but as wives and mothers (see e.g. Bernstein 1994: 171; Moore 1988: 58–9). Increasingly however, women marry men whose families no longer control land, which restricts their access even further (see Pottier 1994a).

Today's problems regarding land access in Africa, for women and poor men, contrast with pre-colonial times, which were more – but not entirely – egalitarian (Davison 1988: 10–11; Raikes 1988: 92). Even in pre-colonial times there was differential access, for dominant lineages and groups often cultivated the best land, and senior men secured long-term rights as against the short-term rights for women and junior men (see Davison 1988: 11–12 for examples). Despite such differential treatment, women's rights in land were fairly well assured.

For a fuller picture of women's contemporary land rights in sub-Saharan Africa, or what is left of them, it is customary to consider whether a community is organized along patrilineal or matrilineal principles, as the two 'systems' tend to have opposed prescriptive rules. In societies that are patrilineal and virilocal, married women access land

mostly through their husbands or senior kinsmen, while women from
that minority of societies that recognize matrilineal inheritance principles *may* have more direct access through their lineage membership
(Davison 1993: 420). When land is transferred matrilineally, much of
it still passes from men (mothers' brothers) to men (sisters' sons), but
provisions may be made to have some land pass to women as well.
Direct access by women, however, does not automatically mean that
the land will be sufficient. Women may have a high degree of security
of tenure, yet, as Hirschmann and Vaughan (1983) found in their study
of Zomba district, Malawi, land availability may differ significantly
between and within villages. In their sample of seventy women, 57 per
cent said they had insufficient land and suffered food insecurity as a
consequence. Even when they did have enough labour and cash for
fertilizer, these women were still unable to grow sufficient staple food
to feed their families (Hirschmann and Vaughan 1983: 89–90). Land
scarcity, in other words, eroded the basis of their economic independence.

It would also be unwise to assume that matrilineal principles imply
that women always inherit unopposed. As Berry warns,

> [even] in matrilineal (or cognatic) descent systems, where many women
> farmed land belonging to their own descent groups and husbands ob-
> tained land through their wives, women's rights to alienate land were
> circumscribed by those of the descent group. Thus, in Ghana, cocoa
> farms which women established for themselves tended to pass into the
> control of their lineages over time (Mikell 1984: 206–11, 1985: 23–7).
> Men's rights to dispose of land through mortgage, sale, gift, or bequest
> were also subject to the interests of the lineage, but senior men espe-
> cially exercised more authority within descent groups than women or
> junior men, and hence exercised greater influence over transactions in
> family land. (Berry 1993: 116)

A woman's labour input, on the other hand, can make a difference
and boost her claims. In Ghana, assistance by wives and children on a
husband's or parent's farm can be rewarded with the right to inherit
at least a portion of it. Rights are strengthened further when the woman's assistance, or that of her children, takes the additional form of a
capital contribution (Berry 1993: 117, 156, referring to Kyerematen
1971 and Okali 1983).

Berry's emphasis on action and negotiation is a useful reminder of
how analytic typologies such as matriliny and patriliny must not be
treated as if they provide clear-cut rules from which certain people
may then deviate. Harri Englund's study of matrilineal, ChiChewa-
speaking Dedza, where men have begun to consolidate their grip on
profitable *madimba* gardens (*dambos*, or seasonally flooded marshes)

by initiating patrilateral inheritance practices, usefully illustrates how elements from both 'systems' may occur (Englund 1999). His final thought is challenging: the 'problem' of patrilateral inheritance in a matrilineal setting may arise from an overly rigid notion of matri-lineage (Englund 1999: 155). Breaking the rules, so to speak, also occurs when men in patrilineal societies go out of their way to be-queath farmland to their daughters (see Mackenzie 1986: 387, 399–400, on central Kenya; Pottier 1997 on Rwanda). Their efforts, however, often come to nothing, because elders may oppose them fiercely. As Fiona Mackenzie explains, such opposition is grounded in the fear that if the woman recipient in turn bequeaths land to her daughter(s), the land could be removed permanently from *mbari* (i.e. communal) control (Mackenzie 1986: 387, 1989: 104–6).

Examples of how women struggle to realize their rights in land re-gardless of what inheritance 'rules' may prescribe, together with the observations on Gola by Leach, suggest that any enthusiasm about the *general* accessibility of land through continuous contestation needs toning down when looked at from the position of female claimants. Women's interests are not much served by the multiplication of claims. This is not to suggest, however, that women are passive bystanders. On the contrary, systematic and persistent opposition to women's rights may spur women on to collective action. Thus, in Kenya, 'as . . . men pressured Land Boards to protect *mbari* holdings by denying titles to women, Kenyan women began to form informal "self-help" groups to assist one another in acquiring land and other forms of rural property' (Mackenzie 1992: 39). Forms of mutual assistance in women's strug-gles over land are testimony that so-called customary land tenure rules are indeed often ambiguous, and subject to ongoing interpretation. As Berry puts it, people's access to land 'depends on their participation in processes of interpretation and adjudication, as well as on their ability to pay' (Berry 1993: 103–4).[3]

Negotiating access, however, is still very much a man's game. Exper-iences like the Jahaly Pacharr project in The Gambia, reviewed below, show how women face an uphill struggle even when legislation is on their side (see also Hill 1982: 59, on Hausaland). For Central Africa, the litmus test of women's ability to steer processes of (re)interpretation and (re)negotiation to their advantage is post-genocide Rwanda, where women, customarily banned from inheriting land, can now lawfully claim their inheritance (Pottier 1997). Whether they will do so in prac-tice is a different matter, since legal stipulations are easily circumvented in local interpretations of which type of woman the law provides for. Local interpretations of the new ruling are likely to stress that the law applies only to war widows who were 'properly' married, that is, mar-ried with bridewealth – and they, it is known, are a clear minority.

Shipton makes an identical point regarding the widespread assumption that land registration provides personal security:

> The concept of secure tenure in individual titles is treacherously misleading. Untitled lands are by no means necessarily insecure, and such titling more often than not seems to heighten insecurity of tenure. The new system of titles does not expunge customary tenure or what is so deemed, but only adds another legal framework alongside it with its own room to manoeuver. (Shipton 1994: 364)

Research on inheritance legislation and practice in Asia has yielded findings very similar to those recorded for Africa. For Persian-speaking Shi'a Muslims in Badsir district, south-east Iran, for example, Shahrashoub Razavi (1994) shows that women face severe difficulty when attempting to exert their rights. They tend to lose out, both as daughters and as wives, because everyday practices – that is, 'common sense' interpretations by men – make implementing the law next to impossible. As daughters, Badsir women's

> inheritance rights . . . are almost completely disregarded, [because the] *de facto* transfer of land to male progeny tends to occur as the father approaches old age. The land is usually entrusted to the son on a share-cropping basis (very often a 50–50 division of costs and output). . . . Following his father's death [the eldest son] becomes the legal owner of the land, buying his brothers' shares. Occasionally he may compensate his sisters as well, although this tends to be a token gesture. In this way land fragmentation is kept to a minimum. (Razavi 1994: 617)

The widow's lot is no better, at least not with respect to land. Here again, Razavi finds ample evidence of circumvention. Although the Iranian legal code recognizes the inheritance rights of widows, the common obstacle to implementation is the age and marital status of sons. A woman who is widowed late in life and has a grown-up son sees her land transferred to him upon her husband's death (Razavi 1994: 618). To compensate his widowed mother, the son normally supplies an 'allowance' in wheat. As this is hardly ever sufficient for survival, the widow must rely on her own animals to raise cash income and cover subsistence needs (Razavi 1994: 618).

Widows in Bangladesh, where short-distance village exogamy is the norm, face a similar predicament. Again, while women inherit in theory (under Muslim law daughters inherit at half the rate of their brothers' entitlement; Hindu daughters inherit for life only, after which land reverts back to the male line), complex social factors and family politics are at work to 'inhibit women from claiming their formal rights' (White 1992: 53). The discrepancy between legal rights and harsh everyday reality also applies to younger men (brothers). In other parts of South Asia too, women's inheritance rights, whether defined by cultural convention or statutory law, are increasingly – and successfully – contested by male claimants. Bina Agarwal (1994a) explains, like Berry does for Africa, that matrilineal and bilateral systems of land inheritance offer women theoretical advantage only, but not the guarantee that their rights will be realized. Women from areas in India where such inheritance systems once existed, used to receive their fair share of 'economic and social security, and [had] considerable autonomy and equality in marital relations' (Agarwal 1994a: 153). But no longer. Given their 'virtual exclusion from property management (in some groups) and from jural and overall public authority in all groups', these women have seen their circumstances gradually deteriorate first under colonial and then under post-colonial state authorities (Agarwal 1994a: 151). The erosion of 'customary' inheritance practices has come about as the influence of patriarchal ideologies has spread (Agarwal 1994a: 153).

In reviewing the change processes for South Asia's three main matrilineal and bilateral communities (Garos of north-east India, Nayars of south-west India, and Sinhalese of Sri Lanka), Agarwal is struck by the fact that 'women's lack of jural authority in traditional public forums such as caste and clan councils was replicated in the modern State's judicial and executive structures' (1994a: 192–3). Hence, where gender equality is promised as a constitutional right, as it is in India today, the removal of legal restrictions is 'only one part of the story. The other part . . . relates to the many formidable obstacles that constrain women from exercising the rights they currently have' (Agarwal 1994a: 248). Not all is lost, however. Agarwal hints that cultural divisions have not broken down entirely, and that the official 'movement toward bilateral forms of inheritance everywhere in the subcontinent [stands a better chance of being implemented in areas that were] traditionally matrilineal and bilateral' (1994a: 290–1).

To complicate matters, lineage organization in South Asia is only one of several factors which determine whether women can realize their rights to land and other property. Another overlapping factor is whether village endogamy or exogamy is practised, and what 'marriage distance' is involved. In this respect, region and religion determine which residence patterns are common. Where village endogamy and close-kin marriage are practised (northeast and south India, Sri Lanka, Pakistan and Nepal), women stand a better chance of realizing the property rights promised by law (Agarwal 1994a: 152). Conversely, where village exogamy and distant-kin marriage are practised (north and north-west India, and Bangladesh), women's chances are much reduced.

In the same context, we need to guard against over-optimistic accounts of how women control dowry. As Ursula Sharma's (1980) research into women's work and property in north-west India shows, it would be wrong to see dowry, which may include land, as a kind of pre-mortem inheritance. 'Real' dowry is transferred not to daughters, but to daughters and their husbands, even to the husband's parents when still alive (Sharma 1980: 48–50; see also Moore 1988: 69). A dowry transfer in other words, does not actually give the bride any power or autonomy within her husband's household (Sharma 1980: 50; see also Moore 1988: 69). The bottom line is that dowry-receiving women are prevented from 'inheriting land as daughters, except in the absence of sons' (Moore 1988: 68). Adding Sharma's observations on dowry and inheritance to the argument that women are generally unable to realize their rights even where inheritance is prescribed by culture or law (see also Agarwal 1994a; Razavi 1994), one must conclude that the situation of many women in South Asia is remarkably close to that of women in sub-Saharan Africa. Even when allowance is made for 'cultural' differences, women's rights are recognized and realized mostly, and perhaps increasingly, as wives and mothers.

A closer look at legislation and land reform is now called for.

Real Lives, Unreal Policies?

Can states intervene to democratize access to land? Committed socialist states have certainly tried, but rarely with success (Croll 1981; Shipton 1994: 365).

To think about possible obstacles, let us take the People's Republic of China as an illustration. In 1947, after the Communist Party's Agrarian Law Programme entitled women to receive land in their own names (Hinton 1972), peasant women came forward to 'speak their bitterness' against patriarchal relations and landlord oppression (Agarwal 1994b: 94). The frankness with which they spoke suggested 'that what held them back earlier was not lack of self-interest, but lack of the economic and political support necessary to speak out without undue risk' (Agarwal 1994b: 94). Legal entitlement to land certainly was a great step forward for Chinese women, but benefits must also be assessed in the context of other gendered imbalances. Concretely, it has emerged that women's personal entitlement to land did not mean that household labour chores and rewards had also evened out. There remained much scope for patriarchy to assert itself, as Elisabeth Croll (1983a) made clear regarding food production on 'private plots', which received a high profile with the 1978 reforms. In *The Family Rice Bowl*, Croll reflects:

It is one of the conditions of the cultivation of subsistence plots and the rearing of domestic livestock that these activities must not detract from the labour time due to the collective and must therefore be undertaken during the free time of family members or by the auxiliary labour power of the elderly, the women or children who all might not otherwise work full-time in the collective labour force. (Croll 1983a: 199)

If women are to take advantage of laws that offer rights in land, they must, as Agarwal suggests for South Asia, engage in 'both a struggle over *resources* and a struggle over *meanings*. [This struggle is to be] conducted in several different arenas – the family, the community and the State' (Agarwal 1994b: 84). Agarwal's supreme illustration is the Bodhgaya struggle in Bihar in the late 1970s, which began when landless labourers and sharecroppers attempted to reclaim land held illegally by a local monastery-cum-temple. The struggle ended with the transfer of a large portion of the disputed land to the poor and, following a struggle within the struggle, the registration of some of that land (10 per cent) in women's individual names (Agarwal 1994b: 103–5). The moment of victory, in February 1982, showed how the struggle over meanings – initially fought at household and community level – then needed to be fought also on a third level, that of the district and state. For indeed, when it came to registering the title deeds in women's names, the District Officer in charge strongly opposed the idea. It was only when the villagers 'adamantly refused to take any land unless it was given in the names of women' (Agarwal 1994b: 105) that the official gave in. The struggle continued after 1982 until all of the monastery's illegal holdings were redistributed.

Agarwal stresses that many women in South Asia genuinely want to control at least some of the land they cultivate. She takes issue with the view, put forward by Amartya Sen (1990a, 1990b), that South Asian women 'suffer from a form of false consciousness in that they may not have a clear perception of their individual self-interests, and may attach less value to their own well-being than to the family's well-being' (Agarwal 1994b: 82). The notion of a false consciousness is rejected on empirical grounds. When attention is paid to what village women say in contexts where they can speak relatively freely, it is clear that they are much less accepting of gender inequity than their overt behaviour might suggest (Agarwal 1994b: 91). In parallel to the situation in China, Agarwal concludes that change is needed 'not so much [in] women's perceptions of their own well-being as [in] their perceptions of the possibilities of improving their situations' (1994b: 94).

This reference to women's self-perception shows just how important social science research has become. More than ever, researchers face serious moral responsibility, for it has emerged that their conclusions on self-perception may determine how the people in question are perceived by others, including influential politicians and policy-makers. Misleading statements, for example that people are 'vulnerable' or 'stubbornly clinging to tradition', may cause severe harm (see the discussion on 'famine victims' in chapter 7 below). Representations of self-perception, however, are a difficult and sensitive matter, since they are contestable almost by definition; social groups are unlikely to share a single self-image. This said, researchers can and must take the utmost care to ask a full set of relevant empirical questions. Regarding women, Agarwal suggests the following be asked:

> what are women's perceptions about themselves and their economic and social situations within and outside the family? To what extent have women absorbed the ideologies favouring male interest? Does this acceptance differ by women's positions in the social hierarchy (such as by class, caste and so on)? What covert forms does women's resistance take in speech and action? What are the material constraints on women's overt resistance? (Agarwal 1994b: 83)

In view of the earlier reference to male economic impoverishment in parts of Africa, I suggest that the first question in the set be asked also of men. To leave men out of the picture, as the next case study shows, is bound to have negative repercussions even for well-intended, women-focused policy initiatives.

In contrast to the successful bottom-up struggle in Bodhgaya, Bihar, where change was fought for first at the household and the community levels, the Jahaly Pacharr rice project in The Gambia was conceived and implemented from the top down. Judith Carney (1988) reveals the questions policy-makers neglected to ask.

Case Study 3.3: The Jahaly Pacharr Irrigated Rice Project, The Gambia

Launched with considerable media hype, the multi-donor Jahaly Pacharr Irrigated Rice Project in Mandinka land, The Gambia, aimed to promote both gender equity and national food (rice) sufficiency. A specific aim was to correct those past development initiatives in which it had been assumed that household production took place on a pool-and-share basis (Carney 1988: 63). To achieve this, the Jahaly Pacharr project site included vast tracts of land on which women had 'traditionally' cultivated rice for personal income. These tracts reflected the 'tradition of awarding women *kamanyango* usufruct rights to rice land', which dated from at least the eighteenth century (Carney 1988: 66). *Kamanyango* land contrasted with *maruo* land, which was customarily claimed and used by residence groups headed by men. But, and this is what the project team overlooked, Mandinka women were 'awarded' their personal access through men. Men retained control.

A year into the project, it became clear that the chief objective had failed. As it was women-focused rather than gender-sensitive, the project had been 'hijacked' by the men, who felt left out. Men had reclaimed the project land through a subtle semantic manoeuvre: they had changed the local terms of reference. The pump-irrigated plots were no longer to be referred to as *kamanyango*, women's fields, but had become *maruo*, compound land in which women had no individual rights (Carney 1988: 71). One immediate consequence of the shift in language use was that '*Maruo* enabled household heads to utilize family labour, while they reaped the benefits of household production' (Carney 1988: 74). This meant the project had resulted in women losing access to land they used to manage on a profitable own-account basis.

Events following the project launch showed conclusively that more is required than a change in legislation or project policy if women are to realize their rights.[4] What went wrong in the Jahaly Pacharr project was that its launch had not been accompanied by a successful, political 'struggle over meanings' at the household and community levels. The project designers had assumed solidarities where they did not exist; they had introduced their own perception bias. The project had aimed to encourage gender equality through the transfer of a productive resource, but took no responsibility for the equally necessary struggle against a constraining gender ideology (cf. Agarwal 1994b: 81).

Perception bias in development, a complement to local forms of patriarchy, is rooted in colonial history and still manifests itself regularly in the undercounting and undervaluation of women's work (Agarwal 1994b: 91; Brown et al. 1995). Brigitte Reinwald (1997) illustrates the claim, now widely accepted, that local men and colonial administrators often worked in tandem to exclude women and deny them their rights in land. Through research on the history of Siin-Siin women's involvement in peanut production in Senegal, Reinwald shows how local men would 'prove' to administrators that their women were no good at farming. Siin-Siin women, Reinwald asserts, had responded positively when groundnuts were first introduced, but were then marginalized by colonists and husbands alike. A woman Reinwald interviewed had this to say about Siin-Siin men in the 1930s: 'The men refused, by then, to give women the fields to cultivate groundnuts, or if they finally did, they refused, for a long time, to give them seeds. The fields [were] thus sown too late, so the harvest was very poor' (Reinwald 1997: 161). The poor yields then reinforced the view that women were second-rate farmers, which in turn 'justified' their marginalization. The attitude changed somewhat during the 1934 famine, when rice granaries – rice being women's responsibility – did not run empty (Reinwald 1997: 159), but it was too late. By then, women had lost the political 'struggle over meanings', and membership of agricultural cooperatives was restricted to senior men. Non-members, women and junior men, thus became obliged to surrender their groundnut harvests to husbands or senior men (Reinwald 1997: 161–2; see also Sow 1988), never seeing their own labour justly rewarded.

Does planned intervention ever effectively reduce power imbalances? Yes, provided there is commitment and certain conditions are met. By way of a counter to the negative experience with the Jahaly Pacharr project, I turn to empirical research in Kerala, the Indian state generally regarded to be a shining example of effective reform.

Case Study 3.4: Land Reform in Kerala, India

In 1987, Richard Franke studied the impact of Kerala's 1969 land reform in the village of Nadur (pseudonym), central Kerala. He found that Kerala's radical reform programme had resulted in a *de facto* redistribution of land rights and landholdings to large numbers of low-caste tenants and labourers, and that social and economic inequalities had indeed been massively redressed (Franke 1992: 81). Using village baseline information collected by Joan Mencher in 1971, when land reform transfers had scarely begun, Franke found that the reform owed much of its success to the abolition of rice land tenancy and tenancy in (fertile) house garden lands. This had resulted in significant gains for the majority of villagers, and thus produced a general levelling of income inequalities.[5] The latter had 'declined mostly where advocates of land reform wanted: the middle and poorest Nadur households' (Franke 1992: 92). Success on such a scale, however, was unusual for India since, as seen earlier, lower castes rarely benefit from land reform.

But Kerala's impressive redistribution record was countered by two changes in the job market which promoted new concerns and inequalities (Franke 1992: 91, 111). First, many smallholders began to struggle to keep pace with rising professional and other incomes, needing to produce enough income from their plots to ensure the effects of the land reform would not be swallowed up in the next generation (Franke 1992: 111–12). Such pressure has created a new form of tension. In addition, many former tenants now find themselves at odds with their newly hired agricultural labourers. Franke puts it thus: 'Where once the poor were pitted against the rich, now the poor are pitted against the slightly less poor' (1992: 113).[6]

These two consequences aside, Franke is most positive about the results of Kerala's land reforms. Not only were the reforms implemented, but they were accompanied by significant food production increases and fairer food distribution. Life expectancy had also increased, while infant mortality was down. This had already been noted in the mid-1970s when 'Kerala's birth rate of 26 per thousand compared with a national average of 33 per thousand' (Hartmann 1987: 281).

Acknowledging Kerala's immense social progress in the pursuit of social justice, Agarwal nonetheless voices further concern over lingering intra-household inequalities, noting in particular how women from landowning households have sometimes been discriminated against as members of their class. This happened when their households – perceived as bounded units! – had been judged to own land above the permitted ceiling. In such cases, gender discrimination within the household often meant that it was the women's personal land that was forfeited. Women's complaints came to nothing. 'Petitions by women arguing that it is their husbands who should forfeit above the ceiling where the latter also have non-land sources of income, came to no avail (Saradamoni 1983)' (Agarwal 1994a: 175).

Research highlights how disadvantaged classes and groups do benefit from land reforms provided the 'struggle over meanings' is carried through on a variety of levels. The success of a land reform programme such as Kerala's, in which land redistribution was linked to greater accessibility to public resources (especially health care), also shows that the benefits to the majority poor are formidable, an observation which must carry weight in any debate on how food security can be improved through assisted development. While social scientists need to be receptive to the view that landlessness does not inevitably mean destitution, they must be equally mindful of the gains that accrue from effective redistribution. Land reform is worth fighting for as long as the struggle over meanings is also actively engaged in, and it is here that researchers need to shoulder their responsibilities.

Researcher commitment can take several forms, from ensuring fair representation (of circumstances, self-perceptions, ambitions, etc.), through providing research informants with information regarding 'the possibilities of improving their situations' (Agarwal 1994a), to lobbying policy-makers and alerting them to questions that must not be neglected.

Land Reform and Researcher Responsibilities

Researcher responsibilities regarding land reform and its implementation currently receive much attention in the context of political developments in Southern Africa. The seriousness of reform came home
to Zimbabwe's leaders in early 1998, when Robert Mugabe awoke
rudely from a seventeen-year slumber. Soaring food prices, especially
for staple maize meal, and frustration over the fact that 4,000 white
farmers still owned the best third of the land, combined to produce
unprecedented rioting. Mugabe's difficulties remind us how easy it is
for liberation movements to plan reforms when in opposition, only to
forget all about them once political freedom is won.

Tension between, on the one hand, the necessity for redistribution
and justice and, on the other, the 'necessity' of securing political survival
through nepotism, has also made its mark on post-apartheid South
Africa, where the ANC leadership has bowed to World Bank pressure
and dropped its commitment to the principles of land restitution form-
ulated in 1992. In bowing to such pressure, the ANC accepted that land
reform should be market-based, with carefully selected 'beneficiaries'
receiving assistance to purchase land (Bernstein 1994: 173–5). It was
bad news for those committed to structural reform and public action.

However, as the 1998 troubles in Zimbabwe made clear, there is no
smothering the popular expectations that accompany broad-based liberation struggles. Politicians can delay the moment of truth and reward, but not forever. The ANC government will need to accept that
structural reform through public action *is* required, and that agrarian
reform with land redistribution is necessary to redress the history of
disposession. Government will need 'to make available resources desperately needed for livelihoods, to provide conditions in which black
farmers can compete with white farmers, in which a more diversified
and viable agriculture can develop' (Bernstein 1994: 179).

In agriculture, South Africa's history of dispossession continued right
through the 1980s and early 1990s, when an accumulation crisis for
white farmers forced numerous Africans out of the 'white' countryside where they had worked as farm labourers (Bernstein 1994: 169;
Murray 1995: 5–7). The accumulation crisis had been triggered by the
withdrawal of state subsidies and become 'accentuated by generalized
economic recession, drought years [especially 1982–4], and creeping
deregulation and market liberalization' (Bernstein 1994: 169). The eviction of black farmworkers often came without warning, as Colin
Murray learned from interviews in the Orange Free State (Murray
1995: 12–13), where over a quarter of farmworkers and their families
became displaced (1995: 10). The force and speed of the evictions

testified to the continuation of extreme imbalances of power and livelihood security.

Capturing the spirit of Berry's analysis, with its emphasis on continuous contestation of land rights, Henry Bernstein recognizes the possibility that a social dynamic will be unleashed to redress old injustices and newly created ironies (Bernstein 1994: 177–8). Already, rural people's impatience 'with the slow pace of implementation of programmes for land restitution, redistribution and tenure reform' has led to land invasions in a number of districts, as Ben Cousins details for the eastern Cape and Kwazulu–Natal (Cousins 1996: 167ff). Disputes, moreover, are regularly 'compounded by return, or "reverse", migration in the face of high urban unemployment' (Bernstein 1996a: 24–5). How the ANC leadership will react should conflicts over land escalate, which is to be expected given the high levels of urban unemployment and population movement, remains to be seen, but its approach is likely to be conservative in the name of stability and reconciliation. As a result, South Africa's land reforms may come to distinguish themselves by their non-distinctiveness, as has happened in Zimbabwe and most of India.

Whatever happens next, neither the unleashing of spontaneous collective action nor a conservative government stance must diminish the academic commitment. Parker Shipton spells out the task that awaits anthropologists: 'Undoing semantic classifications for land and people – e.g. reserves, communal lands, and homelands for the former, and at the starkest, white, black and colored for the latter – sooner or later becomes the task of scholars and land reformers alike, not just in changed South Africa, but elsewhere in the region too' (Shipton 1994: 363–4).

There is thus a simultaneous need for

> broader comparisons – without losing the local nuance and texture – to reach a broader readership and to help reverse expropriations, minimize farmer–herder violence, dismantle race barriers, or otherwise make a difference. If any *single aim* should be kept in mind, it is fairness. More realistic than equality, less uncaring than efficiency, this ideal rings true to a tropical African spirit. (Shipton 1994: 368–9, emphasis added)

It cannot be said more clearly. But the 'single aim' approach carries a further challenge. Fairness, equality, efficiency – how do these terms translate in locally situated discourses of modernity? More specifically, how are such terms negotiated in the multilayered 'struggles over meaning'? Answers, and they must be locally situated and nuanced, must come from the research of social anthropologists, indigenous and exogenous.

Conclusions

This chapter has shown that grand theories and perspectives on agrarian change need to be combined with detailed empirical study if analytic reductionism is to be avoided. While broad political and economic forces have often made significant inroads into very diverse rural economies, they have not done so in systematically uniform ways. Rather, the interaction of 'global' and 'local' forces (no strict dichotomy implied) has produced a myriad time- and location-specific results, the nuances of which need to be understood and publicized to ensure policy-makers will one day reconsider their belief in simplistic models of change and equally simplistic solutions.

Ironically, in highlighting specificity and nuance, this chapter has also confirmed that certain 'global' trends may be at work, especially regarding land legislation. Women's access to land, we have seen, is usually determined by a complex set of localized rules and regulations, yet *de facto* inheritance appears as a fairly universal phenomenon. Regardless of where they live, regardless of what 'local custom' prescribes, women everywhere experience tremendous difficulty when trying to realize their rights to inherit land. This is not to suggest, though, that women have become resigned to this 'fact', for there is enough evidence to suggest that gender relations remain dynamic. Contestations continue, and may indeed intensify, as women see their everyday tasks and commitments stretched beyond recognition, sometimes in the context of male economic impoverishment. The next chapter takes a closer look at this debate.

How important land is to resource-poor men and women is a research question which we must continue to examine. Off-farm economic opportunities may provide suitable alternatives to working the land, as the ethnography from Pariawan showed, yet the sudden loss of valued land (or even of a type of land) can bring problems that have far-reaching consequences for the management of women's time and for the nutritional status of their households. It is impossible to generalize on the question of 'how much' land still matters, other than to stress that views tend to be wide-ranging and reflective of specific local conditions. Nonetheless, there are regions where long histories of allocative injustice have to be put right. It is in such a context that social science researchers need to understand not only the transformative power of effective legislation, but also, as argued in the final section, the responsibilities they themselves carry.

4

Labour Organization on Smallholder Farms
Structure and Diversity

This chapter continues our enquiry into the relocalization of so-called global changes. As argued in previous chapters, an understanding of how quasi-universal phenomena (for example commoditization and the spread of 'advanced' agricultural technologies) are relocalized, equips us to better appreciate the complexities involved in the food security debate. This time the focus is on how these broader phenomena engage with the dynamics of on-farm labour organization.

Farm Labour Availability: Broad Changes, Localized Responses

Africa and Asia form a broad contrast in how on-farm labour is organized, for Africa by and large lacks that vast pool of landless peasant farmers who readily avail themselves to work as hired labourers in Asia (Berry 1993: 138–9; Richards 1986: 22). Such surplus labour is found throughout South and South-East Asia, where high levels of landlessness have existed for centuries. Historically, and more recently with the introduction of 'Green Revolution' technologies, landlessness has steadily increased to create labour markets in excess of demand. On the eve of India's independence, for example, Hari Sharma (1973) calculated that landless and near-landless labourers already constituted 28 per cent of the total workforce in agriculture. South and South-East Asia, however, contrast with East Asia, especially with the People's

Republic of China, where landlessness is not such a problem. In China, difficulties related to on-farm labour organization are of a different nature.

Persistently facing recruitment difficulties, small-scale farmers in Africa today often belong to 'cultures' that used to ensure labour power through large residential groupings (for example Gola, Bwisha). These groupings shrank around the middle of the twentieth century when new economic and spiritual options came to undermine existing forms of authority. Some explanations for this reduced labour availability argue that the dearth came about 'because members of rural households and communities [had] become involved in a growing number of income-seeking activities and social networks' (Berry 1993: 145), but this, in its acute form, is more of a recent phenomenon brought on by structural adjustment programmes (SAPs) that cut formal employment and public expenditure. These cuts have pushed many people, women particularly, into the so-called informal sector where they would seek to make up the ever-increasing shortfalls in cash. Women's greater involvement in petty trade often changed the pattern of food production by causing new labour shortages (Schoepf and Schoepf 1990: 98–9), even though some women re-entered agricultural production. In rural Tanzania, for instance, SAPs have 'driven a growing number of people – especially the youth – into the casual labour market, [where they] seek work [mainly] in smallholder agriculture or in non-farm "off-the-books" activities' (Mbilinyi 1990: 118).

While the Tanzanian exodus expresses women's resistance to excessive demands on their labour at home – i.e. the 'double day' imposed by patriarchy and the appropriation of earnings by men (Mbilinyi 1990: 117–21) – women's greater involvement in casual labour markets also stems from their ever-increasing cash needs. The two forces, patriarchy and cash shortages, nowadays combine to make women 'work harder to maintain themselves and their families' (Mbilinyi 1990: 117).

Women's *reduced economic security* under structural adjustment is invariably to the detriment of their nutrition and health, and to those of their children, for it is impossible to be both more involved in casual labour markets and still find the time and energy properly to carry out domestic work (Whitehead 1990b: 119; Schoepf and Schoepf 1990: 99). The point has been made for instance for Uganda, where SAPs not only narrowed the range of food crops grown, but did so at significant nutritional and social cost (Nyangabyaki 1991). Among poorer groups, it is women and children who are worst affected (World Bank 1993; see also Barton and Wamai 1994). With national health resources cut as part of the economic austerity programme, tens of thousands of poor women are now pressured into making extra money, mostly through petty trade, in order to meet the new 'cost-sharing' requirement in health provisioning (Bantebya-Kyomuhendo 1994). Many women thus affected are also having to cope with the loss of family labour inflicted by AIDS and with the extra duties they must assume as carers for the terminally ill. This again reduces the time available for tending crops, processing foods and preparing meals.

These more recent factors aside, African women's difficulty in mobilizing extra-household farm labour originates in the emergence of the 'modern' household, which gave rise to or exacerbated gender and age hierarchies. In this respect, Whitehead's pioneering work in Kusasi, Ghana, has revealed that 'whereas men can use the unremunerated labour of their wives (and often of all the women in the household), the only way a woman can use the labour of household men [on her private farm] is by calling small exchange working parties which are remunerated in the sense that she provides food and beer' (Whitehead 1981: 103). Even wealthy senior women lack the power to command unremunerated labour. Hierarchies existed in Kusasi also *before* nuclear households came into being, but they were not problematic since production decisions took place at the community level.

Farmers who command resources and surplus foodstuffs may overcome labour problems through the use of gifts or loans of foodstuffs that create networks of obligation among kin and neighbours. These networks can then be used to access additional farm labour when there is a need, as Haugerud (1988) documents for Embu farmers in Kenya. The strategy, however, requires the production of *regular* surpluses, which is increasingly difficult to achieve. Off-farm income, while itself a cause of reduced labour availability, may be used to overcome the labour constraint.

A further characteristic of contemporary farm labour relations in Africa, often the consequence of people's involvement in off-farm activity, is that the sexual division of labour has blurred. Barnes notes this for Kenya (Barnes 1984: 60). Such blurring may in turn lead to uncertainty and contestation over the control of granaries, previously the undisputed domain of women, and over income from crop sales (Berry 1993: 155). Patterns of conflict have been noted in Zambia, Ghana, and Nigeria (Berry 1993: 155). In north-eastern Zambia in the late 1970s, for instance, Mambwe men regularly contested women's control of the main household granaries after they themselves had lost their foothold in the urban-industrial labour market (Pottier 1988: 114). When hybrid maize (labelled 'modern') displaced millet (labelled 'traditional') as the dominant food crop in northern Zambia, men stepped in to control the hybrid crop. It was a neat example of how the struggle over household resources is simultaneously a struggle over meanings (cf. Agarwal 1994b: 84).

These opening thoughts on farm labour organization in Africa indicate that while farmers face serious structural constraints, they attempt to deal with them in dynamic ways. It follows that understanding new work patterns requires not just an analysis of how gender and age structure access to labour resources, but also an appreciation of local nuance as farmers use their human agency to grapple with new constraints. Nuance is what the rest of this chapter is about.

Modern Agriculture, Polarization and Social Complexities

A central feature of the modern African household is that women's independent farming and land rights have become eroded (see chapter 3). The demise was triggered by land appropriation for cash cropping (by husbands) and backed by male-friendly dominant ideologies and state laws. As a result, women now spend more time producing cash crops for husbands and senior men (Whitehead 1990a: 61). Roberts (1984) provides the context: 'the wives' situation as "unfree labour became increasingly important to the household as commodity relations destroyed other bonds securing non-free labour (e.g. that of sons) to the peasant household"' (Roberts 1984; cited in Whitehead 1990a: 61). The destruction of these 'other bonds' not only undermined women's independent farming, but gave rise to a stereotyped view, still alive, of how gender relations in Africa have developed. Drawing upon analysis by Esther Boserup (1970), this stereotyped view claims that 'the economic changes of the twentieth century have relegated rural women to food production within an under-resourced "subsistence sector"', and that this relegation is responsible for Africa's food crises (Whitehead 1990a: 54). The same stereotyped view holds that men, in contrast, moved into cash cropping, the 'modern sector', which was better resourced and more lucrative. The portrayal of a production dualism based on gender, Whitehead argues, gave the erroneous signal that women were not involved in the modern sector and damaged women's economic security. The image of an under-resourced, feminine subsistence sector gave technocrats the justification for proposing remedies that centred on improving subsistence techniques and productivity, but these failed to address 'the complex and often negative impact of development on rural African women' (Whitehead 1990a: 56). It is thus that the invisibility of women's work continued both in indigenous ideologies and in the minds of policy-makers.

Other dualisms also need to be looked at critically as has recently been shown regarding cash payments to labourers. What does the use of cash signify? Have labour relations once embedded in 'gift exchange'

become fully 'commoditized'? Is labour now bought rather than reciprocated? Do relations with farmworkers now resemble the impersonal
ties betweeen employer and employee, as is sometimes claimed for
South and South-East Asia? Caution is advised. Dichotomies such as
free/unfree labour, gift/commodity economy, collective/individual ethos
may be popular ways through which we make sense of a fast-changing
world, but they are to be handled with care. As Harri Englund (forthcoming) demonstrates for ChiChewa-speaking Dedza, southern Malawi,
the meaning of cash payments to agricultural labourers must be linked
to notions of personhood: who recruits, who is recruited and for what
reasons, needs investigating. Heeding the critique that Westerners have
a habit of imputing definite moral qualities to the use of money (Parry
and Bloch 1989), Englund refuses to accept that labour is necessarily
bought or sold when cash changes hands. Paid agricultural labourers,
he shows, are not recruited at random. When wealthy villagers recruit
labourers for a wage, they mostly choose close relatives to 'make their
valued relationships visible' (Englund 1999: 159). True, an element
of self-interest is in evidence, since recruitment which shows generosity may need to be reciprocated, but it does not make sense to use
terms like '"contractual" and "individualized" as descriptive labels
for such labour arrangements' (Englund 1999: 152). While money
changes hands, the relationships remain personal. (Englund's analysis
links in nicely with the argument that land alienation has not occurred
in Africa on a significant scale, cf. chapter 3). Part of the problem,
Englund suggests, is that social analysts have been too hooked on the
construction of overly rigid typologies, matriliny and patriliny being a
prime example.

The 'buying and selling' of labour may be more applicable, however,
to South and South-East Asia where agriculture has been
commercialized, and land and labour dispossessed, for centuries. In this
context, communities appear to have become polarized, especially since
the Green Revolution (GR) boosted yields while reducing the cost of
labour. This benefited larger farmers and squeezed poorer ones out of
production and into the expanding but poorly paid wage market. Agricultural innovations made rural capital artificially cheap. Writing about
the Philippines, Banzon-Bautista (1989) argues that the International
Agricultural Research Centres (IARCs), in this case the International
Rice Research Institute (IRRI), designed 'for the private benefit of the
farmer and owner of capital, whatever the social consequences . . . or
the national cost to a debtor nation importing petroleum fuels and chemi-
cals' (Banzon-Bautista 1989: 139).[1] Displacement also marked change
in Indonesia, where the agrarian structures remained 'unreformed' despite Suharto's 'New Order' commitment to peasant productivity.[2] Again,
the GR's major benefits went to larger farmers who 'rationalized'

through saving labour. They substituted the sickle for the finger-knife (*ani-ani*) traditionally used in harvesting, and bought rotary or toothed weeders, which replaced hand weeding; diesel-powered rice hullers, which replaced hand pounding; and (in some areas) threshing machines that substituted for hand flails. Tractors also took the place of hand hoes and animal-drawn ploughs (White 1989: 255).

The massive labour displacement brought on by the new farming technologies made it attractive for analysts to conceive of *polarized communities*. Thus for India, the introduction of commercial agriculture, coupled with the failure to implement land reforms, came to be portrayed as having produced a broad split between landed and landless classes/castes: the landed classes finding their economic position strengthened; the resource-poor becoming poorer, more marginalized, more proletarianized (Sharma 1985: 58). Beneria and Sen (1981) argued that what happened in rural India after independence reflected the single most powerful tendency of capital accumulation: small producers were separated from the means of production, especially land, which made their conditions of survival more insecure (Beneria and Sen 1981: 288). Such developments led Byres (1972) to suggest that labour relations would in future 'depend on the cash nexus; that, in place of vertical alliances with landowners and bigger farmers, the labourers and small farmers [would] seek security in horizontal alliances with other members of their own group, or with outside political authorities; in other words that increasing "proletarianization" [would] take place' (cited in Harriss 1977: 225).

While such a broad transition-to-capitalism framework remains useful, the need for nuance has by now also been established. As chapters 2 and 3 have shown, broad structural changes impact in different ways in different locations – depending on cultural conventions, for instance, or on the availability of off-farm employment, or even on the range of crops being produced. Regarding hybrid crops in India, a contrast must be drawn, for example, between wheat- and rice-producing areas (Harriss 1977: 238–41). Presented here in some detail, the contrast provides initial ammunition for doubting the applicability of the concept of strict polarization.

Detailed ethnography on social differentiation in mechanized wheat-growing areas does not support the notion of a clear-cut polarization in which all transactions would be impersonal and cash-based. This can be seen, for instance, in India's north-west, which is a showpiece of hi-tech production achievement. The region's record for social and land reform being poor, it is easy to see why the image of polarization became attractive. Indeed, the twisted land reforms and the prospect of 'improved' agriculture in Haryana and Punjab have resulted in the large-scale 'eviction of tenants and [the] resumption of tenanted land for cultivation with hired labour' (Sen 1982: 35). Such developments suggest polarization. The possibility of a neat dichotomy between 'haves' and 'have-nots' is countered, however, by the fact that small-scale farmers have grown in numbers, since 'improved' wheat technology can be tried out in small doses (Sen 1982: 48). Wheat strains being hardy, farmers can get some results even when applying only half the inputs required. This, as Lerche's case study in Uttar Pradesh so clearly showed (Lerche 1995; see chapter 3 above), reduces the possibility of a strictly polarized world, but without closing the door on the possibility of increased social differentiation.

The concept of polarization has also been rejected for mechanized rice-growing areas. One of the earliest anthropological studies of the impact of GR technology on a rice-growing village is John Harriss's account of Randam in Tamil Nadu, which Harriss studied in 1961 and 1971 (Harriss 1977). The introduction of electric pump-sets and HYVs in the 1960s had drastically altered labour organization. In broad terms, the new technology had increased the amount of wet land available and made multiple cropping possible, which in turn had created *more work overall*. The pump-sets, however, had reduced the availability of water-lifting work for men, and lowered their input in threshing. Despite some compensation, such as nurseries needing more men to pluck seedlings, opportunities for paid male labour had stayed 'roughly constant, or might even be reduced' (Harriss 1977: 228). This stagnation had caused the exodus of several scheduled caste (Harijan) households, forced off the land after chalking up debts they could not repay. Harriss acknowledges that socio-economic disparities in Randam had definitely increased – between small farmers and bigger farmers, and among the smaller farmers themselves – but there was no question of a wholesale transition to cash-based, impersonal labour relations. 'Vertical' relations of patronage, with their *personalized* rights and duties, had persisted as well (Harriss 1977: 242).

The question whether rural relations of production are evolving into employer–employee relations has also stimulated debate on Thailand. Again, while some writers perceive polarization, others recognize widening socio-economic cleavages complicated by important cross-cutting factors. Thus Anan (1989) perceives, much like Stoler (1977) does for Java, how 'long-established forms of individual bargaining within relationships of patronage [had] given way to more antagonistic relations between employers and unattached and mobile labor' (Anan 1989: 19); a move facilitated by the availability of off-farm employment, especially in Bangkok. The need for nuance becomes clear, however, when analysts question the usefulness of a single-factor explanation. Thus, while accepting that labour relations have generally turned into capitalist ones, Philip Hirsch (1990) argues that it is too facile to suggest that a strictly polarized world would have emerged. He observes, crucially, that land is no longer the single criterion on which *local perceptions* of change hinge. Villagers increasingly 'differentiate according to cash as well as land holdings' (Hirsch 1990: 27). This injection of nuance reinforces the plea, made very explicit by Murray Leaf (see below), not to focus exclusively on displacement when assessing the impact of the GR.

This is not to deny that conditions in rural Thailand are dire, as can be seen in the deteriorating returns to labour for millions of sharecroppers. Where they have persisted, sharecropping arrangements are now regularly revised and renegotiated, but mostly to the detriment of tenants. Negotiations are strained because sharecropping is less and less on parental land, its 'traditional' locus. (Too many parents have lost their land for the 'traditional' system to continue.) The upshot is that landowners now claim shares of up to two-thirds of the harvest, sometimes also demanding cash (Anan 1989: 120). Generally though, landlords will remain 'careful not to demand more than half of the harvest from main-season paddy as rent, because this rice is so essential for sustaining the life of their tenants' (Anan 1989: 111). Landowners know they still need the loyalty of a stable core of tenants if they want to avoid reliance on difficult-to-control hired labourers. Again, 'vertical' personal relationships persist alongside, or dovetailed with, new impersonal relationships regulated by cash.

But tenurial developments in rural Thailand have done little to improve the livelihood security of poor producers. While 'some poorer villagers [have managed] to hang onto small plots of land for the subsistence production of the locally consumed glutinous rice, using as much family and exchange labor as possible', many others have joined the ranks of a swelling agricultural wage market or have diversified into nonagricultural employment (Anan 1989: 98). In either case, the returns to labour are pitiful. Agricultural wage rates have become so abysmal that labourers now regularly 'go under' (Hirsch 1990: 115). Rates paid to young men in woodcarving may sometimes be attractive, but casual off-farm work for women (for example bamboo weaving for teenage girls) is restricted and paid poorly in the extreme, as is petty trading and selling prepared foods, something poorer women do (Anan 1989: 115).

Thai studies, we note in passing, still offer comparatively little empirical data on actual bargaining processes at the household level; a point also made for India (see chapter 3 above). The calibre of household-level research in the rural Thailand, and the wider region of Southeast Asia, needs boosting. Hart, Turton and White have called for better analysis of gender and intergenerational issues regarding 'diversification which, particularly among the poor, often entails shifts in the division of labor as well as complex patterns of migration and labor circulation that both reflect and shape national and international patterns of accumulation' (Hart et al. 1989: 10). Gerke's research on Java, reviewed below, was a decisive response, but more research of its kind is needed.

Changing Technology, Work Patterns and Rewards

Commoditization and new farming technologies have brought changes that vary significantly over regions (also within regions) and over time. Berry recognizes this, for instance, with reference to the remuneration of women who work on their husbands' cocoa farms.

> In the cocoa economies of West Africa, women who worked on their husbands' farms without pay expected their husbands to contribute more to household expenses or give their wives money for trade when their cocoa farms began to bear. However, the extent to which wives were actually able to realize these expectations varied among women and over time. (Berry 1993: 155)

Women's age and the developmental stage of their households (Goody 1958) determine expectations, as does the nature of their conjugal contracts. As seen earlier for Bwisha, Congo-Zaire, such contracts are affected by generalized poverty. In the absence of bridewealth, which lowers the level of mutual trust between spouses, the prospect of remuneration is bleak. Where bridewealth has been completed, where husbands and wives 'understand each other' and both feel economically secure, women are more likely to share in their husbands' cash windfalls (Fairhead 1990). That women are not always excluded from resource management and its rewards has also been documented for Botswana, where Pauline Peters recorded the frequency with which men consulted wives over livestock management (Peters 1986: 145–50). These consultations did not entitle women to control all the fruits of their labour, nor was there gender equivalence in the rewards, but they did raise women's chances of achieving food security for themselves. Callear has developed a similar argument for Wedza district, Zimbabwe, again in the context of male outmigration (Callear 1985: 226).

Despite the regional (and temporal) variations in on-farm patterns of recruitment and reward, structural obstacles that limit or deny women their just reward remain real enough. They are, moreover, exacerbated when development policies ignore gender relations and impose ethnocentric assumptions, as happened in the Jahaly Pacharr project (see chapter 3 above). Interventions that typically fail to serve women are agricultural extension projects that target men and ignore women's pivotal role in production; nutritional schemes that 'teach mothers' but neglect to address the structural constraints to which women are subjected (Wheeler 1986; Whitehead 1990a, 1990b); and structural adjustment programmes that omit to consider the implications for women (Elson 1991; Lockwood 1992; Mbilinyi 1990).

Women's struggle for fair remuneration is not helped either when the status of a new crop is ambiguous, as it tends to be. This is especially so when conflicting demands are made on a crop that can be grown for both food or cash. Thus, when hybrid maize displaced millet in Zambia's Northern Province, the new crop was perceived both as a food crop and a national cash crop which would make the country self-sufficient in its staple food. Because of its national importance, hybrid maize was labelled a crop for men (by men), but as it was the new household staple, women associated it with other crops they controlled. This caused much friction. In addition, where familiar food crops acquire new meanings there is again scope for uncertainty, contestation and tension. Fairhead (1992a) puts this in perspective for Central Africa: 'Ambiguities arise in particular because men may consider that they control household wealth (which in earlier times did not encompass food, since food was not marketed), whereas women have always considered the disposal of food crops as their concern' (Fairhead 1992a: 30). Likewise, when the government of Zambia put a price on cassava in the late 1980s, women in Luapula feared that if they made money from this crop, their control over it would be challenged by husbands. Men were likely to claim that growing cassava was now a cash-oriented activity (like maize-growing) and therefore within the male domain (Gatter 1993: 163).

Men tend to get the best deals out of 'development' initiatives. In areas of mechanized, high-input agriculture, it is regularly observed that women lose out on the new jobs and remain confined to the more traditional, low-input, low-value jobs. This is well documented for India's 'advanced' wheat-growing regions, where GR technology altered the sexual division of labour in two basic ways. First, as seen in Haryana and Punjab, mechanized agriculture displaced women labourers from familiar tasks such as wheat threshing, corn shelling, sugar cane crushing, sowing and weeding, while most new tasks fell to men. Men thus continued to earn on a regular basis, albeit in smaller numbers. The narrowing of the range of women's tasks caused women to 'crowd' into casual seasonal jobs where competition was high and wage rates were depressed, a phenomenon typical of capitalist labour markets (Sen 1982: 46–7). Today, women are unwilling partners in this 'crowded' market; they take part mostly as members of enterprising households with restricted access to land and credit, and which struggle with the 'finance intensity' of the GR (Sen 1982: 30).

Gita Sen's observations concur with those made for other wheat-growing regions, for example by Miriam Sharma (1985) and Jens Lerche (1995), both of whom researched in Uttar Pradesh, north India. Lerche noted for Pariawan, the study village, that the agricultural labour market had contracted to peak seasons. Outside these seasons, would-be labourers went in search of work to the nearby towns (Lerche 1995: 493). Such off-farm work brought benefits to many Chamar 'households', but not necessarily to their women (see chapter 3 above). Murray Leaf too, despite his positive assessment of GR impact, did not fail to record that whereas the wages of experienced and skilled agricultural workers (men) went up fivefold between 1965 and 1978 (Leaf 1983: 254), the rates for weeding and transplanting 'increased rather modestly from [two rupees] a day plus one meal and two teas to Rs 5 plus one tea and two meals' (1983: 251). Such imbalances between the genders confirm that the GR overvalues men's work and devalues that of women (Sharma 1985: 83; see also chapter 6 below).[3]

Writing about Arunpur, Sharma observed likewise how mechanized agriculture squeezed low-caste and resource-poor women out of agriculture and into the more laborious, less secure wage market (Sharma 1985: 76). Although Sharma does not use the term 'crowding', the situation she describes matches Sen's analysis. Despite the lower risk involved in growing 'improved' wheat, numerous poor peasant farmers, men and women, have lost their peasant status to become dependent on periodic wage labour. Sharma confirms that work opportunities for the dispossessed are now restricted to (two) harvest periods. Opportunities total about thirty to sixty days, during which 'women, men, and children all work approximately 12 hours a day (sunrise to sunset) and with about an hour free for lunch' (Sharma 1985: 77). Poor men were less adversely affected (Sharma 1985: 65).

Poor remuneration for women agricultural labourers must also be understood in the context of certain positive changes wrought by India's labour movements. Mencher makes this point for 'advanced' rice-growing regions, where labour movements secured reasonable working hours and more decent rates. The better conditions, however, far from improving the agricultural labourer's lot, led landlords to cut back on the amount of work they would offer (Mencher 1985: 366–7). These cutbacks increased competition among poor agricultural workers and generally lowered their incomes. For landless women in Tamil Nadu, Mencher adds that they could not compensate for such losses by drawing upon other sources of income. The effects on family welfare were dire, especially on child nutrition (Mencher 1985: 366). This kind of situation becomes alarming when one takes into account that 'the proportion of income contributed by wage-earning women to the household [was generally] far higher than that of their earning husbands' (Mencher 1985: 365).[4]

In sum, the technological benefits of 'improved' agricultural production have been compromised by losses in social equity and social security. The squeeze is felt by women more than by men, and particularly by women from households that are poor or that struggle financially to keep on top of production costs.

But before we accept that this bleakest of scenarios applies throughout South and South-East Asia, two further questions must be considered: To what extent has 'improved' agriculture increased the number of seasons, and therefore the amount of work throughout the year? And what about women's prospects in petty trading? Studies regarding the longer-term impact of GR technology on women's lives emphasize that compensation for displacement (for example 'crowding') exists because of the overall increase in work: the extra seasons and harvests (Gerke 1992; White 1992). And likewise, there is evidence that 'some' dispossessed women have successfully moved into trade. Such studies are still few and far between (and how many is 'some'?), but they must be taken seriously.

Thus, for the Bangladesh village of Kumirpur, where she researched and where new rice technologies were adopted, Sarah White concludes that the introduction of mechanized irrigation, along with HYV seeds and other external inputs, negatively affected three main areas: forest cover, diet and income from familiar sources. In this, poorer women were disproportionately affected, because they 'lack[ed] the means to purchase alternatives to hitherto free resources' (White 1992: 50). Poorer women also suffered more because the GR-induced changes meant the loss of several income sources; sales of locally produced milk, dung sticks, fruit, vegetables and canal fish were all down (White 1992: 49–50). These consequences are not to be taken lightly. Despite such depressing outcomes, not all was gloom-and-doom in Kumirpur. On the positive side, villagers applauded the net increase in agricultural wage-labour opportunities. Notwithstanding the ever-low returns for such work and (as in Java) the presence of migrant labour parties at harvest time, household members *from all rural classes* agreed that there was now (late 1980s) more work available throughout the year and that households dependent on income from agricultural wage labour were better off than they used to be (White 1992: 62). Exceptions to the low-pay policy also existed, with certain households actually enjoying a rise in wages. White elaborates: 'there is evidence that the terms of exchange have shifted in the workers' favour: landowners now often seek out workers, rather than waiting for them to come and ask for work as in the past' (White 1992: 62).

Solvay Gerke's research on the activities of poor landless women in Java (Gerke 1992) comes to similar conclusions. Her starting-point is that research on the impact of the GR in Java/Indonesia in the 1970s occurred at a time when rice production was severely depressed (due to plant-hopper plagues) and the practice of a third harvest, which meant more employment, had not yet been established (Gerke 1992: 95). By the time of her own research in the late 1980s, the hopper plagues had gone and the third crop had become firmly rooted. Researching a good decade after the initial impact studies had been conducted, Gerke found that the negative effects 'were not as severe as it had been assumed earlier' (1992: 95). New plants, production increases and more harvests had brought some prosperity – and more positive research analyses (cf. Manning 1988a, 1988b; Maurer 1989; Schweizer 1987, 1989).

These production increases, Gerke suggests, 'might be the reason why the expected polarization did not occur'. She accepts, though, much like Lerche does for wheat-growing Uttar Pradesh, that the gap between landholders and landless is wider than it was ten years ago, but counters that both groups are better off today (Manning 1988a: 72). For some labourers, recruitment has also become more secure.

> It is for example common for a small group of labourers to be permanently employed by a middle-man (*penebas*) for the harvest, which provides them with a secure income. Schweizer (1987) mentioned that 'the harvesters now earn a smaller wage in the "tebasan" [i.e. the exclusionary market] than in the owner-harvest, but this disadvantage . . . was clearly more than offset by the additional work [of a third harvest] and the increased yield' (Schweizer 1987: 66). (Gerke 1992: 95)

When opportunities for agricultural wage labour increased in the second half of the 1980s, both the landless and the landed became better off. In this, Gerke echoes Sarah White's verdict on Kumirpur village, Bangladesh, that 'the aspect of increased employment availability should not be underestimated'. The point is similar to what Murray Leaf argued for the wheat-growing village of Shahidpur (Leaf 1983), and in line with Joachim Voss's portrayal of better land/labour utilization in Sagada, the Philippines (Voss 1987).

Gerke's more upbeat analysis does not mean that she is scathing about the findings from the earlier research. She fully accepts that the GR has had 'obvious negative consequences for the poor', poor women in particular. She acknowledges the heavy social costs brought on by the replacement of (rice) hand pounding and the decline in traditional forms of labour exchange, negative consequences first recorded in Ann Stoler's research in the Javanese village of Kali Loro (Stoler 1977).

Before the GR, Java had known relatively 'open' markets in which many local people were rewarded in kind. With the GR, rural labour markets began to foster 'exclusionary practices', for example *tebasan* and *kedokan* (White 1989: 255). This resulted in a general loss of rights, especially secure harvesting rights within a context of mutual cooperation, known as *gotong-royong*. The 'old' system crumbled in 'progressive' villages when middlemen (*penebas*) stepped in with teams of male harvesters who used sickles and were paid in cash rather than rice (Stoler 1977: 691). These labour-saving practices eroded the patronage system and the relative livelihood security that had been part of it. Stoler saw the beginnings of a process of reduced work opportunities, particularly for women in harvesting, and a general weakening of the bargaining position of all poor people. Patron–client ties, she concluded, were being transformed into employer–employee relations; labourers now performed for households with which they had no long-term social or economic ties (Stoler 1977: 681). In Kali Loro, poor (landless) people still retained harvesting rights on their patron's land, but rights farther afield were being denied.[5] This conclusion, along with the claim that polarization had set in, runs parallel to certain analyses of agrarian change in India (Sen 1982; Sharma 1985). The social cost of the transition to GR agriculture fell disproportionately on women from poorer households, since 'rice harvesting is by far [their] most productive source of income' (Stoler 1977: 686; see also Hüsken and White 1989: 255).[6] Stoler remarks that possible alternatives – for example mat making and petty trade – were so poorly paid that they attracted only women from larger landholding households who commanded relatively large amounts of capital and whose basic rice requirements were fully met.

Importantly, Gerke acknowledges that many agricultural labourers continue to suffer from the restructuring of relationships in the wake of the GR. But, she argues, there is an equal need to be aware of the more recent, more positive developments in 'improved' agriculture. Thus, by the late 1980s and early 1990s, Java had more and better rice harvests, while many of its displaced women agricultural labourers had branched out successfully into petty trade. In this respect, Gerke found women to be more adaptable than men. 'While male activities have traditionally concentrated on rice cultivation, women have always been involved in a greater variety of income earning activities in the small-scale trade sector and in food production (Stoler 1976: 125)' (Gerke 1992: 95). The 1980s especially were a decade of great expansion in the trade sector, 'and many women were able to earn a small living through trading activities' (Gerke 1992: 95–6).

But women's opinion on whether the new conditions in agriculture were to be welcomed differed according to age. While younger women approved of the shift from rice-paid to cash-paid labour opportunities older women deplored it. Older women commented that:

> the high yielding rice varieties and the new technology are punishing the poor landless people and small landowners. [As one woman said:] 'Now, you have to pay for everything, you have to buy the seed, you have to buy the fertilizer, the pesticides . . . and if you don't have land of your own, you will not get any rice, you have to buy the rice too. There are no *derep* people anymore' [i.e. people who help in the harvest for a share]. (Gerke 1992: 100)

Younger women wage labourers did not care too much about the changes: 'payment in cash for all types of agricultural labour [had] become "usual". Most of them [were] content with this development' (Gerke 1992: 101).

The importance of extra harvests and extra work, and the benefits that may accrue to women's work, were not often highlighted in early research on the GR, with some exceptions (Harriss 1977; Leaf 1983). For the rice-growing village of Randam, John Harriss stated firmly how 'improved' rice-cropping had increased the work available to women wage labourers, especially in relation to transplanting, weeding and harvesting. Women also continued to do 'as much manuring work as men and contribute[d] to threshing' (Harriss 1977: 228). The prospects of work for men were not so good; work for men had stagnated or declined. This went against the general drift of analysis by Joan Mencher, whose overview of gendered access to work in GR Tamil Nadu showed that women were losing out relative to men (Mencher 1985).[7] Increases in agricultural wage labour were also reported by Murray Leaf, whose work on Shahidpur (Leaf 1983) will be considered shortly.

Not 'It': The Multifaceted Side of Modern Farming Technology

More recent analyses of the impact of GR farming (Gerke 1992; White 1992), which stress gains as well as losses, have a forerunner in Murray Leaf who, back in the 1980s, advocated a broader conception of 'the Green Revolution'. After researching the wheat-growing Punjabi village of Shahidpur (pseudonym) in 1965 and 1978, Leaf presented a rosy picture of the changes. On revisiting Shahidpur, he found that there was now 'so much more work . . . that on an annual basis [the rewards in cash and kind added] up to substantial increases' (Leaf 1983: 251). The information Leaf presented, alas not broken down by gender, evoked the existence of *a village community* in full economic and social development, and was a plea for broadening the focus of analysis, i.e. for moving away from the single issue of displacement.

An important aspect of Leaf's follow-up study is that he reports positive changes at the community level. (Lerche also did this, cf. chapter 3 above.) Most noteworthy is that the village council, the *panchayat*, had transformed itself during the interim years into 'a corporate entity in its own right'; the council now worked to help the village as a whole (Leaf 1983: 241). Evidence existed in the construction of a village school, public wells, and in the greater accessibility of credit. Whereas the local cooperative bank used to give credit only to people with suitable capital security, the same bank in 1978 provided credit against future crops, thus serving a wider section of the community. So impressed was Leaf with these changes that he felt confident that small farmers were now 'in a much better position to assume developmental risk' (1983: 261). Farmers, Leaf asserts, experienced an interdependent world, not a dependent one. Whilst there could be no doubt that Shahidpur in 1965 had been 'far closer to being self-contained' (1983: 239), Leaf was convinced that by 1978 farmers did indeed experience a healthy interdependence. These positive impressions, I suggest, could be related to the technical point noted earlier that improved wheat technology is comparatively easy to adopt. This technicality may explain why most landholding villagers in Shahidpur said they controlled the new technology and felt at ease with having essential services located outside the village.

Leaf's argument, though, begs several questions. And especially *who is actually talking here*? Leaf uses an undifferentiated 'farmer' category and takes 'the household' (undifferentiated) and 'the village' to be appropriate units of study. This is troublesome. Choice of these units does not invalidate the conclusions reached, but calls for additional, more diversified information. What, for instance, are the views of landless labourers, those who stayed and those forced to leave; what are the views of women, those who survived as cultivators and those forced into the casual-seasonal labour market; what are the views of the young and the old? And how secure is 'the market' which provides Shahidpur with the goods it must now import? In the absence of a more differentiated approach to labour inputs, wage rates and family budgets, and of an analysis of locally situated discourses of modernity (i.e. in-depth analysis of the concepts of dependence and interdependence), it is difficult to fully share in Leaf's enthusiastic conclusion that the improvements in general welfare 'have gone at least as much to the poorer villagers as to the wealthier' (Leaf 1983: 268). The ultimate question has to be: Is social reality revealed here or are we instead seeing the researcher's own mind at work?

These serious reservations aside, Leaf's argument must be treated as an important counter to those analyses that regard the agrarian scene under GR conditions as invariably a retrograde step. His focus on more work overall – also stressed for other GR areas (Gerke 1992; Harris 1977; White 1992) – deserves our attention, as does the focus on community benefits. The notion of an interdependent world, moreover, is close to Voss's argument (Voss 1987, discussed below) of how Sagada, a community in the Philippines, engaged with labour and commodity markets *on their own terms*. Importantly too, Leaf's optimism is in tune with the recent reassessment of biodiversity losses in West Africa, losses that 'suddenly' appear far less dramatic than previously assumed (cf. chapter 6 below). Particularly refreshing is the fact that Leaf guards against a monolithic conceptualization of the Green Revolution. It is methodologically unsound, he argues, to reduce the GR phenomenon to a single facet or relationship. Leaf is suspicious of studies that focus solely on the displacement of labour by mechanization, pointing out that labour displacement 'can mean very different things in different places depending on the other opportunities available to those displaced' (Leaf 1983: 228). An exclusive focus on agricultural labour displacement fails to appreciate repercussions that carry social benefits, as Gerke and White have confirmed.

The issue here is how people use human agency in the face of change and uncertainty. Basically, when confronted with structured constraints and hardships, poor farmers do not resign themselves. This is well illustrated, for example, in farmer reactions to the high cost of 'improved' agriculture in Pampangan, the Philippino village where Banzon-Bautista (1989) researched. By the end of the 1980s, several peasant farmers who struggled financially (12 per cent of the village) reconsidered the wisdom of a clean break with past farming practices. Closing rank with those who had been sceptical about the hi-tech approach from the start, these farmers cut their chemical inputs and began combining modern with more traditional rice varieties (Banzon-Bautista 1989: 147).

Farmers' active response to new technological possibilities has also been highlighted for the Sagada Igorot area in Northern Luzon (Jefremovas 1993; Voss 1987). The Sagada ethnography is a fine example of how 'global' change must be understood as 'relocalized' change (cf. chapter 1 above).

Case Study 4.1: GR Agriculture in Sagada, the Philippines

Sagada Igorots came to grips with 'global change' in the 1970s when they kept the terms and type of their incorporation on a locally favourable, non-capitalist basis (Voss 1987: 123). Indeed, over the past few decades the basic structure of community relations in Sagada has been maintained and reproduced, especially through ritual pig-feasting (1987: 128), an institution now partly commoditized. Migrants who come home for the festivals may now buy a pig rather than raise it, but the entry of commoditized pigs remains strictly regulated. Pig-feasting has acquired a new vitality and become more frequent.

Taking a stance against deterministic models of agrarian change, Voss argues that regulated commoditization in pig-feasting has benefited the community: labour and land, both under-utilized since the cessation of feuding and headhunting in the 1970s, are once again utilized productively (1987: 135). It is precisely the increase in ritual pig-feasting – which means more gift/debt relationships – which accounts for the better utilization. Better regulated access to land *in turn* facilitated the introduction of HYV crops that enhance soil fertility. (Note this interesting reversal of the common perspective that GR technology is always imposed from the outside.) Thus, Sagada's

> rice fields are now used during the four-month fallow period to produce a crop of legumes for sale on the market. Far from undercutting subsistence rice production, this enhances it by increasing the nitrogen content of the soil. Also, many of the lower fields which previously produced only one crop of rice per year now are able to produce two crops, because of the introduction of faster maturing rice varieties. (1987:135)

Far from being a threat to people's livelihoods, commoditization in Sagada has reinvigorated the indigenous redistribution system and produced benefits for all. That Sagadans continue to maintain their non-capitalist orientation is a convincing demonstration that healthy interdependence (cf. Leaf 1983) is possible *provided the right conditions prevail.* Today, by skilfully combining market and non-market relations, Sagadan farmers produce abundant vegetables and are able to absorb the risk of seasonal glut without loss of economic independence. As Villia Jefremovas shows, a surprisingly high number of producer-sellers are 'able to "ride the green tide" without sinking into the massive indebtedness and virtual tenancy seen in other parts of the Cordillera Central' (Jefremovas 1993: 1). Jefremovas refers to more recently populated areas, such as Mandaymen (Russell 1987), where producer-sellers are tied to middlemen who deny them better prices and lower commission rates (see also chapter 5 below). In Sagada, by contrast, various forms of cooperative and mutual-help institutions underpin the ability to 'ride the green tide'. Known as *ob-obbo*, these institutions can be the obligation to give a certain sum of money or form of help in a crisis or life cycle event, or they can be an agreement to exchange labor on a day-for-a-day basis with friends, kin and neighbors. [This] 'social safety net' enables many Sagadans to underwrite their economic activities, remain independent and achieve a measure of success in various undertakings. (Jefremovas 1993: 2)

A fairly egalitarian society, where landlessness stands at under 1 per cent, Sagada is coping well with the opportunities and pitfalls of modern economy and agriculture. The encounter is *on their terms*, i.e. on terms that honour, even reinforce, community and clan ownership of resources and rights.

If much of this chapter argues in favour of an analysis which focuses simultaneously on the importance of structured constraints and power imbalances, and ways in which these constraints can be absorbed, perhaps overcome, through human agency, we still need to appreciate that countervailing strategies require energy, and that there are limits to how energetic/innovative one can be when structured constraints begin to hurt. Women's labour burdens, and the implications for self-perception, are a special concern here. Before we look at how poor women may strategize to overcome excessive hardship, it is useful to reflect on how their workloads are structured.

'Double Days' and Women's Self-Perception

How serious the concern over women's labour burden is is firmly stated by Solvay Gerke herself. Despite the upbeat assessment of how Javanese women cope with the longer-term effects of the GR, Gerke is most concerned that enterprising women may be paying the price in terms of how they manage their time, because 'running a small trade business or looking for so far unexploited working opportunities require more initiative [and time] than harvesting and pounding in agriculture' (1992: 96). Consequently, women will only improve their economic security, and that of their households, if they can appropriate the extra time and resources required without opposition from men. Impoverishment may help free up time and remove certain constraints (cf. Kabeer 1990; see also Agarwal 1994a), yet husbands and senior men may not sympathize with women's claims if the basis of their own authority is threatened as a result. Facing such a threat, imagined or real, men may in turn threaten women, most likely with a mixture of economic and moral argument, and physical force perhaps, as happened to Ma Cousine in chapter 2. And yet, as the literature on women and structural adjustment in Africa so clearly shows, many women now work longer days, within and outside their homes, in an effort simply to make ends meet. The incomes they bring home regularly exceed those of men. Optimal conditions for women are not easily secured, not even by policy initiatives in communist states like China.

Women's 'double days' have been the focus of research in Asia too, where work intensity is often closely linked to class/caste positions. Miriam Sharma (1985) gives us an informative illustration. Writing about Arunpur in Uttar Pradesh, India, Sharma juxtaposes the wealthy joint families of the Bhumihar caste, whose common stake in land keeps them together, with the small nuclear households of Chamars, who own little or no land. One consequence is that Bhumihar brides join households full of people who have control over them: mother-in-law, elder sister-in-law, father-in-law, husband, husband's elder brothers, and so on. A Bhumihar woman thus remains physically in seclusion, 'confined to household chores, and must observe purdah (veiling) before all males elder to her husband' (Sharma 1985: 73). In Chamar nuclear households, in contrast, there are fewer people who have control over a woman's life. After marriage, 'a Chamar woman moves freely, and her work as a daily wage labourer (when available) puts her in the position of being an important provider' (Sharma 1985: 77). With an independent source of income, the Untouchable Chamar woman has 'greater independence, voice in decisions and – ultimately – status in the *household*', but not in society at large (Sharma 1985: 78).

Under these conditions, the Chamar woman does not experience her independence as enviable. Rather, she feels short of hands, never able to escape the drudgery of the day's multiple routine tasks (Sharma 1985: 75). Suffering truly 'from a double day of work' (Sharma 1985: 76), the Chamar woman's lot resembles that of poor women in the high hills of Nepal (Pradhan 1985) and Chinese peasant women who stay home to produce domestic sidelines but fail to earn workpoints and social prestige (Croll 1983a, 1983b, 1994). It is different for Bhumihar women. In their large joint households, daily chores are divided up 'so that the burden, although undoubtedly falling heaviest on the youngest bride, is somewhat lessened all around. At times of sickness or emergency, a woman may always find another pair of (female) hands to take over the chores' (Sharma 1985: 76).

Facing these multiple forms of hardship and exploitation, Chamar women in Arunpur would prefer to relinquish their comparative independence and higher status in the household, and go into purdah (Sharma 1985: 82). False consciousness? No, not quite. The woman who is 'free' to make certain economic decisions is by definition also poor and low-caste. As she sees it, her independence equals poverty, which is a price 'too high for such "freedoms"' (Sharma 1985: 83).

In China too, it is women who bear the brunt of the production tasks, especially when their households are not large. Government attempts to reduce the domestic demands on women's labour have been multiple since 1949, for instance regarding food provisioning, processing and cooking, but these policies have been more successful in the cities than in the countryside (Croll 1983a: 312). For rural women, the 'double day' continues. Moreover, it is not just that state interventions have failed to reduce the burden; some interventions, both under Mao and since the 1978 reforms, have directly promoted the 'double day'. In developing her thesis, Croll first corrects the often-made assumption that Mao's regime of communes and collectivization had effectively destroyed the *jia* estate (landed property) and thereby the economic basis for the power of the (male) household head. The assumption that 'the household' had died under 'the commune' proved false, because Mao had retained the individual rural household as a major production unit. Collectivization thus produced the opposite effect of what was intended: '[The] economy of the domestic group no longer relied on the exploitation of the family lands or estate but on the waged and domestic labour of each member of the domestic group. [Unsurprisingly, therefore] parents perceived . . . a direct correlation between the size of the family and its income and welfare' (Croll 1983b: 471).The premium on domestic labour under Mao promoted not smaller domestic units, but larger ones; elaborate (stem or joint) household forms based on intergenerational interdependence. These were also fostered after 1978, because the one-child policy and ban on hiring labour (Croll 1983b: 468–70) continued the desperate need for household labour. Expanded household forms were ideally equipped 'to distribute [their] labour between collective wage-earning and private production' (Croll 1983a: 310).

What did this mean in terms of intra-household gender relations? How did households respond to the call that women join the collective labour force and participate in public activity? Households (meaning men) responded by keeping one woman out of wage labour, either full-time or part-time on a seasonal basis (Croll 1983a: 316). Alternatively, in female-headed households women might 'go to work late and return from the fields early, perhaps contributing a total of two to three hours less per day than full-time male workers and therefore earning fewer work points' (Croll 1983a: 316). And here precisely lay the catch. What mattered to women's status was not the 'invisible' domestic work they undertook, but the wages they brought home and the work points they earned. Rural women who stayed at home ended up with 'less mobility in employment and less access to the collective decision-making arena' (Croll 1983a: 316–17). Like poor Chamar women in India, they gained some credit in their homes, but it was not what they wanted as there was no let up in the 'double days' they worked. Self-provisioning in non-staples and domestic work combined to make very substantial demands on women's labour (Croll 1983a: 317).

Following severe decreases in the availability of arable land in the first half of the 1980s, caused by 'an expansion in village and township enterprises and housebuilding' (Croll 1994: 98), the government of China reconsidered its rural production strategy by redressing the balance between village collective and household. This new 'readjustment' (*tiaozheng*) campaign meant that villages reclaimed responsibility for lands and once again carried major production costs in return for control over labour allocations, inputs and profits (Croll 1994: 100–1). While the 'readjustment' episode was by and large welcomed as a means of reducing the excessive demands on peasant labour (Croll 1994: 100–1), it also caused considerable frustration in that households now had to meet the expense of costly agricultural inputs such as fertilizer, agro-chemicals and seeds. The cost of these inputs, to be met annually, is so heavy that, as Croll points out for Henan (researched 1987) and Sichuan (researched 1988), it is 'perceived by many of the poorest villagers to outweigh any of the advantages of reform' (Croll 1994: 103). 'Readjustment' has done women no favours. If anything, 'the recent reforms [have] made their daily routines even more demanding' (Croll 1994: 165).

Struggles with Patriarchy: Still Scope for Bargaining?

Policy interventions that ignore women's economic contribution (for example in colonial Senegal, see chapter 3) or praise it in order to tax it (for example in 'reformed' China; also countries with SAPs), frequently result in a strengthening of 'local' patriarchal ideologies. Paradoxically, however, concurrent economic recessions that impoverish men may force women into positions that challenge the very power-base on which male authority rests. Walking this tightrope, women may be reluctant to openly challenge husbands and other senior men, as is seen in work by Raikes (1992) and Kabeer (1990), or they may take the view that enough is enough, and vote with their feet (Mbilinyi 1990). In this section we look at ethnographies that tell us about the relationship between poverty and patriarchy.

While patriarchy remains pervasive in Africa, cracks in the system are appearing, a major crack being caused by generalized poverty and men's ensuing inability to meet bridewealth expectations. (It is through bridewealth that control over a woman's productive and reproductive capabilities is transferred to men.) Men's problems may make women take matters in their own hands, yet, as ethnography from Kisii (in Kenya) shows, women may prefer a more conservative approach. In Kisii, women who have the means may now offer to pay off their own husband's bridewealth. This gives women a better say in decision-making and the distribution of rewards (Haakonsson 1985, cited in Raikes 1992: 90), but open confrontation is avoided. Kisii women are not out to take revenge on husbands and reverse existing forms of domination. Raikes explains:

> [Since] a woman's sons are not legally the father's until he has started to pay bridewealth, her security in land, as holding it in trust for them, awaits the same transaction. Until then, she can be turned out without recourse or compensation. Thus women have a bit more autonomy [especially in choosing husbands] and a lot less security. [Where women are able to] save up and pay their own bridewealth for this reason . . . [they use] their economic status to pressure the men they [live] with to pay bridewealth and regularize their status. . . . The reasons given included respect in the community and freedom from the harassment, theft or removal of property which single women tend to suffer. (Raikes 1992: 90–1)

Poor women in purdah in Bangladesh face similar problems and also avoid open confrontation. As poverty deepens, poor women's dependence on men (husbands, sons, sometimes brothers) 'becomes increasingly difficult to sustain and women are forced to adopt strategies which represent a break with their former dependent status' (Kabeer 1990: 139). Breaks are particularly evident in agriculture, where 'hitherto strictly enforced rules preventing women engaging in field-based stages of rice production are showing signs of crumbling' (Kabeer 1990: 141). Poor women have also 'entered in large numbers into public rural works projects, into small workshops and mills, and into petty trading activities in the bazaar economy' (Kabeer 1990: 142). Kabeer accepts that the concept of the 'patriarchal bargain' (Kandiyoti 1988) applies, yet stresses that the 'breaks' are not subversive: 'as long as male support is forthcoming, women's survival strategies will adhere as far as possible to social convention so as not to jeopardize their claims on male family members (Kabeer 1990: 139). Poor women in purdah, Kabeer contends, feel uncomfortable when poverty dictates that norms and relations be challenged within their *personal* lives; they thus 'challenge' husbands by force of circumstance, but there is no collective struggle for structural change. On the contrary, there is compliance whenever possible, as is seen when women sacrifice their nutritional status by giving preference to husbands and sons at mealtimes. In sum, women prefer to engage in activities that do not overtly challenge the boundaries of purdah, for example share-rearing small livestock, gleaning rice, or mat weaving at home (Kabeer 1990: 141).

Also writing on Bangladesh, Sarah White (1992) confirms that poverty pushes women to challenge deep-seated conventions. She writes: 'Strict segregation of actual men and women in the "male" and "female" markets depends on the household having the full complement of able-bodied and co-operative members of both genders that the culture assumes. In a large and perhaps increasing number of cases, this ideal is not fulfilled' (White 1992: 67). Kabeer (1990) and White (1992) both argue that the structure of male domination is extremely strong and that women, whether better off or poor, continue to work a 'double day' (White 1992: 60). Both are also committed to fighting the stereotyped portrayal of poor women as passive and helpless. But when it comes to assessing the full meaning of women's breaks with orthodoxy, a fundamental difference arises. For Kabeer, women's survival strategies and challenges are strictly personal and therefore 'incapable of transforming the position of poor women in the interlocking hierarchies of class and gender' (Kabeer 1990: 146). Women's strategies merely provide them with 'small areas of freedom from personalized forms of male control rather than freedom from patriarchal controls in general or from the constraints imposed by class relations' (Kabeer 1990: 145). White sees it differently. She too accepts the force of 'tradition', but she uses a different lens. While accepting that gender inequalities are structured through male control of the interlocked markets for land, labour and credit, White is eager that we should understand how these relationships between men are often mediated through women. Specifically, '[w]omen's work sustains male participation in the major markets and the networks which women foster serve to convey all kinds of information, including some about transactions from which they are formally excluded'(White 1992: 66). From this perspective women exercise power through being brokers; their struggles are not merely personal, but structural too.

There is still a dearth of empirical data on how gender roles are (re)negotiated in South-East Asia, but that they are, and that women sometimes reclaim lost territory, is beyond dispute. For example, writing about east Java after women were massively displaced as harvesters, Hesti Wijaya (1985) revealed how certain poor women took up sickles themselves to compete with male harvesters, before making them redundant. Again, it was poverty that made women challenge an 'established' practice (only men could use sickles), but the challenge was not just personal. Wijaya commented: 'Use of the sickle by women used to be considered as improper or "male", but pressure to survive and the threat of losing a means of livelihood encouraged these women to break common practices which have probably existed for centuries' (Wijaya 1985: 182).[8]

Despite the dearth of data, early research on Java did speak of social complexity and flexibility, thus hinting that 'bargaining with patriarchy' was a real possibility. Ben White's review (1985) of several micro-studies carried out on Java was insightful on this point. In a passage reminiscent of the argument by Wheeler and Abdullah (1988) on household food security (see chapter 2 above), White concluded that

> the sexual division of labor within the household is in practice not so clearcut as ideology suggests. Men, for example, will sometimes stay at home to babysit and cook a meal while adult women and girls are off harvesting, or trading at the market. Similarly, attempts to study household decision-making patterns have found that wives are neither so excluded from decisions in the extradomestic domain of production, nor so wholly in charge of the domestic (reproductive) domain as is implied by the normative segregation of these spheres of influence in community ideology. (White 1985: 132)

The scope for 'bargaining' appears real enough in this passage, yet the kind of domestic revolution required if 'expanded opportunities' are going to boost poor women's economic security, and that of their households, may not so easily get off the ground. Perhaps it is a question of age and generation (Gerke 1992), perhaps not. It may be too that the desire/pressure to maintain the status quo is very deeply ingrained (Raikes 1992; Kabeer 1990; Schoepf and Walu 1991). Whatever the motivations that prompt women to 'break with tradition' and explore new economic avenues, durable solutions will require more than the sympathetic ear of a few high-ranking policy-makers. As Agarwal (1994b: 84) emphasized in writing about land, the intra-household struggle over resources is also a struggle over meanings, and one to be fought on many levels. One level is not enough. Gender emancipation in China reached many spheres of life, especially public life, but has yet to touch the household, which is perhaps the most crucial level at which meanings are fought and forged.

Of African women who fight prejudice and patriarchy with some measure of success, it can be suggested that they do so both in their personal lives and on a collective basis. Bwisha women in eastern Congo-Zaire, for instance, glean their husbands' coffee fields for personal recompense but, as this hardly counts as structural subversion, they also engage in countervailing group strategies by joining extra-household organizations: churches, saving groups and cooperatives, all of which offer hope that some economic independence can be recouped (Fairhead 1990). In Rwanda too, in the mid-1980s, women joined cooperatives and campaigned successfully for fairer workloads and rewards (Pottier

1989b) and, as mentioned earlier, Tanzanian women are also increasingly defiant in the face of oppressive relations and injustice. 'Increasingly, peasant women and young people have refused to provide unpaid labour for husbands, fathers and other household "heads"' (Mbilinyi 1990: 117). In instances where they have marketing advantages over men, women may also market crops themselves or find ways of clawing back some of the profits their men make (see chapter 5 below).

A common strategy through which African women attempt to combine their collective and their personal struggles is the conversion of minor food crops, which women control, into major crops; a process which de-emphasizes the grain crops of men (Fairhead 1990, 1992a; Leach 1991, 1994). Fairhead details the process for Bwisha:

> The new food crops (cassava, bush beans, soya and colocasia) which have been adopted since the mid-1970s, and which now predominate for many households in Bwisha, were in fact all introduced by women as inter-crops.
>
> Women plant cassava wherever they can get away with it. . . . They plant colocasia in coffee groves, on the fringe of banana groves, and on odd plots near the house. In Bwisha, as Guyer (1986: 100) has argued elsewhere, field and inter-cropping types which women control have become the backbone of the food system, whereas crops which men help produce have greatly diminished in importance. (Fairhead 1992a: 31)

This storage-in-the-field strategy, which strengthens women's grip on the products of their labour, finds a parallel in the practice whereby Bangladeshi women sell the small livestock they share-rear

> to a middleman who comes to their homestead, even though he gives a lower price than the bazaar. [This] arrangement gives them greater control over the income. Relying on a husband (or other male intermediaries) to procure a higher price in the bazaar carries the risk that they will not receive the full returns for their labour. (Kabeer 1990: 144)

Small livestock (sheep or goats), like intercrops in Africa, are more likely to be regarded as women's property. And yet it would seem that these parallel strategies differ greatly in terms of their meanings: purely personal (and conducted from the homestead) in Bangladesh; both personal and collective (and conducted from the field) in Bwisha, Congo-Zaire. The contrast makes sense in view of the broad typology Kabeer set up between cohesive and not-so-cohesive conjugal units (Kabeer 1994: 116; see also chapter 2 above), yet there certainly is scope here for a more in-depth analysis of the meanings attached to women's strategies. Such an analysis would also consider how meanings may vary within a given locality, perhaps reflecting class and age, and over time.

Conclusion

Rather than summarize the many challenging arguments this chapter contains, let me make a suggestion regarding the future direction of research. Studies of labour organization on smallholder farms, or of agrarian change generally, stand to benefit from the post-structuralist feminist critique of the essentialist portrayal of so-called 'Third World' peasant women (e.g. Mohanty 1988; Parpart 1993). Like the construct 'woman', so the notion of the 'Green Revolution' (or commoditized agriculture) and 'its' impact have for too long remained focused on vulnerability – on the displacement of labour and land, on polarization – at the expense of seeing a plurality of experiences, strategies and outcomes. Parpart's argument that the 'vulnerability' of women in the 'Third World' is today 'neither so clear, nor so pervasive' (Parpart 1993: 456) must resonate in future appreciations of how poor women and men engage with the multiple components of modernized agriculture. The time has come for studies of agrarian change to drop the single-focus lens. The methodological challenge, as Leaf explained back in the early 1980s, is to understand the GR not as 'it', but as a collection of varied experiences. Work has begun: by Gerke (1992) for instance, who looks simultaneously at displacement and new opportunities; by Englund (1999), who argues that agrarian change cannot be understood in isolation from the study of personhood; by White (1992), who appreciates the new work opportunities despite obvious ecological costs; by Voss (1987) and Jefremovas (1993), who highlight strategies that show peasant farmers to be creatively engaged with 'global' change.

The challenge ahead is to further explore these 'alternative' perspectives, using a multi-focal lens, to bring them into mainstream analysis. But, and here lies the real challenge, this exploration must be achieved without detracting from the hardships that are also experienced, and with full appreciation of the power imbalances and hierarchies that are sustained and continually recreated. In this respect, research needs to clarify whether anti-poverty strategizing is merely personal or rather structural and collective in its impact.

Being critical of single-lens approaches to poor people's encounter with 'improved' agriculture does not, however, mean that one celebrates the free-market principle. While there is a need to correct monolithic approaches to agrarian change, there is an equal need to keep a clear focus on the potentially heavy social costs that transnational agribusiness inflicts. The next two chapters deal with the structure and diversity of markets.

5

Playing the Food Market
Actual Markets, Moralities and Social Engineering

For the past two decades an appeal to economic stabilization based on free-market trade has shaped development policy in the Bretton-Woods institutions (theWorld Bank and the IMF). Most international donors have followed suit, eager to 'get prices right' for all countries with debt-related balance of payment difficulties. At the centre of the approach is a set of measures presumed to be advantageous to smallholder agriculture (World Bank 1981, 1986). The set includes devaluation, the lifting of trade barriers, reduced public expenditure and curbs on state control in agricultural markets.

In the early 1990s, however, it became clear that this experimental set of corrective measures, known as 'macroeconomic structural adjustment', was hitting the poor. Unwarranted assumptions about how markets worked on the ground had left peasant farmers mostly worse off than before the experiment. The central assumption had been to believe that the removal of price controls and state subsidies would make economies optimally efficient through the impersonal play of supply and demand, thus giving small producers automatic access to more resources and better opportunities (Hewitt de Alcántara 1992: 2). Free-market economists and policy-makers had viewed 'the market' as natural and universal but threatened by backward cultural institutions, which included the state apparatus itself. Government interference with free-market forces, they believed, systematically 'distorted' market signals.

Within this abstract ahistorical framework there was no need to provide small farmers with the basic infrastructure and support services which they require before they can benefit from price incentives (Hewitt de Alcántara 1992: 2). Of this necessity several development economists were nonetheless well aware (Lipton 1977; Pinstrup-Andersen 1986). Crucially, programmes for structural adjustment (SAPs) were designed and implemented without any knowledge of how markets in 'the real world' were driven by complex processes of social and economic interaction.

This chapter has four parts. First, we discuss how food and crop markets, still the most common type of market (besides labour markets), are mediated by local culture and the exercise of power. This means that food and crop markets interlock with other markets – especially for land, labour and credit – and that degrees of interlocking can be mapped out on a continuum going from incomplete to complete integration. Second, we appreciate that actual markets are embedded in moral economies. Markets and debates about market organization are inherently about ideology and social engineering, about what kinds of people there should be. Attempts to create a certain type of person for entry into a certain type of market, however, do not necessarily achieve the intended goal. As historical evidence shows, colonial markets and ideologies spread and made their mark, but the resulting change was more diverse and autonomous than envisaged. So we ask: what are markets for and who benefits? Next, we examine the conditions under which small producers and rural traders (petty and middlemen) establish their working relationships. Finally, we ask how 'romantic' notions of farmer–trader relationships, as found in the theory of free-market liberalization or in the policy view that traders are parasites who sap the vitality of pristine, self-contained farms, relate to the political and cultural embeddedness of actual markets. Here we consider and critique the policies to which these romantic notions have led.

Given that all markets can be shown to be regulated by definition, we conclude that policy interventions should aim at *better* regulation, not *de*regulation (Bernstein 1996b). Space does not allow me to spell out what a programme for better market regulation might entail, but the debate continues in the next chapter where we discuss the international trade in genetically engineered seeds.

Embedded Markets

The chapters on land and labour have established how the increased cost of modern agriculture puts many smallholders at risk, especially when they run up serious debts early on in the farming season. Where small farmers control only limited assets and there is full market integration (as in Java or Bangladesh), the cost will be prohibitive and displacement results easily. In contrast, where resources are shared out more equitably, as in Sagada or in those parts of sub-Saharan Africa where land remains accessible, there is a better chance that small farmers accommodate the cost of 'improved' farming.

The logical extension of this argument is that levels of indebtedness determine the marketing options farmers have. We expect to find a varied picture regarding producer–marketeer relationships on the ground, going from totally unfree to (fairly) voluntary, flexible and 'equilibrating'. Put differently, terms of trade and trade channels are defined by local power structures. The diversity thus produced explains why it would be misleading '[to] speak of "the market"', as if there were a single integrated exchange environment' (Hewitt de Alcántara 1992: 7). To do so would be to discount variations, networks of micro-markets, that are very real indeed and may exist within a particular locality.

Aware of the range of structured variations that 'real markets' exhibit, anthropologists in the 1990s have battled to explain why markets cannot be understood in the terms of abstract economic theory. Specifically, their research and writings have focused on how 'deeply the notions of globalizing economic exchange (such as "commodity", "money" or "markets") are embedded in political processes, social institutions and cultural images at the local or regional level' (Gould and von Oppen 1994: 6–7).

For many anthropologists, though, the frenzy about 'real markets' was more like a rediscovery. If there was discovery too, it was perhaps in the realization that the seemingly more abstract markets of the Western world could be shown to be just as 'embedded' and regulated as were those that existed in remote places half a century ago. Thus, economic life in Tiv country, central Nigeria, in the 1950s (Bohannan 1953; Bohannan and Bohannan 1968) can be shown to have had much structural affinity with contemporary economies within the OECD. In Britain and other OECD countries, writes John Davis,

> governments legislate to curb axiomatic self-interest, and to create markets which approximate to the idealized model. A hierarchy of officials ... are devoted to creating markets where our local rules of fair trade are maintained with the ultimate authority of ministers and national bankers. Economists, expert in regulated markets, advise both traders and statesmen on how to stimulate a perfect market in the real world, to maintain competition and to control the free play of self-interest. It is a quite extraordinary exercise of power and ingenuity, sublety and skill. (Davis 1996: 57)

Davis uses the ethnography of Tiv markets and of 'tribal' markets in north-western Morocco (cf. Fogg 1940, 1941) to demonstrate that the inherent dangers of the marketplace (insecurity, violence, unfair trade) are here too overcome by well-established rules of conduct and penalties for infringement. The parallels with contemporary, 'modern' economies are so striking that we can only conclude that *marketplaces everywhere and at all times are regulated* through political, cultural and legal conventions.

The next step in understanding 'real' markets is to accept that those who make market policy – today and in the past – have more on their minds than 'pure' economic transactions. Gould and von Oppen put it succinctly:

> debates about market regulation or liberalization are not simply about the mechanics of economic transactions. Such issues are embedded deeply in normative discourse about social relations and political values. Competing images of 'the' market and its role express fundamental distinctions between contested notions of 'the good society' and the kinds of social bonds and associations upon which it should be based. (Gould and von Oppen 1994: 3–4)

From this perspective, the desire for commodities, once believed to be 'culture free', is understood to be equally influenced by culture, i.e. socially regulated in dynamic ways (Appadurai 1986: 29–30, paying tribute to Gell 1986). Consumption used to be regarded as 'private, atomic or passive', yet has become 'eminently social, relational and active' (Appadurai 1986: 31). For this insight we also thank Douglas and Isherwood (1981) and Baudrillard (1975, 1981). The converse applies as well: gift exchange is no longer considered as 'pure', disinterested and divorced from politics, but as strongly calculating. Referring to Malinowski's Trobriand ethnography (cf. Malinowski 1922), Appadurai reflects that a ceremonial *kula* transaction

> is not easily categorized as simple reciprocal exchange, far from the spirit of trade and commerce. Though monetary valuations are absent, both the nature of the objects and a variety of sources of flexibility in the system make it possible to have the sort of calculated exchange that I maintain is at the heart of the exchange of commodities. (Appadurai 1986: 19)

Once thought to be clear opposites, 'gifts' and 'commodities', like 'primitive' markets and 'modern' ones, have shaded into one another, their contours blurred. Both are now understood to be equally embedded in 'culture' and produced by power relations. One implication is that commodity relations too are regulated by moral discourse. This is reflected, for instance, in the Kenyan Luo concept of 'bitter money', which refers to money that makes certain modern transactions look morally suspect. In southern Luoland, gold, tobacco, land and cannabis 'are not necessarily considered evil or dangerous in themselves. What makes [them] dangerous is the selling, and the implicit disrespect or denial of someone else's rights or claims to [them]' (Shipton 1989: 28–9).

The argument that commodity relations are imbued with moral discourse can be extended to the 'detached' opinions of those neo-liberal economists who set market policy and attach conditions to World Bank/IMF loans. Their ideas too are manifestations of power embedded in cultural morality.

Market Moralities and Social Engineering: The Limits of Induced Change

One of the strongest manifestations of market 'embeddedness' is that markets are shaped by, and in turn help shape, notions of morality and personhood. Markets everywhere are about people as moral beings. Megan Vaughan demonstrates this with reference to colonial possessions in Africa and the Indian Ocean, where markets 'cannot function without some degree of consensus on acceptable and unacceptable behaviour' (Vaughan 1996: 61). Relying on institutionalized patterns of socialization, the colonial markets Vaughan analyses thus emerge as incorporating 'ideas, not only about the economic behaviour of societies and individual persons, but also about the very nature of the person' (1996: 61). Her analysis supports the growing awareness that empirical study of 'the market' illustrates time and time again how 'the economy' is best understood not as a material entity, but as a space of power and signification which produces 'human subjects and social order of a certain kind' (Escobar 1995: 59).

The idea that markets are culturally structured with categories of people in mind has spawned several volumes of empirical, historically situated studies (see Dilley 1992; Gould and von Oppen 1994; Davis 1996; Harriss-White 1996; Vaughan 1996). The general thrust of all these studies is that agricultural markets are regulated by definition. To add a further illustration, complementing the previous discussion on land and labour in South Asia, Harriss-White's (1996) analysis of food/crop markets in West Bengal and Coimbatore shows markets to be regulated by caste, gender, ethnicity and physical location. As they interact in specific localities, these attributes produce a *structured* diversity and complexity that goes undetected in abstract models of 'the market'. Regarding women's participation in food markets, Harriss-White specifies that:

Gender interacts with class and caste to structure agricultural markets in a 'plurality of oppressions' (Bardhan 1993). Women traders are socially restricted to rural locations, periodic markets and petty sales. . . . They are generally low caste and poor. Poor cultivating- and out-caste women make up 70% of the deliberately casualized commercial workforce and handle the bulk of the physical work. By contrast, women in asseted households are used as a means of accumulation of trading capital via the transfer payments made at marriage. (Harriss-White 1996: 34)

The link between economy (including forms of exchange and trade) and personhood has excited anthropologists ever since fieldwork began. In his appreciation of Malinowski's pioneering work, John Davis recalls the Trobriand scene of the 1940s, a space where 'how' you exchanged by and large determined 'who' you were. Exchange, trade and righteousness were inextricably entwined.

A good Trobriander was one who had a portfolio of exchanges going, and did them well. People who wished to be thought of as good Trobrianders – good men, good women, good gardeners, good magicians – had to play an appropriate range of pieces from the repertoire, and to do so fairly honestly, and with reasonable success. The set of expectations was sustained by moral, legal, religious sanctions. (Davis 1996: 49)

And of course, 'who you were' also determined who you could exchange with, i.e. 'how you exchanged'. 'Who' and 'how' were interrelated.

It was no different for the colonial officers who – as legislators, policy-makers, researchers and philosophers – 'brought civilization' to Africa. They too carried a portfolio and played set pieces from the repertoire. Among their more ambitious pieces was the duty to create good colonial citizens, that is people prepared to play the liberal trading game. Vaughan's (1996) historical reconstruction of policy and economy in two French island possessions in the eighteenth century (Ile de Bourbon, Ile de France; now Réunion, Mauritius) shows how it worked – and failed.

Case Study 5.1: Markets and Moralities in Colonial Africa

France's economic philosophers, then as now, preoccupied themselves with 'human nature'. Their reforms aimed 'to produce not only prosperity, but also loyal subjects' (Vaughan 1996: 66). Debates on how this combination could be achieved revealed an interesting duality of

opinion, a duality replicated in contemporary debate on economic reform and macro-economic structural adjustment. Indeed, just as we
now have supporters and opponents of structural adjustment, so too
did French economic philosophers fall into two camps. While some
believed that the combination of prosperity and loyalty to the State

> would be best achieved through the continued use of subsidy and the
> encouragement of agricultural production which, by its nature, would
> tie the 'habitant' to the soil and, materially and symbolically to the King,
> others moved towards a more 'modern' version of economy and society
> in which money as well as land could be the source of capital, and in
> which the individual's freedom of action within the market economy
> was the only certain guarantee of their ultimate loyalty. (Vaughan 1996:
> 66)

This debate, however, applied only to 'free men', not to women, despite women's real interest in landholdings; nor did it apply to slaves.
Women and slaves, the latter in particular, were properties, not persons. And as properties, slaves were legally (though not 'in reality')
barred from owning property or transacting in the market, as one
commodity could not possess or exchange another.

When Britain imposed indirect rule on African societies, it too produced a discourse for justification which linked markets and moralities. As conceptualized by Victorian economic philosophers, the
challenge of colonial rule was to end the inhuman slave markets and
'to introduce the African to the responsibilities, as well as the opportunities, of free commerce' (Vaughan 1996: 68). The challenge, not
surprisingly, came with a particular anxiety about what kind of people 'the Africans' were and how their long-term loyalty to the Crown
could be secured. Yet the challenge itself was clear as crystal: 'Before
they could benefit from the freedoms of the market, Africans had first
to be transformed into the appropriate kinds of persons' (Vaughan
1996: 68).[1] The task of creating the right kinds of African people and
of socializing the youth was delegated to African agents, local chiefs
and elders, rather than to the state. It was thus that 'traditions' were
invented.

Grand and resilient, these 'traditions' did not, however, work as intended; administrators could neither determine the relationship that
would develop between people and markets, nor could they prevent
the creation of a range of new identities. Ordinary-but-real African
people forged their own moralities of the market (Vaughan 1996: 71).
An illuminating account of how colonial (and post-colonial) administrators in Africa attempted to engineer social types suitable for the

modern economy and its markets is presented in *Cutting Down Trees* (Moore and Vaughan 1994), which charts northern Zambia's history of agricultural intervention and policy discourse. In colonial northern Zambia, administrators, local chiefs and academic researchers fashioned a close association between cutting trees (a practice referred to as *citemene*) and Bemba masculinity, in which the cutting of fields from the forest came to be viewed as symbolic of male/Bemba autonomy and contestation. The product of many converging discourses, the construction of a Bemba identity – fiercely autonomous – then warranted that 'appropriate' action be taken. Through taxation and forced resettlement in fixed villages, 'the Bemba' could be disciplined and prepared for entry into the modern world and migrant labour market (Moore and Vaughan 1994: 19).

As a neat example of the Foucauldian thesis that social identities are not natural givens, but engineered through interlocking discourses that involve outsiders as well as some of the individuals concerned (see e.g. Foucault 1986, 1991),[2] the story of how 'The Bemba' were created and disciplined continued after independence. *Citemene* lived on as a symbol representing primitive agriculture, evoking anything but the complex set of adaptive processes that existed and had been researched and recorded, while the *citemene* farmers were still in need of discipline. As in the late colonial period, the remedy again came in the form of resettlement programmes that promoted 'modern' village life by advocating settled agriculture (see Bratton 1980). Hugely unpopular because poorer villages could ill afford to lose the advantages *citemene* offered, the schemes were doomed from the start (Moore and Vaughan 1994: 139).[3] While agricultural 'experts' still failed to appreciate these aspects of *citemene*, while anxious administrators still tried desperately hard to create the 'correct' moral climate in which accumulation could take place, many farmers voted with their feet and left the resettlement areas.

Kinship relations are another striking manifestation of how experiences, values and meanings may fuse creatively to escape the official preoccupation with personhood, morality and governmentality. Rather than destroy the institution of kinship, as evolutionary models of change predicted, market 'penetration' often strengthened kinship ideology (Vaughan 1996: 73). My own research in northern Zambia in the late 1970s, a period of crisis following the slump of copper on the world market, demonstrated how adaptability and social creativity (rather than homogenization) were the hallmark of the Mambwe people's encounter with markets. At a time when the region's high divorce rate could easily be mistaken for (further!) social and moral decline, Mambwe women used kin and presumed-lapsed affinal relations to make the most of new market opportunities, particularly in cross-border trading, and to exercise control over men's ability to accumulate (Pottier 1988: 149–50). (The situation parallels Sarah White's (1992) claim that 'male' markets in Bangladesh are mediated by women.) The control which (some) women exerted over the men who traded on their behalf was reinforced by a notable change in the pattern of village residence. As many divorcees returned to settle in villages where they had male kin, their villages developed cores of agnatically related women. This did not fit the patrilineal model upheld in the 1950s; it was not what modern administrators had ordered.

Further evidence of the vitality of African kinship ideologies in the face of commoditization can be found in *The Real Economy of Zaire* (1991), in which Janet MacGaffey confirms that difficult-to-control markets and borrowing at usurious rates may put a premium on the cultivation of trust between people who share close kinship and/or ethnic ties (MacGaffey 1991: 32). Berry observes likewise: 'Instability contributes to the proliferation of institutions and social memberships, as well as their continued salience for access to goods and opportunities' (Berry 1995: 309–310, quoted in Vaughan 1996).

So far in this section, the point made is that markets and market participation developed in ways not entirely planned for in the grand scheme which morally inspired colonial administrators had prepared. Colonialism did alter African economies in certain standard ways, mainly through commoditization and 'appropriate' laws (see e.g. MacGaffey 1991: 35–6), but the economies affected did not become homogenized to the degree intended. Despite the introduction of uniform facilities/obstacles (monetization, taxation, laws and policies that discriminate against women . . .), market opportunities also resulted in an eruption of unique, situated responses.

'Real market' studies in Kivu Province, Congo-Zaire, illustrate this mix of predictable and not-so-predictable developments.

Case Study 5.2: Kivu Markets: Universal Constraints, Unique Responses

Participation in food markets often reflects trends in wage-labour markets. This seems almost universal. Very obvious in my Mambwe study, where men who lost their position as industrial migrants entered the domestic grain market, the link is also demonstrated in Fairhead's work on Bwisha, where 'food markets developed spontaneously in the deregulatory and chaotic aftermath of independence' (Fairhead 1992a: 29). The spontaneity, however, had much to do with a dramatic decline in the opportunities for (male) migrant wage labour, after which agriculture-at-home became the chief avenue to wealth. The changes prompted Bwisha households to sell crops for cash, 'even when production should be consumed by the household itself' (Fairhead 1992a: 29). This fuelled tension between women and men over the right to sell and made women vulnerable to male domination in times of severe food scarcity (Pottier and Fairhead 1991).

This reality on the ground, however, carried its own contradiction. Despite male domination, Kivu's women participated regularly and fairly freely in the monetized markets, and especially so after they developed production strategies that gave them greater control over marketable produce. This meant investing more in tubers and root crops, which women controlled (unlike grain). In Bwisha by the late 1980s, most men (i.e. the 75 per cent that are poor and unprotected because they lack the 'right connections') experienced travel on the roads to market as very risky: they were exposed to direct expropriation by the authorities. Women, in contrast, had different experiences, more like those of the other 25 per cent of protected men. Fairhead writes:

> [Women] are relatively free of direct expropriation on the roads and in the markets. They resent legal taxation strongly, and can be very aggressive towards officials who attempt to impose it. Women tend to walk to markets in groups and physically to protect each other against the officials they encounter on their journeys. Newbury [1984] has documented a revolt by women over increased taxes elsewhere in Kivu, and shows how, just as in Bwisha, their liberty gives them certain marketing advantages over men. (Fairhead 1992a: 23)

What Catharine Newbury documented was a situation in which men had become fair game for the gendarmes who prowled about the markets. Men's response had been to 'hide behind women' and to let women transact in the markets on their behalf, especially when profitable groundnuts needed selling (Newbury 1984: 46-7).

Situated Responses versus Structured Constraints

Despite the ingenious ways women may have devised to play the market well, structural obstacles continue to prevent them from reaping full benefits. And poor women often get hit hard. Schoepf and Walu (1991), for instance, recall the struggles of one Mama Mongongo, who sold cooked food to Kinshasa's unskilled workers, policemen and watchmen. Not only did these men take food on credit (with debts hardly ever being paid off), Mama Mongongo was also virtually forced out of business when her rent rose from 500 *zaires* per month in 1987 to 2,500 in 1989. Far from anecdotal or trivial, her testimony under-scored the fundamental contradiction that no matter how long her working day, no matter how resourceful she might be, there was always an obstacle to undo all of Mama Mongongo's effort.

Rent is a big issue indeed. Reflecting on how Africa's problems are so often presented as food problems, Jane Guyer (1987) objects to food being 'singled out, in disproportion to its contribution to an increasing gap between incomes and the cost of living' (Guyer 1987: 44). Specifically, she argues that

> When one examines recent budget studies and cost of living indices, it is evident that the cost of housing has been rising steadily throughout the post-war period, but receives far less attention than the food component of urban expenditure. . . . [Taking rent in Nairobi as an example, the average rent by 1980] was more than double its 1975 level, whereas food was only sixty per cent higher. (Guyer 1987: 44)

The structural vulnerability of small urban traders has also been exposed in cities like Bogotá, Colombia, where Caroline Moser recorded and compared petty trader activities in 1970 and 1978. At the time of her second study Colombia was hit by massive inflation, which amongst other things meant 'increases in market stall rents, transport costs and house rents as well as comparable food price increases' (Moser 1980: 377). Moreover, Bogotá's wholesale marketing system had been modernized to give more economic power to a few privileged groups. Petty traders found that the benefit of speedier transactions and better quality of produce were easily offset by increased travel times and transport costs, which reduced profit margins, while the expansion of supermarket chains made small-scale market prices uncompetitive (Moser 1980: 381). Poverty had worsened too, because of the 'lack of access to capital, increased competition resulting from unemployment and rural-urban migration of unskilled workers, and the prohibitive drain on resources of house rent, medical expenses, and education' (Moser 1980: 378). These bad times meant a shift in demand from increasingly expensive fruits towards cheaper vegetables and staples, for example, potatoes were 'in', plátanos 'out' (Moser 1980: 377). With so many small-scale sellers already living on the poverty line in 1970, it was no big surprise that the reforms had squeezed poorer sellers out of the market. The process of exclusion speeded up further when many of the area's low-income residents, the most loyal clientele, left after land speculators offered them 'attractive terms' for moving out. (That familiar story of 'what sorts of people there should be' just continues.) Moser concludes that small-scale entrepreneurs working in an economy which is externally oriented can do so only in a dependent, subordinate manner.

The perspective that commoditization and market incorporation have a mostly negative impact on resource-poor producers and traders is aptly outlined by Maureen Mackintosh:

> As markets spread through and transform rural areas, so individuals come increasingly to depend upon the workings of markets for survival, by selling goods or their own labour to buy food. The net result is an increase in the *vulnerability* of many people, especially those who own few resources bar their labour. Small farmers, pastoralists, labourers, crafts workers become vulnerable not only to drought and pests but also to changes in prices and quantities on volatile markets. Previous payments in kind are transformed into cash: 'more modern perhaps, more vulnerable certainly'. Old methods of insurance against disaster weaken or disappear. (Mackintosh 1990: 43)

Taking a leaf from Amartya Sen's book (1981), Mackintosh adds: 'As a result, famines can be caused, or more sharply reinforced, by the normal workings of the market' (Mackintosh 1990: 43).

While this political economy framework is broadly applicable, it is still necessary to ask further questions and to proceed to an analysis in which real-life experiences are understood in their specific contexts. Questions about specific response, about 'relocalization' (see chapter 1 above), are needed. In the case study above, Bwisha women in the late 1980s were dependent on a market controlled by international capital; 'local' prices were set by traders who controlled international money (US dollars) and who operated in several large cities including Kinshasa. As these long-distance traders could afford to be generous, their prices drained the area of its food and made local purchases more expensive. The situation caused dilemmas for producer-sellers (how much to sell and when? how much to buy and when?) and made people despair at times. But, and here comes the need for nuance, producer-sellers showed no signs of resignation. Bwisha women responded to the tightening market noose with various initiatives, for example, by joining extra-household saving groups and by growing more of the intercrops they controlled. *Elles se débrouillaient.* As MacGaffey remarked for Zaire as a whole, 'the reality on the ground is that, despite the severe economic crisis, a population of 35 million people . . . finds the means to survive, with some people thriving and becoming wealthy' (MacGaffey 1991: 13).

The spread of global markets does not have a bulldozer effect on local institutions, nor on people's identities, nor in fact on their determination to secure livelihoods. This is not to deny that markets do not at times create vulnerability, but rather to argue against a monolithic conception of 'the market'. Simply put, the stranglehold of interlocking commoditized markets *is real*, but not so strongly integrated

markets do provide opportunity as well. The efficiency with which informal channels funnel food in bulk and on a regular basis to Africa's
major cities is a prime illustration of the existence of opportunity. As
Guyer appreciates:

> low production at farm levels, high levels of management by the state,
> and the pressing conditions in the international economic context . . .
> must not . . . eclipse the continuing, and perhaps increasing importance
> of all those forms of organisation which continue to funnel food from
> rural areas to cities. In terms of actually feeding the cities, as distinct
> from generating a commotion about it, the non-state sector is still crit-
> ical. (Guyer 1987: 45)

While women can become 'the casualty of market control' (Robertson
1983), 'many cities, from Accra to Bangui (see Adam 1980) and Lusaka
(Muntemba 1982), depend to a significant degree on goods produced,
processed and/or traded by women' (Guyer 1987: 45).

The efficiency of informal food channels has also been praised in
South-East Asia. For Davao City, for example, a seaport on the island
of Mindanao in the Philippines, Barth highlights that households engaged in food trading frequently pursue 'a mixed economy of agriculture, trade, and other types of supplemental activities' (Barth 1984:
38; see also Swetnam 1980: 35). Their mixed-economy strategy implies
close cooperation between spouses (over 70 per cent of marketeers are
married) and is known to be an efficient way of food provisioning. Un-
fortunately, as is so very common (for example in Peru and Tanzania:
see below), middlemen are vilified as social parasites (Barth 1984: 41)
and excluded from official plans for food market development.

This raises the question of how small-scale trade networks achieve
supply stability. What is the relationship between the traders and the
rural producers? Which conditions make for a good relationship? And
can mediocre conditions be regulated better?

Farmer–Trader Relations: Not Biting the
Hand that Feeds You?

Traders influence regional and household food security because they
control not only the flow of foodstuffs, but also the prices at which
foods are bought and sold. The influence can be positive, argues Gracia
Clark on the basis of research in Kumasi (Ghana), provided that traders operate in flexible ways, and that farmers combine trade with a
sound production strategy (Clark 1991: 227). (That the two must be
combined has already been noted for Bwisha, above.) Clark's findings
are in line with Guyer's observation that flexibility is key to achieving

long-term food security (Guyer 1987).

In the setting of Kumasi, researched at a time of severe food scarcity (1978–84), Clark learned how women traders had worked out ways to iron out supply and price irregularities (Clark 1991: 231). Flexibility was indeed the key. In the first instance, traders refrained from hoarding, thus avoiding artificial shortages and inflation. Instead, they 'lengthened' the harvest seasons by offering reasonable prices to farmers over a longer time-span. This removed the excessive costs urban shoppers would otherwise have had to face. Supply and price fluctuations became larger than the normal seasonal fluctuations, but never unmanageable. Traders also ensured that the local markets on which rural farmers relied for buying in food continued to operate at near-normal levels.

The traders' constructive response was made possible because they themselves had been consulted in district plans for crop specialization by micro-climatic zone. Traders were thus optimally informed about produce availability. They also made use of a vast network of producers with whom regular contact was maintained, which again enhanced their knowledge about supply sources. But farmers too felt secure. The traders being so numerous, any smallholder who felt exploited in any way could easily shift to another trader. This safety in numbers put a premium on fairness: traders needed to be fair if they themselves wanted to stay in business. Another important aspect of Kumasi's effective food-trading system was that the source of cash was truly local. Hence there were times (of seasonal glut) when traders would depend on credit extended by farmers. And as farmers could ill afford a bad name, they too needed to be fair (Clark 1991: 236–7). In short, the effectiveness of Kumasi's food supply channels rested on farmers and traders recognizing and realizing the mutual benefit that accrued from flexibility and fairness. Traders with strong local ties and limited cash flows were aware that fairness was in their own best interest.

The same argument has been advanced by ethnographers like Solvay Gerke and Hans-Dieter Evers (both working on Java) and Timothy Finan (on Brazil). On the basis of his longitudinal research in a fruit and vegetable market in north-east Brazil, a setting in which both petty traders and farmers faced uncertainty, Finan comes out in support of the notion of 'equilibrating relationships'; a concept coined by Plattner (1985). Viewing these relationships as social stabilizers that counteract the danger of increasingly uncertain markets, Finan stresses that they are 'socially recognized, long-lasting, and [entail] mutual responsibility. Linguistically, these social and economic ties are distinguished as *freguês* relationships (the term *freguês* in Brazilian Portuguese means roughly "customer," but with much heavier connotations of obligation than the English term permits)' (Finan 1988: 695). In this situation, which resembles conditions in Kumasi, smallholders and middlemen alike face multiple uncertainties, including risks previously unknown (Finan 1988: 698). Farmers face escalating costs for inputs and labour, and volatile prices, while petty traders 'face varying costs and risks' at different stages of marketing (Finan 1988: 700). Risks to traders commonly include irregular product flow, the perishable nature of goods, variable prices and customers defaulting. It is the shared risk environment, and the perception that risk-taking is mutual, which explains why equilibrating relationships become significant and possible.

But how far can resources and generosity stretch when both parties feel vulnerable? Evers (1994a, 1994b) addressed the question during research in Java. Javanese petty traders, he argues, are bound by an enforceable code of honour, a strong sense of obligation, but they also experience traders' dilemma. The dilemma is that 'traders cannot disentangle themselves from the values of sharing and cooperating with fellow villagers and consequently find it difficult to accumulate the necessary profits to expand their business' (Evers 1994a: 5, 1994b: 70; see also Alexander 1987). The contradiction is between the need for profit and the moral requirement that no undue pressure be put on debtors in need or on needy relatives and neighbours (Evers 1994a: 8). The choice is between losing cash or losing social esteem. Local traders can afford to lose neither.

Now – and this is where the Javanese scene differs from Kumasi – the typical strategy through which traders in Java attempt to solve the dilemma is by adopting physical and socio-cultural distance. In this way, 'separate moral economies come into existence that might stress cooperation but not sharing across moral boundaries' (Evers 1994a: 8). The strategy is most visibly 'at work' in situations where migrant trading communities operate, a phenomenon found throughout South-East Asia (Evers 1994a: 9). Migration aside, the formation of religious and ethnic groups is another strategy through which distance can be created to reduce traders' dilemma. Java's Santris, alumni of Islamic religious schools, are a case in point (Geertz 1963). These traders convert material wealth into symbolic capital as a way of disengaging from moral obligation. This is observed also in India, where trading castes protect their enterprises through religious purity and ostentatious charity. Indian migrant communities abroad may continue the strategy, as Evers illustrates for Chettiar moneylenders in Singapore. Chettiar moneylenders 'assume the aura of sanctity and moral superiority to achieve trade success' (Evers 1994a: 12) and manage funds collectively through the temple (Evers et al. 1994: 205). When distance is thus created, individual traders cannot be accused of amassing excessive personal riches. On the contrary, their moral superiority and continuing commitments to the community – in the form of community spending and charity – are manifest and applauded, especially during festival times.

Where the creation of difference is not practised, trade patterns are more likely to resemble those found in north-east Brazil or in Kumasi, Ghana, where trade involves a mass of small entrepreneurs trying to make ends meet despite the dilemmas they face. What saves the traders, under those conditions, is the restricted scale of their operations and profits. It is through restriction, through the 'minuscule quantities in which commodities are sold to the final customer' (Alexander 1987: 59), that the dilemma is resolved. Evers insists, however, that small scale and low cash flows do not mean mediocrity, and he praises the initiatives traders take. But in doing so, he also reminds us (implicitly) that market opportunities exhibit a 'plurality of oppressions' (Bardhan 1993) structured around class and gender imbalances. Java's petty trade, Evers writes, is typically 'carried out as subsistence trade where market women just sell enough to enable them to buy daily household needs from their meagre profits. There is absolutely no profit margin left that might give rise to demands for sharing or redistribution' (Evers 1994a: 13).

In contrast to interpretations that equate petty trade with an 'involuted' agrarian economy (Geertz 1963) or with crisis (Scott 1976), Evers proposes to view the spectacular boom in petty trade in Java, between 1961 and 1980, as indicative of growth and strong adaptive capacity. Traders face a dilemma they resolve 'by sharing initiative rather than poverty' (Evers 1994b: 71). This positive verdict includes praise for 'the efficiency of supplying a very rapidly growing population, especially in urban areas, with fresh food and even remote villages with other consumer items to satisfy their daily needs' (Evers 1994b: 71). This is congruent with positive assessments for other parts of South-East Asia and Africa (Barth 1984; Guyer 1987).

We have now reached a point we also reached in discussing agricultural labour markets. Regarding the latter I argued for the full recognition of creative responses to displacement and against the essentialist portrayal of the displaced as helpless victims. Yet, simultaneously, I urged that the recognition of how people use human agency must not be at the expense of ignoring the structured obstacles that severely limit the deployment of a creative response. It is the same with people's investment in petty trade. Evers rightly celebrates that resource-poor traders share initiative, in the same way that Clark and Finan celebrate the capacity of resource-poor traders and farmers to overcome the vagaries of the uncertain environment they share. Their emphasis on trust and initiative, rather than antagonism and helplessness, is valuable.

But such an emphasis must not overshadow the incidence of poverty, which is a structured phenomenon. Let me put it bluntly. Why is it that Java's market women work long days for such meagre rewards? Why is it that agricultural women labourers are on rates well below those paid to men? Celebration of initiative and human agency, I have no doubt, need to be better researched and reported, yet they must not detract from the continuing need for a clear understanding of how entry in markets on favourable terms is socially restricted (Harriss-White 1996; Mackintosh 1990).

There are consequences here for policy-making. Exposed to the celebration-of-initiative perspective, policy-makers may well conclude, as many have done, that the appropriate policy response is to make small amounts of credit available to hundreds of thousands of resource-poor traders, women especially. Sometimes, though, this has happened without ascertaining whether the conditions that prevail in households enhance or impede the likelihood that women will make full use of the credit. Problems may arise, as shown for Grameen Bank projects in Bangladesh, because of strong gender inequalities. Such problems, however, can be overcome by keeping credit limits low and earmarking them for economic activities undisputedly controlled by women (Goetz and Gupta 1996; Rahman 1992). Loans for activities that women control are more likely to be used for the purpose intended and less likely to be appropriated by husbands or senior men. Many of the gender issues discussed in chapters 3 and 4 – particularly where they deal with the *practice* of land distribution and inheritance – indicate that little is to be gained from making credit available unconditionally. Moreover, as already seen, interventions are open to interpretation (see Gatter 1993 on Zambia; Carney 1988 on The Gambia), which may mean that activities women control could come to be redefined. For such reasons, a 'credit plus' approach (cf. Berger 1989) is to be preferred.

Micro-credit schemes will achieve their best results in situations where access to resources is not socially restricted. The previously outlined 'social safety-net' in Sagada, northern Luzon, where resources are still allocated communally, provides that kind of situation.

Case Study 5.3: Contrasting Market Regimes in Northern Luzon, the Philippines

The social safety-net in Sagada guarantees that vegetable producer-sellers, especially in the small and medium range, can enter the market with some confidence. Petty traders here can use cooperative and mutual help in harvesting and packing, and can bank on good gender

cooperation. They also gain 'flexibility . . . . by staggering their planting and harvesting' and/or by mixing low-value, low-input crops with
high-value ones that require credit (Jefremovas 1993: 3–5). This again
confirms that farmers do not distinguish between their market decisions and their production decisions. *'Playing the market' successfully
always entails mixing effective strategies both in the market and on
the farm.*

Sagadan vegetable producers work in teams that honour equitable
relations. Frequently this involves cooperation between spouses. In the
case studies Jefremovas presents there is no trace of gender exploitation, but lots of evidence that positive cross-gender and cross-family
relations are being fostered. Take, for instance, Andrew and Rachel,

> who began gardening at the time of their marriage in 1981. Andrew
> was 21 at the time. Rachel's father established a series of gardens on the
> land that Rachel inherited and planted the initial crops, while Andrew's
> parents paid for the seed, fertilizers and pesticides for the first season.
> Andrew's elder brother, a skilled gardener, gave him advice and the
> whole family provided labour. The couple have continued to grow veg-
> etables using the proceeds of previous harvests supplemented with cap-
> ital provided by their parents at no interest. Like [others do,] they make
> use of a system of reciprocal exchange with fellow gardeners which
> enables them to borrow inputs during emergencies. These they return
> in kind and without interest during the growing season. (Jefremovas
> 1993: 6)

The strength of Sagada's community ethos is such that available resources offer every would-be trader the possibility that a bundle of
effective strategies for market participation can be secured. A range of
guaranteed community rights and secure access to land through inheritance (for men and women) top the list, and provide much room for
manoeuvre and independence.

For more recently established communities in the Cordillera Central, in contrast, the prospect of entering the market successfully looks
much bleaker. This applies to the Mandaymen region, for example,
which Susan Russell (1987) has studied. Unlike the egalitarian orientation of Sagada, which allows would-be petty traders to absorb risk
by drawing upon community resources and support, petty traders in
Mandaymen are tied to *non-local* middlemen in what is effectively a
tenancy arrangement. To borrow from Evers, the situation is one in
which traders have solved their dilemma by creating distance. The
agreements that are entered into are, from the small trader's point of
view, both non-voluntaristic and self-perpetuating.

Lacking the 'social safety-net' Sagadans can draw upon, peasant
farmers in Mandaymen enter into arrangements with middlemen with

whom no affective ties exist. Deals are 'raw' and imply that large amounts of future harvests are mortgaged to cover the purchase of essential agricultural inputs: improved seeds, fertilizers and pesticides. Russell found that '[67 per cent] of farmers depended on middlemen for production credit, while only 10 per cent availed themselves of bank loans' (1987: 146). The high cost of informal borrowing, which the non-local middlemen can keep high as alternatives forms of borrowing are not considered, puts a serious brake on farmers' capacity to make independent market decisions (1987: 140). Being incremental and almost impossible to cancel out, indebtedness is the lever middlemen and wholesalers use to exert their power and secure continuity for their own profitable participation (Russell 1987: 150).

The structure of indebtedness in Mandaymen is such that market relations there must not be described as voluntaristic or equilibrating. Access to essential inputs, for production and petty trade, is too skewed for the notion of equilibrium to apply. As the markets for land and credit interlock, poor farmers in Mandaymen are left with no room for manoeuvre; the situation rather resembles that of Birbhum, India, where displays of power pervade relational contracts. Birbhum contracts, essentially verbal, are not entered voluntarily (Harriss-White 1996: 35).[4]

To conclude, the quality of the relationship between smallholders and petty traders can be mapped out on a continuum from equilibrating and voluntaristic to highly exploitative and self-perpetuating. Exactly where a farming community or household stands is determined to a large extent by the degree to which the various types of market interpenetrate. Where the markets for land, credit and produce are firmly interlocked and controlled by a nucleus of overlapping elite groups, small producers do not enter into voluntary or fully 'equilibrating' relationships. Where, on the other hand, market integration remains incomplete, as in most of sub-Saharan Africa where land remains fairly accessible, it is less likely that the trader–farmer relationship will be labelled exploitative. Richards (1986) illustrates the more benign nature of trader–farmer relations when he argues that the loans of cash or rice which resource-poor farmers in Mogbuama (Sierra Leone) receive from their patrons are not detrimental to their livelihoods. The loans do not bind peasant farmers to middlemen in that never-ending cycle observed in Mandaymen (Russell 1987). Mogbuama farmers seek loans of cash or rice when self-help and reciprocity have failed, at which point they expect their patrons to step in and fulfil their duties. The interest that farmers pay on such loans, Richards claims, must not be considered excessive: 'rates on rice loans are no higher than is necessary to prevent rice leaving the village during the "hungry season"' (Richards 1986: 127). Importantly too, the same patrons can be relied upon when a more serious crisis looms. During the 1982 hungry season, for instance, which was particularly severe, 'local merchants agreed to a ban on rice transactions outside the village for the duration of the hunger period' (Richards 1990: 213). This meant that Mende villages retained their capital – cash and rice – and recovered quickly when the hard times ended (cf. Prindle 1979, discussed in chapter 7). What gives Mogbuama farmers some leverage over their patrons is that the latter need supporters when seeking political office. The interdependence means that fairness must prevail – as Clark (1991) observed for Kumasi.

Commodity markets offer opportunities which need to be realized. The conditions under which opportunities are least likely to be realized are those in which interlocking markets prevail, in which case the redistribution of assets and profits is all too severely curtailed. The question of market participation, then, as Swift (1989: 12) also appreciates, is not a simple for-or-against commodity relations, but rather a question of how market relations – as evolving social and moral constructs – can be improved in the interest of better food security.

Beyond Market Romanticisms?

The Bretton-Woods institutions have been criticized for using a neo-liberal conception of markets quite out of touch with on-the-ground realities. Their defence of privatization and market deregulation in the face of so much evidence suggesting that all markets are regulated by definition, and through a variety of institutions, only one of which is the state, qualifies at best as romantic (Bernstein 1996b; Harriss-White 1996), at worst as 'unequivocally evil' (Miller 1995: 147). Both criticisms apply. That 'free-market romanticism' (Bernstein 1996b) is far from innocent is indicated by the World Bank/IMF claim that the recipe of privatization and deregulation is of the highest moral quality; it will save the poorest of the poor. The claim is made explicit through slogans that advocate 'market discipline'. Among the strongest market efficiency claims made is this statement by Cammann (1992):

> Marketing systems are vital to the poorest of the poor, to women, to the landless and the uneducated. . . Markets offer them every day a chance to acquire the minimum means they need for survival. . . [They] offer a variety of approaches towards the promotion of self help among the farmers themselves. . . Markets should ensure a livelihood for the rural masses, limit exploitation and lead to a sustainable, efficient and self controlling system. (Cammann 1992: 1–7, quoted in Harriss-White 1996: 28; see also Mackintosh 1990)

What makes this kind of statement morally unacceptable is that it relegates the struggles over power and resources to the category of 'externalities' (see also Raikes 1994).

Empirical research, as is clear by now, emphasizes that economic activity is neither autonomous nor natural, but *regulated* through cultural norms and practices. This makes 'the search for a normatively neutral theory of "the market" . . . well nigh futile' (Gould and von Oppen 1994: 4). The empirically derived perspective is therefore opposed to that of the free-market economist who views markets as disembedded, natural and universal, and believes salvation will come from 'rolling back the state' and moving towards full privatization. To roll back the state is not the same as to deregulate, since the impact of state removal may indeed be minimal.

Free-market enthusiasts must shed their romanticism. First, they need to accept that market exchange takes many economic forms and meanings (Harriss-White 1996: 40). Second, they must accept that state and market do not exist as separate, substitutable entities (Harriss-White 1996: 38; Hewitt de Alcántara 1992: 12). Rather, there exists a plurality of market circumstances and rationales, and *therefore a need to widen the range of policy options*. Third, 'private trade' and 'free trade' must not be confused. Referring to Birbhum District, West Bengal, where moneylending merchants operate in a hierarchy of tied credit and commodity relations (Harriss 1992: 72–3), Hewitt de Alcántara argues that 'even a thriving private commercial sector, promoted in the rhetoric of market reform, in itself constitutes no guarantee of renewed development within the present recessionary context' (Hewitt de Alcántara 1992: 7).

When market liberalization was imposed on Birbhum, poor people were unable to take advantage. What resulted was increased poverty and a massive expansion of 'unlicensed and therefore illegal petty traders, often women and often relying on family labour' (Harriss 1992: 72). As the markets for land, labour, credit and goods are firmly interlocked in Birbhum, and controlled by powerful elites, adjustment measures had a devastating impact on the livelihoods of small traders. Adjustment measures liberalized the activities of the elites, but banished the poor into illegality.

The point is this: 'petty traders operating at the lower levels of networks dominated by moneylending merchants are likely to participate little if at all in any increasing profits obtained by their powerful merchant patrons' (Hewitt de Alcántara 1992: 8). The more correct response then, as Bernstein proposes, is to abandon the preoccupation with 'less' versus 'more' regulation and to consider new policy options 'in terms of better versus worse forms of regulation' (Bernstein 1996b: 122).

Better Regulation?

Blame for rural stagnation or commercial inefficiency is easily attributed to 'the state'. This can be short-sighted. While certain state marketing boards or food corporations may have kept producer prices low 'in order to feed a growing urban population at the least possible cost', thus marginalizing agriculture (Bates 1981), it is equally true that pan-territorial pricing, 'even at relatively low levels, protects [farmers] . . . from extreme variation in income associated with [factors] ranging from unpredictable climate to oligopolistic trading practices' (Hewitt de Alcántara 1992: 10).

Analysts, then, must not assume that state intervention in rural marketing is necessarily damaging to rural producers and that free-market forces will invariably be of benefit. In some situations, the answer may well lie in better state regulation, rather than less. Hewitt de Alcántara backs this argument by recalling the history of agrarian reform in Mexico, which shows that state monopoly in the disposal of cash crops (and in rural banking) was clearly detrimental to resource-poor producers. The 'free-market' alternative prescribed under structural adjustment, however, turned out (as also happened in Birbhum) to be not free trade but private trade in a context of interlocking markets. Poorer peasants in remote regions were so harshly affected that many called for the return of extensive state-run trading programmes into disadvantaged areas. In their experience of structural adjustment, interlocking private markets were a good deal more exploitative than state monopolies (see also DeWalt and Barkin 1991). What Mexican peasant farmers from disadvantaged rural areas were calling for was better policy options, better regulation.

Under different circumstances, however, better regulation may mean that states or development agencies should refrain from intervention. For regions where markets are not strongly integrated and where farmers and traders recognize that their working relationships are mutually beneficial and essential to survival, intervention from the outside is likely to be less than welcome if it challenges these relationships. To eliminate the presumed parasitic middlemen may in such situations not be what smallholder producers want. Policy interventions aiming to cut the number of middlemen 'in the chain' – often based on the equally fraught/romantic notion that the small farmer is self-sufficient and must be shielded from contact with exploitative traders – are regularly subverted by the 'beneficiaries' themselves. As the following two case studies make clear, small-scale producers may, provided the conditions are right (that is provided markets offer choice and are not too tightly interlocked), prefer a measure of 'exploitation' over the 'privilege' of direct access to markets that offer better prices. The two examples show that less intervention from above ('above' being the state in example 5.4; an NGO in example 5.5) may be the better option at times. This contrasts with the example of rural Mexico where isolated small producers requested more intervention.

In the first illustration, the government of Peru attempted to secure better prices for small farmers by bringing them in direct contact with urban consumers. In the second case, Oxfam (UK) attempted to give Tanzanian fishermen a better price by (again) encouraging them to take charge of market operations rather than rely on traders. In both these cases, the presumed beneficiaries quickly dropped the 'better price' strategy and reinstated the petty traders with whom they used to deal.

Case Study 5.4: Huaraz, Peru, mid-1970s

In the mid-1970s, the Peruvian government launched its 'from the field to the cooking pot' programme (*de la chacra a la olla*), through which it aimed to reduce the chain of intermediaries in food trading. Poor rural producers were to become better-off producer–sellers. Branding marketeers as social parasites and blaming them for the country's failure to make food available at affordable prices, the government launched regional fairs and expected the producers of primary foods to turn up in large numbers.

The Peruvian initiative flopped, as it pleased neither the producers nor the consumers. The regional fairs – such as the one at Huaraz, which Babb (1987) researched – were poorly attended. The women food producers who initially turned up did receive higher prices for their produce, but they had to pay for transport to and from the fair, and were spending a good deal of their time 'just being there'. It was not worth the trouble. Soon they stayed away. What peasant producers preferred was 'to sell in large quantities to sure buyers rather than slowly to the public' (Babb 1987: 142). Doing away with intermediaries, they felt, was not the answer. Contact with sure buyers interested in buying large quantities, and with whom risks in an uncertain environment could be shared, provided more security in times of need, as when illness struck or harvests were poor (see also chapter 7).

Case Study 5.5: Mkolani Fishermen, Tabora, Tanzania, 1992

In 1992 Oxfam (UK) made a loan available to fishermen at Mkolani, near Kabila village, Tabora region, to buy new nets and transport facilities (bicycles, cooling box), so they could take matters into their own hands and break free from the traders who bought up the daily catches. Mkolani fishermen set up their own cooperative, a YEG (Youth Employment Group), and cut out the traders in order to secure a better price for their fish. This, however, lasted only for a little while and sales to traders, now covert, soon resumed. Allison Tierney (1997) writes:

> Despite saying [to Oxfam] that they wanted to be independent of the traders, it soon became clear that the individual YEG members preferred to sell their fish to them. Several members covertly sold fish to the traders when they were supposed to be contributing to the YEG catch, and this resulted in some disputes within the group... This persistent selling to traders became a problem which the YEG leaders tried to control with a system of fines as punishment, but this only caused individuals to leave the group. When the younger members were out of the way [i.e. after they moved to another fishing site] the leaders also sold to traders... Trader–fisherman interaction was [only] temporarily modified by the effect of the loan. (Tierney 1997: 187)

Fishermen found it more convenient to 'work from home', as it were. Taking charge of fish marketing was a chore they could do without, it meant extra work and extra risk. Just like the small food producers in Huaraz, Peru, the Mkolani fishermen knew there would be no shortage of traders coming to the lakeside. 'The fishermen are confident that the demand for fish always outstrips supply. Traders buy as much of it as they can; villagers are always keen to sell fish if it is available. ... The result is that there is little incentive for fishermen to increase their workload by marketing their fish themselves' (Tierney 1997: 232).

Together the case studies confirm, firstly, the need for understanding markets empirically in their specific spatial and historical contexts and, secondly, the need for better regulation, i.e. for tailoring policy options to the degree to which markets are interlocked.

Conclusion

While these case studies from Peru and Tanzania (and also north-east Brazil and Kumasi-Ghana) would appear to support Plattner's concept of 'equilibrating relationships', it remains essential to ask further, highly specific questions before this concept's value and applicability can be accepted. In particular, attention must be paid 'to the wider institutional constraints that limit the choice of contractual arrangements' (Russell 1987: 139). Free access to resources and the market is not to be assumed. Equally important, cutting out the middlemen or opening the door to private traders are policy decisions that make no sense when introduced without prior knowledge of existing production and trade relations.

In view of the 'real markets' debate, the policy concern should be to find ways in which policy options can be widened in accordance with the needs of specific, socially and historically situated settings. The exact shape of the 'better' regulations will then depend on context, that is, on a thorough examination of actual markets. Better regulation, the argument so far suggests, will be of the kind that reforms interlocking markets and restores ownership (that is control over land and labour allocations) to those who work the land and sell its food. Only when the markets for land, labour, credit and goods are reasonably delinked can there be any hope that 'real' equilibrating relationships will come into play.

But there is a further issue. Better market regulation is also needed internationally, as smallholder farmers see their own production decisions increasingly 'regulated' by powerful transnational interests. Despite the attempt to appreciate the positive consequences of the adoption of 'Green Revolution' agriculture (see chapter 4), the power of the multinational companies demands that we take a closer look at the transnational trade in agricultural seeds. The trade has swept across the globe and been the focus of much debate: on farmer identity, on autonomy and on property rights.

6

The Politics of Identity
Agri-business and
Agri-culture

The poet Gower complained about 1375 that farm workers were
now demanding wages and food above their station in life: 'Labourers of old were not wont to eat of wheaten bread; their meat
was of beans or coarser corn, and their drink of water alone . . .
Then was the world ordered aright for folk of this sort.'
Wilson, Food and Drink in Britain

The close relationship between social identity and resource control is
a theme already introduced. In this chapter I extend the debate to
consider the claim that scientifically improved agriculture has eroded
on-farm genetic diversity and dented farmer self-perception to the point
of self-effacement.

Farmers worldwide have actively managed their genetic resources
for as long as they have grown crops. Everywhere they have interacted
with natural habitats and seed stocks to produce a formidable range
of crops and diversity within crops. This varietal diversity offers security against climatic vagaries, diseases and pests, and provides the means
to meet various basic requirements (Johnson 1972). Andean potatoes,
for example, 'traditionally' include varieties that are good to eat, good
to store and good to market (Rhoades 1986; van der Ploeg 1990: 197–
202).

The interaction between farmers, micro-environments and crops has
been dynamic throughout history: seeds have evolved, along with
farmer expertise in crop architecture and breeding. Today, critics of
scientific agriculture claim that this process of continuous adaptation
and experimentation *at the farmer's pace and for her or his own ac-*

count is threatened by the 'business' of development. Labour and seed are at the heart of the claim: farmers are losing control over the allocation of resources, including their own labour, and over the products of that labour, which is the food and seed they produce.

This chapter briefly tells the story of agricultural seed and asks whether the spread of genetically engineered, commoditized seed has indeed made farmers lose control over the production process. Specifically, we ask whether farmers are losing control over seed production and, if so, what the consequences might be for the way they perceive themselves as producers and human beings. We begin with some general thoughts on development intervention, bureaucracy and power.

Power, Bureaucracy and the 'Superiority' of Scientific Knowledge

A central aspect of the development 'business' is that its protagonists have produced a powerful discourse which is both diagnostic and prescriptive. Sometimes referred to as 'devspeak', this discourse defines development problems in terms set by Western scientific interests and knowledge (Apthorpe 1984: 128; Hobart 1993; Long and van der Ploeg 1989: 229) and invites developers to ignore, devalue and delegitimate local knowledge. Within the same logic, developers must present themselves as knowledgeable and in possession of the very inputs required to reverse undesirable situations. It is also customary for developers to carve up social realities into 'manageable' sectors: health, environment, population, agriculture, food security, and so on.

The business of carving up reality and labelling the components is characteristic of Western scientific knowledge, and a central feature of the standard approach to development intervention. The approach typically leads to separations that do not correspond with local-level perceptions (for example of food security and environment, see chapter 2 above) and can thus damage long-term survival prospects. A tampering with local people's values and life-worlds may also occur, often in an attempt 'to bring the dynamic of local initiative into line with the interests of public authorities and to reproduce the image of the state (or other agencies) as being the key to development' (Long and van der Ploeg 1989: 236). In the world of farming, the most common 'hidden agenda' implies that ecological and technological heterogeneity must make way for standardization. Development programmes thus do more than simply transfer material inputs and knowledge; just like markets, they provide both goods and normative and evaluative concepts. Within this *meaning*ful world, political and scientific elites have universally acquired the power to determine which problems exist and which solutions should be offered. Development programmes can therefore be conceptualized as instruments for the exercise of 'governmentality' (Foucault 1991).

To justify their acts of streamlining, planners and policy-makers mostly embrace the assumption that modernity and the life-worlds of 'Third World' farmers represent two opposed epistemologies: respectively, scientific and non-scientific. As Fairhead notes, their most fundamental belief is that Western scientific knowledge has more authority and justification than so-called non-scientific, indigenous knowledge (Fairhead 1993: 200). Even when this crude distinction is rejected in principle, as it nowadays is within international agricultural research (see chapter 8), an essential dualism still persists. The typical dichotomy is between plant breeders (Western-trained scientists) who work fast and local farmers whose capacity for experimentation is comparatively slow. In the context of bean cropping in Rwanda, for example, scientists working for the International Centre for Tropical Agriculture (CIAT) argue that 'farmers do cross and select, but at an extremely slow rate: breeding accelerates the process' (Sperling and Scheidegger 1995: 12).

What matters to the present argument is that 'speed' has been *selected* – always an arbitrary act – as the variable *par excellence* with which to judge performance. Speed, of course, is only one aspect of any given farming operation or 'system' defined in the broad sense. 'Speed' is today's icon; 'slow speed' stands for the totality of 'Third World' practices and knowledges, in the same way that colonial developers in northern Zambia singled out the slash-and-burn technique to represent the sum total of the *citemene* system (cf. Moore and Vaughan 1994).

The 'superiority' of the Western scientific approach to farming demands that a reductionist view of farming knowledges and practices be adopted. This reductionist view separates local knowledges (plural!) from the specific social, economic and political contexts in which they have emerged. It eliminates uncertainty and dispute from local resources management, and conflates practice and knowledge(s). Farmer knowledges are thus perceived as grounded in a single rationality: knowledge (singular!). Fairhead observes how this knowledge is then viewed as extant 'stock', unambiguous and under-exploited (Fairhead 1993: 192–9). In adopting the perception, scientists are prevented 'from grasping how farmers flexibly alter their practices to suit their diverse social and ecological circumstances' (Fairhead 1992b: 14), but they (and the policy-makers) do not experience this incapacity as failure; rather they claim not to have any need for the information. This attitude expresses the 'superiority', including the moral superiority, with which Western science is presumed to be endowed.

Critics of this 'superior' Western science claim that its generalizing, simplifying tendencies have the power to erode the on-farm diversity which has emerged over thousands of years. Let us look at the critique and (some of) the evidence in support.

Crop Genetic Diversity Under Threat?

The appreciation that genetic diversity is an ever-evolving insurance strategy to maximize production and improve nutritional intake under variable circumstances (Cooper et al. 1992) has developed only recently, mainly in the 1980s, and this after many decades during which, it is said, this same on-farm diversity became eroded (Moock and Rhoades 1992). While the extent of this erosion, along with the image of the farmer–victim can be questioned (see Guyer and Richards 1996), conventional research wisdom has it that ecological and social worlds have their richness reduced under the impact of a homogenizing world economy. The process began with the expansion of colonial markets that favoured cash crops over food crops, and later intensified with the Green Revolution. The latter, it is claimed, erodes not only the range of local crops and varieties, but also the community ethos and the knowledges that sustain them. The standard charge is that commoditization and Green Revolution technology have eroded crop genetic diversity by making environments uniform (Amanor et al. 1993). Uniform environments eliminate landraces (local crop varieties) and their wild relatives, thus reducing the genetic raw materials available for *future* crop breeding. Concern about the future has become apocalyptic. Take Zimbabwe, for example, where just two hybrid varieties now account for 90 per cent of all maize planted. Their introduction has displaced many traditional varieties of millet and sorghum (ODI 1993). In Kenya too, landraces that took generations to develop and were well adapted to environmental stress are rapidly being displaced by 'improved' cultivars (Kiambi and Opole 1992).

Peasant farmers appear to be under no illusions: they seem to know what is happening to the crop genetic diversity they used to manage; they also know who to blame. In an interview in Buhera District, Zimbabwe (September 1993), elders stressed that traditional crops, especially fingermillet (*rapoko*), were declining because local farmers now looked down upon them. 'For these modern farmers, *rapoko* seed is like shoe polish', one elder said (Mararike et al. 1995). Elders linked the decline of fingermillet to the crop's reduced ceremonial value, which in turn can be attributed to the rise of Christianity and its attack on ancestor worship. The latter point is important because it shows how the displacement of local crops and varieties is indeed meaningful: it is not something which happens in isolation. Displacement, the elders' statement implied, was a process that involved, consciously or otherwise, the streamlining of local knowledges and initiatives. Elders reflected further that modern forces, which they readily personified, were responsible for bringing into the area crops not suited to the soils. The consequence was a threat to local genetic resources. Another elder told the interviewers (Zimbabwean sociologist, agricultural extension worker, myself) that

> You, you are the witches. You are taking us back, you are not making us develop. In times past, my family used not to have problems because I grew the traditional small grains. You are the people who are killing us now, you are taking us back because you are telling us to grow crops that are not proper. Even the fertility that you sell is not good for the small grains. We believe that the 'Number One' crops are the small grains. They are our ancestral spirit, our bank. . . . Ah, you people, you let us throw them away. (Mararike et al. 1995: 63)

The small grains gone, and I was to blame! My initial reaction may have been one of guilt, but I was quickly reminded of a very similar conversation in Rwanda in the mid-1980s, between a local agronomist and a few male farmers, when 'the small grains' had also been the topic under discussion. On that occasion, however, and to please the agronomist, farmers had praised the loss of the 'small grains' (small-sized beans), which, they said, had at last been replaced with HYVs. On hearing the conversation I had felt not guilt but glee. The agronomist got to hear what he wanted to hear – and that the recent harvest had contained a good mix of large and small beans, which I knew about, was none of his business (Pottier 1989a). On second thoughts, then, might the Buhera elders not have been telling us what we 'needed' to hear? ('You modern people, you got us in trouble. Now, get us out of it, do something!') I was not in a position to judge the Buhera elders' words. Not being involved in long-term fieldwork in Buhera, the best I could do was ask what farmers really meant when they said the hybrid maize had displaced many traditional varieties. The questions that came to mind remain useful: Displaced to what extent? And irreversibly so?

Biotechnology, with its radical outlook on the order of life processes, is another backdrop against which the words of the Buhera elders can be understood. The 'bio-revolution' does not just tamper with the fabric of life, but also aspires to restructure fundamental perceptions and values. Environment, human values and relationships, and intellectual property rights are all drastically reconfigured under the spell of biotechnology. The brainchild of powerful petrochemical and phar-

maceutical companies, biotechnology has grown up with its own private logic and ethics, and a strong desire to subject others to its own
outlook on life. By the mid-1990s, Transnational Enterprises (TNEs)
reportedly controlled one quarter of global economic activity, with
global mergers rocketing to the value of $US1.6 trillion for the year
1997 (Mooney 1998: 134–5). Truly, biotechnology had become a tool
to control the world.

The bio-revolution has sparked off a whole series of debates, mostly
to do with concerns over power and profits, safety, ethics, ownership
and patenting, and the relationship between university research and
business. Two themes especially have attracted the attention of anthropologists: biotechnology's impact on smallholder farming and livelihoods, including community ethos and morale (see e.g. Shiva 1992;
van der Ploeg 1989, 1990), and the legal-judicial argument about the
ownership of products and processes (see e.g. Mooney 1993). We look
at the latter first.

New Seeds and Intellectual Property Rights

Biotechnologists claim that the landraces which evolved over thousands of years are valueless 'primitive' cultivars when compared with
the 'elite' varieties created by transnational seed corporations and
IARCs. What gives the seed its value is laboratory treatment. Value
derives from 'the long, laborious, expensive and always risky process
of back crossing and other means required to make genetic sense out
of the chaos created by the foreign germplasm' (Witt 1985: 71; see
also IDRC 1994: 57). Biotechnologists thus place the contribution of
corporate scientists over and above the intellectual contributions of
peasant farmers worldwide, whose time and expertise are considered
to be free and valueless. It was not until 1987 that the notion of farmers' rights, as against plant breeders' royalities, was recognized (Juma
1989: 173).

Critics point out that such claims distort reality. Far from being
genetically chaotic, landraces consist of improved and selected materials that embody the work and ingenuity of farmers past and present.
There is therefore a need to guard against abuses of a discriminatory,
possibly racist nature, and hence a parallel need to invest in broad
public debate (Fowler et al. 1988: 227). The power of the seed corporations, however, is such that they are constantly backed by (they breed,
you could say) new legislation that enables them to win legal arguments as if *they* – and not the peasant farmers worldwide – are in need
of patent protection. Farmers in the developing world ('the South') are
thus reconstituted as ungrateful, 'primitive' competitors whose contrib-

utions should be confined to the supply of valueless raw materials. Vandana Shiva (1992, 1993a, 1993b), a leading critic, has explored important consequences of this process of social reconstitution (reviewed below), showing how the analysis can be linked to developments and outcomes in human reproductive technology.

Besides being a (perceived) threat to the maintenance of genetic diversity worldwide, biotechnology especially threatens to erode the control smallholders have over food production, that is, production according to their own knowledges and circumstances or what van der Ploeg has called the *art de la localité* (van der Ploeg 1989, 1993). The 'poisoned apple', so to speak, is patented seed, which is produced and reproduced scientifically, and cannot be reproduced on-farm. Even if peasant farmers should overcome the technical constraints of reproduction, they may be doing so illegally. The ultimate threat, then, is that farmers stand to lose not just their control over production inputs, but, through legislation, may be denied the right to experiment and innovate. At no other point in history have small-scale farmers in the South, and increasingly worldwide, had to face legal anxieties over the seed they plant. Today such anxieties are real, as 'some forms of Intellectual Property (IP) could make it illegal for farmers to sell seed to their neighbours or even to save seed for the next planting season' (IDRC 1994: 47).

Modern plant breeders' argument for protection is that international genebanks provide an invaluable service to 'the world community', since their collections can offset the risk of permanent genetic loss almost anywhere in the world. So resource-poor farmers should be grateful. The claim is contestable, though, even on technical grounds; *ex situ* genebanks are 'fixed in time' and therefore a flawed response to conservation needs. Since *ex situ* seed samples are unaffected by the processes of sustained adaptation to changing conditions, it can be said that what genebanks do is preservation, not conservation. Seeds stored *ex situ* may in fact not be viable when planted twenty or thirty years after the point of sampling (Amanor et al. 1993; Salazar 1992). This was demonstrated when 'the international community' intervened in Rwanda to restore the country's capacity for ecologically adapted agriculture following the 1990–4 war and genocide. The experience confirmed that germplasm taken from *ex situ* genebanks is prone to rapid erosion (Pottier 1996).

The international genebank approach, moreover, looks suspect in terms of its political uses. Genebanks are unlikely to focus on poor people's crops, which are rarely deemed economically viable (Kiambi and Opole 1992), while 'big money' deals can invalidate the claims to guardianship and moral integrity. Mooney (1993) documents examples of companies that have patented varieties derived from germplasm held in IARC genebanks in return for substantial reward, while the original innovators and maintainers of the germplasm, the small farmers, went unrewarded. The company Agrectus Inc., for example, was awarded a European patent to cover all forms of genetically engineered soybean plants and seeds, irrespective of the genes used or the transformation techniques employed (*New Internationalist,* February 1995). Such alarming developments demand that all institutionalized attempts at conserving biodiversity be set within a broad political and economic framework. The final irony, and a realistic possibility, is that by depriving small-scale farmers in the South of the right to innovate, the North has embarked on a self-destructive course of action.

The challenge is to ensure that control over genetic diversity reverts to community levels, while local knowledges become validated and positively linked to science (Amanor et al. 1993). To narrow the gulf between internationally recognized breeders and informal innovators, a culture for mutual respect and collaboration needs to be developed. Thus the North must recognize that 'abundant genetic diversity will be the key to human survival. If diversity goes, we will soon follow' (IDRC 1994: p. xiv). And recognition must lead to appropriate rewards. For its part, the South must accept that the 'new biotechnologies can use biodiversity in ways it has never been used before' (IDRC 1994: p. xiv). Agriculture's new biotechnologies are not inherently evil. Ways must therefore be found so that industry's concern about IP for biomaterials can be combined with the launch of a strong multilateral framework through which nation-states can manage their resources and negotiate access (IDRC 1994: p. xv). 'The task is to allow the two to cooperate without violating their rights or capacities' (IDRC 1994: p. xviii).

Anthropologists can contribute to the call for a 'culture for mutual respect and collaboration' in several ways, but most contributions will be variations on familiar research activities. First, anthropologists need to continue, in their many research settings, the search for 'a new balance in our appraisal of the very nature of knowledge about the world, a balance which will no longer overvalue formal, official science and undervalue indigenous knowledge' (Pratt and Loizos 1992: 2–3). Second, this search must be accompanied by a determined attack on the images and misrepresentations that create and sustain power imbalances (cf. Moore and Vaughan 1994; Pottier 1996). This could mean supporting local demands for the right to 'greater access to a more generous idea of development' (Rangan 1996: 22). It is indeed ironic, as Haripriya Rangan reminds us, 'that contemporary scholarly voices should clamour for a "post-development" era just when voices from the margins – so celebrated in discourses of difference and alternative culture – are demanding [such] rights' (1996: 22).

The challenge not to overvalue formal science but to create more respect for indigenous knowledges is no easy matter, though. There is the problem that indigenous knowledges must be valued without becoming 'frozen', that is without detachment from their specific social contexts (Fairhead 1993); there is the further problem that the search for a 'culture of mutual respect' requires a rethink of the populist dichotomy between (good) farmers who till and toil and innovate for love, and (bad) scientists who exploit cheap labour and resources. This dichotomy parallels the view, critiqued in the previous chapter, that commodity markets invariably extract without any benefit ever going to poor producers. The critique suggested that participation in 'real markets' is somewhat different, more varied. Markets constrain, yet they also offer, under certain circumstances, advantages that allow new vitalities to be discovered. 'Real seed markets' should be no exception, for here as well farmers can use their human agency to overcome potential dangers and reap benefit (for example, wheat farmers in the Punjab; rice growers in Central Luzon and Sagada, discussed above in chapter 4). Essentially, this means that the availability of 'improved' seed – like the spread of commodity markets – is not in itself either good or bad. Depending on a range of factors, but mainly on the power relations that prevail at national, community and household level, farmers may be able to pick and mix, as it were, and respond positively to the new opportunities without ditching their own seed patrimonium.

This perspective has become more attractive following the recent argument that biodiversity in West Africa is not as eroded as has been assumed. Guyer and Richards (1996) suggest we need not be pessimistic, and argue against the common assertion that commoditization has irreversibly reduced the range of crops grown on smallholder farms. For Guyer and Richards, and for the contributors to their edited volume (*Africa* 66, 1), the notion of irreparable damage is a verdict to be studied, not assumed. The debate on biodiversity, they contend, has fallen victim to 'crisis talk' and must therefore be reinstated: 'As has been suggested in critiques of relief assistance to Africa, there seems some danger that a crisis-oriented mode of thinking creates a discourse that ends up as a tool for the realisation of its own worst nightmares' (Guyer and Richards 1996: 2).

The alternative to crisis talk is to appreciate 'the multi-stranded character of human strategies for the management of biodiversity (as one among many types of diversity) and the multiplicity of ways in which those types of diversity are conceptualised' (Guyer and Richards 1996: 3). The appreciation is not unlike the approach Murray Leaf developed regarding the 'Green Revolution' (see chapter 4 above). As Netting and Stone (1996) and Guyer (1996) argue on the basis of their respective on-farm observations, the point is 'that smallholder farming practices are rich in complexity and subtlety and that we should not conclude too quickly that apparent simplifications, under the stimulus of commoditization, are necessarily permanent and irreversible' (Guyer and Richards 1996: 10).

Regarding her research in the Yoruba town of Idere, western Nigeria, Guyer contrasts the 1968–9 scene with that of 1988, and concludes that the notable increase in *individual* tendencies towards crop specialization, caused by an attractive and rapidly growing urban market, has not been accompanied by a similar tendency at the *community* level. For the latter, Guyer notes that the level of diversity in cropping has hardly changed, if at all (Guyer 1996: 72). Looking at the Idere hinterland as a whole, Guyer concludes that the changes induced by greater market involvement 'have not, then, homogenized the micro-ecological variations among the small villages that make up the Idere hinterland' (1996: 79).

Analysing the relationship between swidden agriculture (in central Nigeria) and mechanized agriculture, Netting and Stone (1996) confirm that mechanized agriculture – which indeed manages only a relatively small number of species – does not necessarily erode local agro-diversity levels. For Kofyar smallholders on the Benue plains, who migrated 30 km. south of their 1960s home villages (Netting 1968), Netting and Stone argue the exact opposite:

> the cumulative effects of maintaining more than one farm (one in the migrant plains and one in the hills, for example) can mean that each smallholder household now manages a wide spectrum of crops, semi-domesticated wild plants and animals than the single farm in the hills in the 1960s. . . . There is no simple negative correlation between 'modernization' and agro-diversity, as is sometimes assumed. (Netting and Stone 1996: 64)

Netting and Stone agree with Ellis (1988) that maintaining agro-diversity in the farming repertoire reduces risk and provides a modicum of insurance against the uncertainties of both the market and the state (Netting and Stone 1996: 55, 65). But there is some 'small print' to be considered. If modern Kofyar agriculture has successfully maintained its agro-diversity, this has been possible because of two conditions: access to multiple micro-environments, and secure land tenure; both are vital. So once again, secure access to land is stressed.

But there is a caveat. Maintenance of biodiversity levels does not mean that food security levels have been equally well maintained. On the individual farm in Idere, the shift towards narrow-spectrum farming for the market means that 'a varied diet is now no longer planned and guaranteed entirely through self-provisioning. In fact farmers' budgets show that more food is now purchased: 27 per cent of total expenditure was devoted by men to food and minor household needs in 1988, as against 13 per cent in 1969' (Guyer 1996: 81). This reliance on cash does not bode well for food security: 'An increased richness of agricultural variety does not necessarily mean that the variety of *dietary inputs* has also increased' (Guyer 1996: 71; emphasis in text).

In sum, while we must not assume that diverse, secure, 'traditional' farming practices have always and everywhere made way for a specialized, risky 'modern' agriculture (Guyer 1996: 64), we must not forget either that the maintenance of biodiversity requires certain specific conditions, for example secure land tenure, that are not always present. Nor does this maintenance imply that a healthy diet is necessarily achieved. With this mixture of good news and bad, and given that there are 'real seed markets' out there, there is vast scope for increased research on plant diversity and food security.

Another area where the search for evidence needs stepping up regards the relationship between the HYV seed markets, with their many dependencies, and farmer confidence. What needs detailed, situated examination is the claim that the modern dependencies have eroded small farmers' self-esteem.

New Seed, New Selves: A Threat to Farmer Self-Esteem?

In 1970, when Norman Borlaug was awarded the Nobel Peace Prize for creating 'a new world situation with regard to nutrition', the Prize Committee agreed that the kinds of grain which were the result of Dr Borlaug's work would speed up economic growth and be a source of prosperity for all (Doyle 1985: 256). The optimism rested on the view that modern science was a universal, value-free system of knowledge which would, with time, displace all other belief and knowledge systems, and do so legitimately.

Two decades later, the 'miracle seeds' industry came in for serious criticism by eco-feminists who took umbrage at its representations and perceptions. Eco-feminism recognizes that biotechnology (and modern science generally) is driven by an unacceptable dichotomy between, on the one hand, activity/creativity/culture, faculties viewed as typically male and, on the other, passivity/materiality/nature, viewed as typically female and outside of science (Shiva 1992: 152–3). At the cutting edge of the debate, Vandana Shiva argues that this dichotomy has drastically altered perceptions of 'seed' and 'farmer', and done so universally. Regarding seed, biotechnology has obliterated the view that seed would be 'active in a passive earth', which was an ancient patriarchical representation, to promote the opposite (and worse) view that seed is raw material, passive and valueless. In terms of agriculture, the new perception means that activity/creativity/culture has moved from the farm to be relocated in the laboratory (Shiva 1992: 154). In a parallel move, and to complete the logic of biotechnology, the farmers who initially created that wealth of crop genetic stock have become devalued as well (Shiva 1992: 154).

This universal devaluation, Shiva maintains, is the end result of centuries of colonization. The patriarchal construct of a passive earth, which negates the earth's regenerative capacity (Pilger 1989), started to flourish some 500 years ago when ambitious explorers and their influential backers came to regard all foreign land as *terra nullius* (land 'vacant' and 'waste') and started to colonize it (Shiva 1992: 154). In the process, the church and the military worked as a team: 'The morality of the missions justified the military take-over of resources all over the world to serve imperial markets. European men were thus able to describe their invasions as "discoveries", piracy and theft as "trade", and extermination and enslavement as their "civilising mission"' (Shiva 1992: 154).

The demotion of land as *terra nullius*, Shiva maintains, then led to changes in land use which accelerated the depletion of on-farm genetic diversity; habitats containing important genetic resources disappeared. By way of an example, Worede (1992) argues for Ethiopia that large tracts of grazing land, being important sites for the wild and weedy relatives of major food and fibre crops, are threatened by extensive ploughing, itself the result of pressures to achieve national food security. For Shiva, the 'Green Revolution' merely extends the 500-year-old process of colonization and degradation: 'By treating essential organic inputs as "waste", the Green Revolution strategy unwittingly ensured that fertile and productive soils were actually laid waste; the "land-augmenting" technology has proved to be a land-degrading and land-destroying one' (Shiva 1992: 156).

Humans are also being degraded. Firstly, farmers are caught in a dependent relation which is self-perpetuating. That is to say, hybrid seed has to be purchased over and over again, as it is incomplete and does not reproduce itself (Shiva 1992: 157). Secondly, 'Third World' farmers are now labelled '*competitors* in terms of innovation and rights to genetic resources' (Shiva 1992: 160). The impact on farmer confidence and self-perception, Shiva argues, has been devastating. As a result of patent protection and market dependence, the 'Third World' peasant farmer is now labelled 'a supplier of free raw material, [which] makes him totally dependent on industrial supplies for vital inputs such as seed' (Shiva 1992: 160). Shiva's analysis is powerful and applicable, especially as the argument on agriculture is extended to health technology, but not without its flaws.

Among the more convincing applications in agricultural anthropology is Jan Douwe van der Ploeg's portrayal (1989, 1990, 1993) of the Andean potato farmer who has been bombarded with 'scientific potatoes' to the point of absolute bewilderment. The ethnography deserves a detailed look.

Case Study 6.1: Potato Farming in the Peruvian Andes

Experimentation by small-scale potato farmers has become strained by the availability of 'improved' crop varieties and the infrastructure set up to promote them. One major reason for the strain is that farmers need time for proper experimentation; a condition 'scientific' farming denies. The main dislocation, however, is that farmers have lost control over the key production factors – land, labour and seed – with severely damaging consequences for their confidence and self-perception.

Before the 'improved' potatoes became available, Andean farmers promoted crop diversity and ecological complementarity. They managed various ecological 'floors' and improved their plots 'by responding to the specific set of conditions that each plot present[ed]' (van der Ploeg 1989: 148, 1993: 211). Most farmers cultivated between twelve and fifteen plots continuously, as well as a number in rotation (1989: 149). Through socially regulated exchange, farmers might obtain up to a hundred cultivars (van der Ploeg 1989: 148, 1993: 212).

This extreme heterogeneity and its underlying knowledges is what van der Ploeg calls the *art de la localité*. Made up of interpenetrating technical and spiritual elements (see chapter 1 above), the framework enables farmers to experiment and adapt at their own pace (van der Ploeg 1990: 186). Resorting to the same dichotomy Vandana Shiva presents, van der Ploeg describes the highland Andean approach as diametrically opposed to that of Western science. The logic which informs scientific research is the antithesis of that which informs practices in the *art de la localité*.

> In the Andean highlands the given phenotypical conditions are – within the framework of the *art de la localité* – interpreted as starting points for the selection and adaptation of genotypes, whereas in the scientific knowledge system the genotype is the point of departure for the specification of the required phenotypical conditions. (van der Ploeg 1989: 155)

The dynamic *art de la localité* of small Andean farmers, van der Ploeg argues, is threatened because of the introduction of 'improved' varieties and the infrastructure set up by state-controlled as well as international programmes in scientific breeding. Prominent here is the Lima-based

International Potato Centre (CIP), a member of the Consultative Group on International Agricultural Research, CGIAR (van der Ploeg 1989: 154). Van der Ploeg's concern is that scientific potato breeding and its infrastructure undermine the system whereby varietal heterogeneity used to be created and guaranteed on the basis of detailed knowledge of field and seed variety. The future looks bleak. Scientific breeding programmes have resulted in 'changes in crop rotation plans which in the long term [appear] to be untenable, not only because of soil fertility problems but also because *reduced diversity* greatly increases market-induced risks. Falling potato prices increasingly threaten the continuity of the [farm] enterprise' (van der Ploeg 1990: 182–3). The cost of modern fertilizer is also highly restrictive, and amounts easily to a third of the overall cost of farm operations (van der Ploeg 1990: 177).

Cost and risk were handled differently in the past. Whatever production factor was lacking on a given farm (labour, land or seed) could be accessed on a reciprocal basis. Under *ayni* (reciprocal) arrangements, missing production factors (basically, the poor lacked land but had surplus labour; for the rich it was the reverse) could be accessed without dependence on commoditized exchange relations (van der Ploeg 1990: 161). By extension, there was some assurance that the impact of specific crop failure or personal misfortune (for example illness) could be accommodated through community relations.

The situation today is less secure. State bureaucracy and credit institutions have introduced 'a short time horizon, high-risk insecurity, and an increasing rigidity as far as buying and selling in different markets are concerned, so that higher costs and lower benefits occur, requiring further extension of credit' (van der Ploeg 1990: 221). The provision of such credit, by either the Agrarian Bank or Proderm, has had a negative effect on labour input; labour has lost its use-value, which in turn has lowered the intensity of cultivation. In short, the restructured organization of farm labour has brought down yields and enhanced vulnerability (van der Ploeg 1990: 199).

Highland farmers now talk of *despachamamamización,* as *pacha mama* (nature) is no longer the guardian of the interests of future generations (van der Ploeg 1990: 156). Guardianship has moved to the agricultural research station, where there is a strong belief that 'traditional' agriculture has reached its limits. A continuous strand in the crisis narratives that inform policy in Peru, this belief was voiced, for instance, at a Proderm seminar in Cuzco in 1982, at which it was argued that without external intervention small-scale farmers would be 'unable to fulfil a meaningful role in any kind of agrarian development' (Kervin 1982, quoted in van der Ploeg 1990: 165).

Demonstration of the inferiority of the 'traditional' food systems (and hence justification for intervention) may require some rigging of statistics. Van der Ploeg points out that his own calculation of mean production under *art de la localité* conditions is around 10 tons per hectare (rising to 25 tons under ideal conditions), whereas official assessments claim the mean to be around 5 or 6 tons per hectare. Such statistical misinformation is an important component in the creation of ignorance within development agencies; ignorance which then 'justifies' the view that it is a waste of time for scientists to show serious interest in local farming approaches and their logic (van der Ploeg 1989: 160).

Maria Salas (1994) reinforces van der Ploeg's criticism of the damage the 'scientific potato' has inflicted. Salas does not compromise:

> The 'scientific potato' monopolizes genetic resources, ignores ecological diversity, privileges the lowlands, concentrates on mechanization and high inputs and minimizes the role of social and cultural knowledge systems. For instance, there is very limited research into the bitter potato varieties, which grow above 4,000 meters. [And yet,] they are a major concern of peasants since the high ecological zones offer them the best conditions for production without chemicals, using foot ploughs, natural manure, etc. They are able to transform the potato into potato-starch which is the best form of storage. (Salas 1994: 66)

This local preference, however, is appreciated neither by the CIP nor by Peru's national research organizations, because 'the nation' prefers a different type of highland potato. Dietary preferences have indeed come to be dictated 'from above', with a little help from PL 480 food aid shipments from the USA (Doughty 1991: 159).

There is also psychological trauma. In challenging the philosophies and techniques developed within the *art de la localité*, Western scientific research has pronounced a death sentence on Andean farmers' life-worlds and identities. Farmers express this trauma by stating that they, like the land, have become 'invisible'. One farmer told van der Ploeg, '[experts] go around as if you yourself did not exist: as if you, as a social being, were indeed invisible' (van der Ploeg 1989: 159, 1993: 221). The insult is doubly painful since commoditized farming has made many farmers slide down the social ladder. Van der Ploeg conveys their feelings of inadequacy when he writes that farmers

> know how to farm but feel themselves forced to 'hasten.' 'Now it is impossible, the world has gone mad,' is the lament of an evening at the edge of a field; 'it doesn't work anymore, the world is crazy.' 'You still work hard, but proud is something you cannot be anymore.' The tension between the existing calculus and the increasingly adverse circumstances results in feelings of powerlessness and dismay, without the real causes being clearly identified. (van der Ploeg 1990: 169)

A Note of Caution

Van der Ploeg's Andean research, which portrays potato farmers as confused, degraded selves, is an excellent illustration of the old adage that 'food is not just something to eat' (de Garine 1971), but good to think with too (see e.g. Appadurai 1981; Lévi-Strauss 1966; Tapper and Tapper 1986). Particularly valuable is van der Ploeg's demonstration of how development agencies may create ignorance through falsifying data, whilst justifying their interventions by mixing in claims to moral superiority. Kervin's mix at the Cuzco seminar resembles the claim of physical and moral breakdown in colonial rural Zambia (Moore and Vaughan 1994) and is echoed in the conviction that what really matters in experimentation is speed (Sperling and Scheidegger 1995). Reductionism is at work here. Just as policy-makers and scientists in Zambia reduced *citemene* to a simple slash-and-burn operation, so policy-makers and scientists in Peru regard Andean farming as simply a matter of insufficient yield and speed. In the name of better yields and increased speed, it has become quite acceptable to omit all other aspects of the 'primitive' approach – for example the relatively secure access to production factors, and the ability to contain uncertainty and risk *within the community*. (The relationship between community-based social safety networks and top-down intervention is a central focus in chapter 7 below.)

But caution must be exercised too, since social science generalizations couched in terms of Marxist dependency theory are flawed by their 'inability to deal with empirical variation' (Gardner and Lewis 1996: 18). Discussion of transformations in land, labour and market relations, in previous chapters, has already highlighted the relevance of the postmodern critique. Gardner and Lewis spell it out neatly: 'While it is certainly important to analyse the structures which perpetuate underdevelopment . . . we must also recognise the ways in which individuals and societies strategise to maximise opportunities, how they resist structures which subordinate them and, in some cases, how they successfully embrace capitalist development' (1996: 18).

Are farmers everywhere affected in the way Vandana Shiva suggests? Have they all become 'Homo Gene-ous'? Or have they (some, many, most) found ways around the problem by selecting aspects of the new technologies without going to the extreme of feeling totally dependent and degraded as producers and human beings? Shiva is not ahistorical, but she hides the heterogeneity that also exists in rural transformations. There is continuity, I suggest, between Shiva's analysis and that of van der Ploeg, and earlier interpretations by Claude Meillassoux in his *Maidens, Meal and Money* (1981). All three opt for a broad 'passive victims' representation, thus denying the 'victims' their social differentiation and human agency. Meillassoux's treatment of women, as Moore reminds us, has been criticized for its failure to differentiate women as a social category and for assuming that 'women's subordination ... is an established and unproblematic state of affairs which does not require further specification or analysis' (Moore 1988: 50).

The problem with Meillassoux is that his analysis raises

> questions which he leaves unanswered. If the reproduction of society depends on the control of women's productive and reproductive potential by male elders, have the women not evolved strategies to deal with this control? If they have such an important role in agricultural production, what happens to the crops they produce? Do they really surrender them all to their husbands, or do they retain control over them? (Moore 1988: 50–1)

Similar reservations must be levelled at Shiva's and van der Ploeg's portrayal of how peasant farmers, women and men, are reproduced by transnational seed companies. Questions resembling the above must be asked. Are farmers totally powerless in the face of the homogenizing activities of such transnational bodies? Do they really engage with these global forces in a uniformly submissive manner? That this is hardly the case in so-called 'Third World' farming, previous chapters have already illustrated. Analyses which put all the emphasis on structural constraints at the cost of highlighting how farmers strategize to make the most of new opportunities have merit, but they are one-sided. Despite the formidable hurdles they encounter, small-scale farmers are not passive pawns at the mercy of globalizing forces. They may claim to have been made 'invisible' by the scientific potato breeders, but surely must not be made invisible twice through a denial of the human agency they exercise.

This critique extends the earlier argument that we need an antidote to the simplistic view that timeless, harmonious ties embedded in gift-giving are invariably being destroyed by commodity markets to make way for purely impersonal relations. Such a straightforward gift-to-commodity sequence and the parallel progression from personal to impersonal relations were not borne out in 'real market' situations: neither for land, nor for labour, nor for commodities. Regarding 'real' seed markets we must heed Miller's critique of homogenization (Miller 1995: 143) and appreciate his contention that hybridity is just as authentic as are the genetic parents themselves. Miller contends that earlier literature on consumption viewed commoditization as destructive of embedded customary relations, and was replete with moral purpose (1995: 144). The analyses by Shiva and van der Ploeg proceed in the same vein: being the embodiment of evil, commoditized seed destroys cultures and social identities on a global scale. The way out of the impasse requires a more active notion of appropriation.

An excellent example of how farmers can develop 'a sense of self that is genuinely transnational' (Long 1996: 45) is that of the Mexican migrants from Oaxaca who work on tomato farms in California. Their manifold, cross-cutting experiences (as workers and militants, as foreign nationals, as members of the Mixtec residents' associations, etc.) have culminated in 'the emergence of a new conception of self which is essentially pan-Mixteca' (Long 1996: 45). These migrant workers may be poor and working under hi-tech conditions they do not control, but they have not become degraded selves. Their selves have proved to be less bounded and more participating and relational (cf. Moore 1996: 7). It is experiences like that of Oaxaca which have prompted anthropologists to reconsider the conventional approach to 'the self' and accept that '[it] is no longer, if it ever was, a singular, self-contained entity, but a participating, relational one' (Long 1996: 7).

An early anthropological illustration of the debate on how 'selves' are to be understood is the analysis of how Bruson, a Swiss Alpine village in the Canton of Valais, came to terms with 'fifty years [of] gradual erosion of village autonomy and an increasing dependence . . . on the outside world' (Gibson and Weinberg 1980: 113). In the mid-1970s, the loss of autonomy and ensuing dependence upon wider administrative structures were experienced as a real squeeze, but there was no long-term erosion of village identity. As Bruson risked being swallowed up by a world it had difficulty controlling, the villagers saw to it that Valaisan culture and their own village identity would survive. Wine, an excellent meaning-maker, became the chief means of countering the danger of cultural erosion. Being one of the few remaining products of Brusonins' own labours, and outside the control of external interference, wine emerged into the public arena as the symbolic medium through which past and present could converge (Gibson and Weinberg 1980: 115). Cafés sprang up. Threatened with the loss of autonomy and self-sufficiency, villagers reasserted their identity (as a strong, autonomous community) by making the most of what they still produced and controlled: 'Wine and the cafés took on new functions. Both private and the newly-institutionalized public drinking became a symbolic medium for validating the social contracts that bind the families in Bruson' (Gibson and Weinberg 1980: 116). Important for our purposes, the demise of the once grand-scale, diversified agricultural base was not experienced as a loss of 'the essence' of people's identities. Whilst agricultural autonomy was enormously important to people's livelihood and self-esteem before 1930, the changes that were introduced through mechanized agriculture were not experienced as destructive for people's self-image. Agriculture was reduced in scale and importance, and many older inhabitants no doubt regretted this, yet new opportunities (cash crops, off-farm work) were fully explored and used to offset the danger of an impaired collective identity.

Conclusion

Dramatic changes in agriculture, disorientating as they are, do not necessarily lead to self-effacement. International capitalism and hi-tech agriculture certainly carry costs that can be heavy – for example job losses, heightened dependency, heightened risk and uncertainty – and these must be recorded, analysed and corrected. The same forces, however, also bring new opportunities, and many people will respond positively to accommodate them.

The influence of transnational markets and images can both disempower and empower (cf. Miller 1995: 153). As Vupenyu Dzingirai wrote of Clara, a village farmer in Zimbabwe who had seen her debts spiral after she bought a modern planter that ended up lying idle in some shed, this farmer did not consider selling the equipment. Debt was only one aspect of her 'self'. Dzingirai reflected: 'Perhaps the symbols of "master farmerhood" could not be dropped; perhaps Clara still wanted to be thought and spoken of as one of the few enlightened farmers in the village' (Dzingirai 1992: 83).

While Shiva's analytic framework and the case study by van der Ploeg expose a full range of interlinked constraints that analysts cannot afford to ignore, the additional challenge for analysts is to test the range of concerns in specific locations and to keep an open mind as to how farmers – truly differentiated, and with their composite selves – respond.

7

Famine Relief, Famine Prevention
Whose Analysis? Whose Solutions? Whose Patronage?

'Don't worry about what I feed my family. You just give me some money and I will take care of it. You don't have to assume that I don't know what to feed my family. The problem is that I happen to be poor, and if you can't do anything about that then get out of here. Don't waste my time.'

farmer, Bangladesh, early 1980s, quoted in McCarthy, 'The Target Group'

Thoughts on Famine

Amartya Sen's *Poverty and Famines* (1981) marked a paradigm shift in famine analysis. Challenging the theory that famine is invariably caused by 'food availability decline' (FAD), Sen proposed instead to focus on 'food entitlements decline' (FED). Famine was not caused by a slump in the overall availability of food, but by the loss of entitlements to that food – either through loss of endowment (failed crops; perished livestock) or loss of the means to access food. 'Supply failure' thus came to be de-emphasized; 'demand failure' took its place. The shift, which meant that poverty and inequality now replaced calamity and God's will, also had implications for market analysis: famine was now the 'predictable consequence of *normal* market processes, given that markets respond to purchasing power rather than to needs' (Devereux 1993: 71).

Sen's approach was a breakthrough, but not flawless. He was criticized, for instance, for portraying famine as caused by the rather *sudden* loss of individual or group entitlements. Critics stressed that famines develop over time; famine is a process, not an event. As famine ethnographies now show, famines indeed come mostly 'at the tail end of a long-term process of increasing vulnerability . . . to food supply shocks' (Devereux 1993: 159). The view that *normal* market processes were at the root of famine, invaluable as a new insight, also overlooked the possibility that well-functioning markets sabotaged in war can trigger famine. Thus, in Tigray, which has a history of chronic food shortages and periodic famine, the 1980s famine was induced by the Ethiopian government severing the trade links on which Tigray depended. Diverting international and internal grain supplies, the government made sure that Tigrayans could not use 'the market' to keep hunger at bay. Ethiopian fighter-bomber aircraft then completed the sabotage by attacking markets inside Tigray (Hendrie 1994: 128–9).

Before we spell out how the new paradigm translates into measures for famine alleviation and prevention, it is useful to recall that the term 'entitlement' has a formidable range of meanings. Richards provides a good summary: 'Entitlement systems are beliefs, created in political practice, about who ought to get what under what circumstances, and the embodiment of those beliefs in legal and economic processes, e.g. land tenure rules, notions of family obligations, wage rates, rules of market transactions, etc.' (Richards 1983: 46). Entitlement, in other words, is about social position and worth; the very preoccupation also found in market ideologies (see chapters 5 and 6). And because these concerns are cultural, we cannot be too surprised that 'rights and obligations' are often loosely, even ambiguously, defined and always open to interpretation.

The emphasis on *entitlement* and *process* in famine analysis has impacted on the way 'relief' is conceptualized. Basically, a consensus has emerged from famine ethnographies (cf. D'Souza 1988) that famines are preventable and that relief initiatives must focus on restoring lost entitlements and not simply 'throw grain at famines'. Better relief can contribute to prevention.

This chapter focuses on relief and prevention rather than on the occurrence of famine itself, because the latter has been thoroughly analysed in Stephen Devereux's excellent *Theories of Famine* (Devereux 1993). The aim of the present chapter, then, is to complement Devereux's overview with a look at actual, conventional relief practices. What happens when a full-blown crisis can no longer be averted? What is the standard relief response? Can it be organized differently?

Actual Famine Relief Practices

There are many reasons why famine relief, including emergency food aid, persists. First of all, wars trigger humanitarian catastrophies at (fairly) short notice. In the event of population displacement by war, food aid remains an appropriate initial response. Second, not all disasters are man-made or fully predictable; some natural and quasi-natural disasters (earthquakes, floods) will continue to provoke displacement, material need and hunger. Such catastrophes warrant the swift transfer of relief, including food aid, as a first response. The third and perhaps most important reason why food aid persists is that it has become a major ingredient in 'normal' packages for international development assistance. The dividing-line between 'emergency' and 'normal' food aid has narrowed.

But why should an injection of external aid be appropriate *only initially*? How could a robust humanitarian response – lots of equipment, material goods, copious quantities of food – be working against recovery? A down-to-earth look at some well-documented famine relief practices explains why. A review of externally induced relief activities in drought-hit parts of Africa, for instance – Darfur (1985–6), Rwanda (1984), Ethiopia (1970s), Somalia (1992) – quickly reveals how time and again external aid imposes a structured response (Harrell-Bond 1986), the rigidity of which thwarts local initiative. All too often, the external response is based on erroneous assumptions. Thus, when drought struck in Darfur in the mid-1980s, officials from international agencies *assumed* that the migrations towards Mawashei they observed were a sign of distress, a 'last ditch migration on the brink of death by starvation'. This was incorrect. The migrations were a regular economic activity aiming to raise income at a time of year when little or no farming was undertaken. Migrants would return to their villages to cultivate in time for the rains (de Waal 1989: 168). After officials blew the emergency whistle and food aid arrived at Mawashei, the sudden availability of free food enticed the migrants to stay on. It was not what they and their people back home needed. A better strategy, de Waal explains, would have been to provide the migrants with seed help, for example, or with grain that could be taken home and eaten to protect local seed stocks. By not returning home, the migrants – now labelled famine victims – failed to carry out essential agricultural activities.

Elsewhere in Sudan too, camp conditions and free handouts discouraged able-bodied workers from resuming regular activity, such as waged seasonal work. In *The Hunger Machine*, Jon Bennett recalls how a government official from the Managil Extension, part of

Sudan's cotton belt, journeyed to Talha in south Omdurman, hoping to persuade the villagers to come to Managil for the cotton-picking season. They had been involved every previous year. In spite of a day wage and free transport, the people of Talha refused. As they had been identified as famine victims and were now receiving free rations of grain and supplementary food from relief agencies, there was no reason for them to find work (Bennett 1987: 77). Bennett's reflections are insightful:

> Talha is not an isolated case. It highlights the complexity of issues sur-
> rounding 'food aid', where and when it should be used, and who sets
> the agenda. Contrary to impressions created by the media, 22 million
> people were not starving in Sudan in 1985. Chronic famine was local-
> ized – its effects were worst felt by particular sectors of society in par-
> ticular locations. True, drastic reductions in food availability, inflation
> and large-scale displacement were to depress the economy as a whole
> but, in many parts of the country, the more naive relief agencies mis-
> took poverty for absolute hunger, and blind enthusiasm took the place
> of professional planning. (Bennett 1987: 77)

The experiences on which Bennett (1987) and de Waal (1989) report are instances where food was delivered in the wrong place and for the wrong reasons. It is equally common, however, for food aid to arrive in the right place, but late and to the detriment of local recovery efforts. Whatever the reason for this lateness (for example transport delays or an initial refusal by government to acknowledge the famine), the consequences are mostly catastrophic. Thus, in Rwanda in 1984, when food aid in response to *localized* drought arrived roughly a year late, the sudden availability of cheap grain (wheat, rice) on the market obstructed local production efforts in areas where rice and wheat had a comparative advantage (Neel 1985: 69). The predictable result: en-terprising smallholder farmers were pushed out of business, their meagre reserves eroded, their households once again at risk. Then, faced with serious income losses, these better-off farmers reduced the agricultural wage work they offered the following season. The domino effect was that many poorer farmers were thus denied access to an important 'normal' strategy for getting by. Somalia underwent the same fate *after* the 1991–2 famine. When Somalia enjoyed its first harvest, this important step towards economic recovery was again marred by the arrival of unnecessary food aid. This was 'the moment when the donors should have been reducing their food aid to Somalia, and turn-ing towards local purchasing programmes and agricultural rehabilita-tion. Instead, the increased and indiscriminate supply of relief food had the predictable effect of driving the price of cereals down to very low levels and providing a serious disincentive to production' (de Waal

1994: 157). Once again, the labour market was hit right at the point of recovery.

The failure of conventional famine relief (and of 'normal' food aid, cf. Doughty 1986) is the very reason why anthropologists tend to argue that communities facing food shortage may be better off when food aid – distributed at fixed feeding stations where migrants are labelled famine victims – fails to reach them. Relying on their own resources, vulnerable communities may stand a better chance of recovery and of preserving their ability to do so in future. Writing about a group of Ethiopian Mursi who at the end of the 1970s drought migrated to resettle spontaneously, not having been reached by organized relief, David and Pat Turton reflect:

> Systematically distributed relief would certainly have saved many lives, especially, one must assume, those of young people. And yet, [this relief] might also, if distributed in 'emergency feeding stations', at which people were obliged to congregate for daily handouts, have turned large numbers of Mursi into permanent refugees in their own country. It might, in other words, have saved lives at the cost of destroying a way of life – a complex mode of adaptation for which there exists no viable short-term alternative. (Turton and Turton 1984: 179)

This Mursi group survived through migration into an area less affected by the drought where it forged alliances and rights. Its social and economic institutions came out of the drought 'shaken but intact', and there was an undiminished sense of cultural identity (Turton and Turton 1984: 179).

If local resourcefulness and resilience can be sapped by the manner in which international relief is dispensed, then questions must be asked regarding both the efficiency of aid organizations and their accountability. For instance, to whom are relief agencies and donors accountable? Is the setting up of fixed, potentially harmful feeding stations deliberate? Are officials merely misreading the situation, for example misinterpreting normal/seasonal adjustments for distress signals, or is something more deliberate and sinister going on? In the late 1970s, Pierre Spitz adopted the position that camp-based emergency programmes during famine could be 'a means of forestalling the development of a political consciousness which might degenerate into social disorder, i.e. rebellion' (Spitz 1978: 885).

Accountability, like any other aspect of famine, is a theme best discussed with a specific context in mind. David Keen highlights the complex matter of accountability in his discussion of relief operations in Darfur, 1985. His study suggests a lack of accountability on behalf of the donor involved, while the implementing agency was up against intractable problems and dilemmas. Here are some details.

Case Study 7.1: Targeting Emergency Food Aid: Darfur, 1985

In 1985 in Darfur, USAID-sponsored famine relief failed to reach the target groups. Keen explains the failure in terms of various bottlenecks at operational and local administrative levels. From the relief workers' point of view, the chief problem was that a good deal of the grain was diverted towards area councils with lesser need but superior lobbying power, while similar diversions occurred also within each council:

> people in bigger towns received more relief grain than the smaller towns, and townspeople received more than villagers. . . . People in richer villages tended, very often, to receive more than those in poorer villages . . . residents received more than migrants, and settled people more than nomads. Very often, this was the antithesis of distribution according to need. (Keen 1991: 194)

The operation's specific failure was that entitlements did collapse; targeting failed to prevent 'distress sales of livestock and labour by the poorest groups' (Keen 1991: 194). A purchase-and-resale policy by government or outside agencies would have prevented the collapse of livestock prices and the simultaneous rise in the price of grain, but it was not to be (Keen 1991: 206; see also de Waal 1989: 133–5; Sperling 1987).

Why did targeting fail? First, regarding the failure to target *by area council*, local administrative priorities differed from those set by the mainly Western relief NGOs. Actual allocations reflected a cultural (Sudanese, we are told) conception of fairness which, among administrators at least, meant that 'singling out certain groups for assistance was somehow unfair, and that food should be shared out among all those in a particular village or area' (Keen 1991: 199). Accordingly, area councils harbouring significantly fewer destitutes than others 'lobbied successfully for a sizeable chunk of the relief grain' (Keen 1991: 196). As donor, USAID was not interested in a proper needs assessment and turned a blind eye, while Save the Children Fund (UK) as implementing agency was powerless to do anything about the injustices it perceived.

In addition, many councils hoarded the relief grain, through which action they first caused steep price rises and then raked in significant revenue. Local authorities favoured employees over destitutes (noted for example for Kebkabiya: Tobert 1985) and discriminated against migrants and nomads. The outcome was that nomads resorted to distress sales of livestock to the benefit of merchants and urban residents. Rather than solve the crisis, the relief operation perpetuated it.

Contemplating these intractable problems, Keen recommends that relief should be designed on the [proven] assumption that targeting will, at best, only be partially achieved. This means allocating relatively large quantities of grain and allocating them *at an early stage*. Leakage of relief grain away from the target group should be anticipated and allowed for, rather than simply noted in retrospect. (Keen 1991: 191–2; emphasis added)

The problem of donor and NGO accountability has worsened since the end of the Cold War and the emergence of the outright commercialization of humanitarian assistance. Now delivered by the market rather than by mandate (de Waal and Omaar 1994), famine relief has resulted in a scramble for resources and media coverage, with the latter regularly projecting out-of-context images of agency need and success. The post-Cold War funding climate has thus led to a dramatic loss of accountability and public debate, while media dependency perpetuates the emphasis on reactive interventions in fixed places (emergency stations). Prevention has taken a back seat.

Other key players – patron governments and grain donors – are also not too concerned about accountability. Devereux reflects how the international trade in food is

one of the world's most inscrutable oligopolies . . . hardly regulated and controlled. . . . Seven families own the seven major grain merchant houses, which have no public shareholders and therefore little obligation to disclose information. This gives them unprecedented power to manipulate the demand for food on the world market to their own needs. (Devereux 1993: 165)

As is well known by now, the interests of 'real' decision-makers rarely coincide with those of the poor, 'because eliminating hunger requires not so much a transfer of food as a transfer of power' (George 1976: 206–13; see also Arnold 1988: 96–118). And since governments wish to stay in power, they must provide cheap food for the urban middle classes and elites, that is groups that have the power to pressurize them. This produces an infrastructure capable of 'silent violence' (Spitz 1978; Watts 1983).

Among the better-documented examples of discrimination against the poor is the Bangladesh famine of 1974, during which poor people were twice selected for exclusion: first, internationally as citizens of the 'wrong kind of country', then internally because of their poverty and lack of political clout. As floods disrupted agricultural production in Bangladesh in 1974, repeated government requests for PL 480 food from the USA were turned down (allegedly) on political grounds, that is because of Bangladesh's trade in jute sacks to Cuba. In response, the government then cut its own public distribution programmes. Food rationing became selective, 'favouring those groups who had the greatest political influence – and the lowest economic and nutritional need' (Devereux 1993: 175), a situation not unlike Darfur 1985. As the crisis worsened, food prices rose sharply while work opportunities and wages plummeted. The famine that resulted claimed hundreds of thousands of lives, not only among poor farmers but also among agricultural and non-agricultural labourers (Crow 1986: 10).

In 1979 and 1984, Bangladesh faced the prospect of a similar tragedy, but disaster was prevented. No longer headed by a 'problematic' government, Bangladesh received US food aid on request. Arriving *on time*, the delivery meant there was no need to select social groups for exclusion. Rationing and rapid intervention through internal food distributions on the open market effectively 'protected vulnerable groups, restrained food price rises and averted a major tragedy' (Devereux 1993: 138). The tragedy that loomed in 1984 would have been on a scale comparable to that of 1974 (Clay 1985: 206).

Despite the difficulty that culturally disparate value systems may seem irreconcilable, a problem compounded by notions of sovereignty, analysts agree that interventions can be effective provided they enable vulnerable people to use their own survival skills to optimum effect. People's *own planning* must be made more reliable (de Waal 1989: 216; Turton and Turton 1984). Concretely, in a situation like Darfur, relief operations should provide rural farmers with grain *before* the rains start and target them *at home*, so they can cultivate instead of sitting idle in camps. What needs to be prevented, then, is that food producers become spatially divorced from the agricultural cycle at a time when their labour is critically needed.

Writing about famine prevention in India, Michelle McAlpin concurs with that view: *working capital* for agricultural and pastoral populations must be preserved despite the hardship suffered, or be rebuilt as soon as the crisis ends (McAlpin 1987: 398). Preserving or restoring capital means moving from free food handouts to a *cash*-for-work situation, the rationale being that even during a famine money must circulate and long-term recovery plans be carried out. In India, as in Sudan and Ethiopia, preservation of assets and livelihoods is a priority which comes before actual food intake (cf. also El Sammani 1990; Wolde Mariam 1986, 1990). Governments and relief agencies must assist sufferers in their own endeavours to achieve this goal.

Better Relief through Bolstering Local Initiative?

The theory looks neat. Measures that bolster existing coping mechanisms and prevent the liquidation of productive assets are measures that can prevent famine. If such policy measures are available, in the form of a purchase-and-resale (livestock) strategy for example, they must come into effect *early on* in the crisis to prevent the collapse of entitlements. In actual practice, implementation is more difficult, as Keen's account made clear. Cultural conventions about who should be helped may disadvantage the most needy, but the question also arises as to which local initiatives can/should be supported.

Politics aside, the matter is complicated further because the actual onset of a famine and the location of its worst impact are never easy to predict. The problem of whether to intervene (and if so, when and how) cannot be resolved in the abstract. While the unfolding of a famine – any famine – may be patterned and therefore broadly pre-dictable, there is always a need to establish, given that drought is mostly *localized*, which areas exactly, and which people within those areas, will be hit. This is a difficult task, especially in areas that are ecologically diverse. In such cases, and even when the political will to intervene is present, it may still be virtually impossible to establish *in advance of the full crisis* who exactly will be most affected. The reason for this, as shown in the ethnography of famine in highland Bwisha, Congo-Zaire, is that while an adverse condition, say drought, may be generalized, its impact will vary geographically, for example according to altitude and crop maturation times (Pottier and Fairhead 1991). In other words, one may have a general profile of social dif-ferentiation and vulnerability for a given area, yet who exactly will suffer – which farmers, which poor, which women-headed house-holds – may not be known until the moment the drought actually impacts.

Little wonder, then, that there is disagreement over 'when' to inter-vene. William Torry reviews the controversy as it applies to relief prac-tices in India, exposing the contradictory views held by two economists, M. D. Morris and N. S. Jodha (Torry 1986). Morris (1974, 1975) claims that farmers in India plan for weather fluctuations by 'accumu-lating assets in good harvests, and drawing down stocks in lean years' (Torry 1986: 12). When harvests fail, farmers minimize risk through belt-tightening measures, asset depletion, inter-household sharing ar-rangements, and out-migration. The problem, says Morris, is that officials habitually misread these 'adjustments', seeing distress in what really are effective ways of coping. Government aid may then be pro-vided when it is not needed. Jodha (1975) takes the opposite view by contending that when small farmers mortgage land or deplete pro-ductive capital to meet current needs, they risk becoming landless, which means they are already affected by acute distress and must receive relief at once.

Given the *localized* nature of drought impact, full answers to the

question of 'whether' to intervene, and if so when and how, will ultimately depend on an accurate, situated reading of the famine crisis; a
reading which will take account of local contexts and their dynamic.
The point is that assets are graded as more or less important to livelihood, and that not all are disposed of at once. Moreover, some early
strategies do not involve asset loss.

An insightful ethnography through which we can learn more about
asset disposal and post-famine asset recovery, and thus about the workings and efficacy of internal coping strategies, is Prindle's account of
the 1971 famine in Tinglatar, Nepal (Prindle 1979).

Case Study 7.2: Famine and its Aftermath: Tinglatar, 1971–1977

Some seven days on foot from Kathmandu, Tinglatar in 1971 was a
village with good productive land and divided by caste: inhabitants
were either (dominant) Brahmins or (subordinate) Bhujels. The latter,
and several poorer Brahmin households, were not self-sufficient in food
(Prindle 1979: 50). As subordinates, however, Bhujels were less concerned about purity, which made them 'generalists' who pursued a
variety of income sources. This social characteristic became advantageous in the famine. Brahmins, on the other hand, were mainly
'specialized' in grain production and thus less flexible in working out
survival strategies.

When harsh times followed the failed August–November harvest of
1971, the people of Tinglatar acted promptly, both at the community
and the household level. Through its most influential resident, the village as a corporate entity attracted loans for every household in need.
This involved internal reloaning on low interest rates. Further action
ensured that existing grain surpluses, held by better-off Brahmins,
stayed in the village and that any land sold in distress would be bought
by fellow villagers (Prindle 1979: 52). The prospect of selling land to
outsiders was real enough, especially 'when several households de-
cided to emigrate during the winter of 1971–72 and the remaining
families simply did not have enough cash on hand to buy [their] land'
(Prindle 1979: 53). But the principle was upheld. 'Despite the fact that
a higher price for land could have been obtained in a free market, the
custom of selling to a fellow lineage member (*hakwalla*), as well as the
pressures exerted by community opinion, ensured that all of Tinglatar's
fields remained under local ownership' (Prindle 1979: 53). As the
crisis deepened, two groups bought the land that became available:
sanskritized elite Brahmins keen to expand their estates and move closer
to the Brahmanic ideal of disengagement from agricultural field work

(Prindle 1979: 59; see also Macfarlane 1993: 117), and 'generalist' Bhujel households who had accumulated wealth through various non-grain activities.

The community-based strategies were supplemented with action at the household level. Households borrowed rice from in-laws living in nearby ecological zones less affected by the severe weather conditions.

> [E]ven before the 1971 harvest was in, practically every household with a grain deficit (i.e. 85 per cent) undertook at least one visit to the wife's village to secure a loan, in cash or kind, from her parents or brothers. In most cases this was feasible only because Tinglatar's marriages were with villages situated at lower altitudes where rice rather than corn and millet constituted the main crop, and the famine's effects were consequently less severe. (Prindle 1979: 54)

On returning to Tinglatar in 1977, Prindle learned that the better-off Bhujel households, the 'generalists', had thrived in the famine. In relative terms, their landownership had increased by 22 per cent, whereas elite Brahmins had gained only 16 per cent. The net losers were the 'specialized' Brahmins.

How to sum up? First, as a corporate entity Tinglatar anticipated the famine and dealt with it proactively. Vital assets (food and land) were preserved to contain not only this famine but also future ones. No one died. The principle of keeping productive capital within the village was also at work in the very different setting of Mogbuama, Sierra Leone, when times were hard (Richards 1986, 1990). Second, the economically better off helped out with self-interest in mind. Tinglatar's 'moral economy' response had been a *situated* response with winners and losers. The big winners in this famine were not the high-status, high-caste specialist Brahmins, but 'the generalists' less concerned about pollution, who belonged mostly to the subordinate Bhujel caste. Thirdly, and a point also made by anthropologists for other famine settings (see below), the internal coping strategies that came into play enabled *the majority* of the villagers to get through these highly insecure times. True, some villagers became destitute and left, but the internal arrangements that came into play ensured the survival and stay of many more villagers than would have been the case had the internal strategies not been deployed. While some died a social death, a way of life was again preserved.

Seeing clear on this moral issue is not always easy. In the case of the Mursi migrants (Turton and Turton 1984), it is easy to accept that a way of life was preserved, that the local response was therefore 'a good thing'. Where, on the other hand, class/caste imbalances prevail and local community-level responses result in the exclusion of the most vulnerable social groups, it becomes more difficult to approve. Prindle saw the social deaths in Tinglatar as an acceptable price to pay, which they may well be if less reliable state patronage is the alternative. But a similar village exodus under different circumstances, when Harijans 'lost their land to urban money' during adjustment to Green Revolution possibilities, made John Harriss comment that their departure was a matter of grave concern (Harriss 1977: 233, 243).

Bolstering Initiative or Bolstering Inequality?

Informal social security networks continue to operate in the Nepalese hills today, despite severe population pressure, soil erosion and fast-declining food production (Macfarlane 1993; Seddon 1993). The chief safety instrument appears to be the institutionalized share-rearing of animals, a practice widespread in both Asia and Africa. Acknowledging the very precarious position of poor households in the Nepalese hills (cf. also Bista 1991: 95), Nabarro et al. write that share-rearing livestock (and share-cropping too) is a local security mechanism that serves the interests of both the creditors and the poor (Nabarro et al. 1989: 70). Share-rearing may be premised on inequality and does not offer the prospect of wealth accumulation, yet Nabarro and colleagues are confident that these local partnerships are the key to peasant farmer resilience and survival.

Analysts and policy-makers who advocate that 'bolstering local coping mechanisms' is the correct approach to take must be prepared to face dilemmas. Supporting a 'local strategy', which is a political act, implies accepting that the poor who survive drought (or other calamities) through local mechanisms may end up worse off and thus more vulnerable when the next calamity comes along. Is such a price acceptable? Anthropologists have offered the following thoughts: first, disasters would impact harder were internal mechanisms not in place; second, possible alternatives, especially state-run relief schemes, are not known to be more effective. The latter argument, reviewed below, has been advanced by Tony Beck (1989), after research in West Bengal, and by Jacqueline Solway (1994) following research in Kgalagadi, Botswana. Although their respective research programmes were carried out independently, Beck and Solway reach very similar conclusions. In both instances, central governments are endeavouring to stamp out traditional, 'evil' practices that exploit the rural poor, but substitute a type of state patronage which looks equally exploitative, and far less reliable in the long run. If deciding on 'which policy?' is a question of deciding between two 'evils' – that is, certain patronage versus uncertain patronage – then the moral issue may be resolved by choosing the lesser of these two 'evils'.

But there is a further issue: how durable are these local safety-nets? Although the issue is insufficiently researched, some useful observations are to hand. Writing within a 'moral economy' framework similar to that adopted by Richards (1990) and Prindle (1979), Soheir Sukkary-Stolba (1989), for instance, writes of Sudan that the hub of the moral system is the Muslim custom of *zakah,* whereby 10 per cent of the annual income of individuals is given to the poor. Important here is the role of the village leader or *sheik,* who is responsible for collecting food from the rich and then distributing it equally among the less well off. *Zakah* is available especially in times of *normal difficulty,* but turns problematic once 'real crisis' sets in (Sukkary-Stolba 1989: 293). Thus *zakah* helped to alleviate much of the hunger in the early part of the 1980s, but it did not last; the role of local leaders came to be *redefined* once the famine deepened. As resources dwindled, the type of assistance offered by local leaders shifted from financial support to the provision of emotional support and advice.

The redefinition of support services in famine may also affect gender relations. In the 1949 Malawi famine, for example, women initially confronted the hunger as members of consumption units that provided mutual support and access to scarce food (Vaughan 1987: 136). As the famine wore on, however, consumption units shrank, sharing became more secretive, and women came to depend more on 'male sources of income, such as what was sent back from migrating workers' (Vaughan 1987: 137). When women lost their direct entitlement to garden produce, their husbands or brothers became the main providers (Vaughan 1987: 146). And since a (migrating) husband's responsibility did not always stretch very far, brothers became more important (Vaughan 1987: 34).

The observations by Sukkary-Stolba and Vaughan may lead to scepticism about the efficiency of 'local coping mechanisms', but that would be a disingenuous conclusion to draw. Their observations, I suggest, are rather intended to be signposts that remind us how each situation needs to be understood in its own right. As with market transactions, local coping mechanisms, too, provide a mixture of opportunity and constraint. They are valuable but not perfect. And there is the further problem of what alternatives are available. What happens, for instance, when governments take over the role of patron?

Local Initiative versus State Initiative

Governments, like developers, mostly work towards what they believe will be a simpler, more rational world. In situations where hunger may arise, they tend to frown upon local coping mechanisms, seeing them as exploitative, messy, unreliable, to be eradicated. But what alternative social safety mechanisms do they propose? Jacqueline Solway (1994) studied the problem in Kaglagadi, Botswana; Tony Beck (1979) in West Bengal, India. Here are their findings.

Case Study 7.3: Drought Planning in Kgalagadi, Botswana

In the decade before the 1980s drought, economic relations among Kgalagadi people, excluding Basarwa, revolved around oxen-sharing and field-sharing. The latter was particularly important when the rains were late. These two types of arrangement and their variants, Solway argues, are effective but can be placed on a continuum going from 'egalitarian to hierarchical, with some amounting to simple field sharing (not share-cropping) and others resembling but falling short of wage labour arrangements' (Solway 1994: 489). Hierarchy was most clearly seen in the returns for the use of loaned cattle, which could be expensive and time-consuming (for example training the oxen on loan, working the patron's land). On the other hand, arrangements for mutual help were 'most rational when subsistence livestock production [was] emphasized over commercial factors' (Solway 1994: 485), as they provided local social security entitlements and a sense of dignity to all concerned.

The overall assessment is that sharing arrangements in Kgalagadi, while no great equalizers, nonetheless

> function to keep the gap between rich and poor narrower than otherwise might be the case. They are relations of entitlement which permit semi-independent production on the part of the poorer majority. As such they are consistent with the Kgalagadi cultural logic of self-construction . . . the ethic of doing for oneself. The Kgalagadi contrast this with other forms of economic activity, particularly wage labour, which do little to contribute to an individual's 'valorization'. (Solway 1994: 487–8).

Two development initiatives by the government of Botswana are now eroding the community-based sharing arrangements: commoditization in the form of cattle ranching, which started well before the 1980s drought, and ARAP, the Accelerated Rain-fed Arable Programme introduced in 1985. With ranching, cattle owners find it more profitable to rear cattle for the export market and to use tractors on the land. The switch had dealt a direct blow to the oxen-sharing arrangements. Regarding ARAP, Solway explains how this programme initially 'sounded too good to be true: farmers would be paid the equivalent of P50 (approximately US$20) per hectare for every hectare they ploughed up to ten hectares, and they would receive additional funds for properly destumping and weeding their fields, for utilizing fertilizer, a planter, and so on' (1994: 489–90).

Although ARAP remained under-utilized, its effects on resource-poor Kgalagadi households were devastating. Not only were ARAP subsidies beyond the grasp of poorer peasants, female-headed households especially, but their availability limited the opportunity to field-share. Women household heads, about one-third of all heads (Izzard 1979), were excluded because 'areas of agricultural land are associated with groups of kin related through the male line; the normative pattern is for women to gain access to land as wives' (Solway 1994: 490). ARAP, then, was not just a strategic response to drought, it was also a conscious strategy by some government officials *to engineer a new social identity for Botswana's rural populace in an attempt to extend government control.* The new social ideal was that

> of individualized nuclear family production units which functioned independently of one another but in conjunction with the state. Horizontal linkage (in terms of inter-household, not necessarily in terms of equality) should be minimized but vertical linkage to the state encouraged, initially in the form of aid but eventually through greater involvement in credit schemes, marketing, taxes, etc. (Solway 1994: 490–1)

Solway continues:

> What appears to be happening . . . is a shift; dependence on the wealthy is being replaced with dependence on the state, one sort of paternalism for another. . . . [The] set of entitlements which allowed people to survive previous droughts and which allowed the majority of people to produce in good years have been undermined to the point that they no longer provide basic social security. . . . [The] vitality of reciprocal use entitlements has been undermined as a result of long-term structural changes tied to commodification, privatization, and class formation. (Solway 1994: 492)

The Kgalagadi system of patronage does have a primary weakness in that certain communal claims for assistance are difficult to honour when the rains are late or insufficient. This weakness is well

publicized every time state officials praise the government's programmes for drought relief. Exposure of weakness in local initiative,
however, usually turns into an attack on the 'evil' of exploitative
local patron–client relationships, which then becomes a pretext for
the government's own intervention. Solway does not quarrel with
the claim that government in the 1980s prevented starvation, which
it did very successfully, but she highlights how drought was being
used as a moral pretext and licence for denying community autonomy
(1994: 491). It is another example of how a way of life can be destroyed through intervention.

While policy-makers may have felt they were 'liberating' rural households from relations that kept them beholden and dependent, the ARAP
strategy could be criticized for being poorly attuned to the realities of
rural poverty, interdependence and debt. Above all, ARAP 'failed to
recognize the good sense which many of the existing arrangements
make in the context of a largely resource-poor rural populace attempting to minimize the risks inherent in producing in a marginal environment' (Solway 1994: 491). As Prindle (1979) and Beck (1989; see
below) do in similarly risk-prone environments, Solway acknowledges
that local sharing arrangements, premised though they are on inequality, are nonetheless firm guarantors of adequate production under
normal-to-difficult circumstances.

Solway's argument exposes the narrow, typically technocratic focus
on problems and solutions, and illustrates the thesis that development
bureaucracy constructs the 'Third World' in a way which strengthens
state power and reproduces the dominance of the West (Escobar 1995;
Ferguson 1990). This construction usually involves the portrayal of
local people as ignorant or evil and exploitative, and incapable of
properly managing their resources. Custodianship can then be transferred to designated development experts (Hobart 1993; Hoben 1995;
Roe 1995). Solway's ethnography offers a counter-narrative which
acknowledges that significant potential for development is locally available.

Solway has an ally in Beck who, through his research in West Bengal, advocates that policy interventions must focus on local power
structures and build upon existing security systems. It would be folly
to replace them. Beck, however, does not feel the state should be
disowned for its social engineering; states must remain partners in
the search for better interventions. The parallels between Kgalagadi
and West Bengal are striking. In West Bengal too, central government has stepped in to replace local coping mechanisms deemed
backward and exploitative. In doing so, government has become
the new patron, but it offers less security than is the case under
'local' arrangements. Beck does not deny that there is hierarchy and

exploitation in the local self-help relations found in West Bengal, but he points out, just like Solway does, that when central government steps in with its own strategy it does little more than undermine the local social security system which the majority of villagers rely on *and need* when the going gets tough.

Case Study 7.4: Poverty Alleviation in West Bengal, India

What resource-sharing arrangements are available in West Bengal? For the village of Fonogram (pseudonym), Beck (1989) reports how very poor households rely heavily on loans from other very poor households. These small 'horizontal' loans, of money or foodstuffs, are an expression of support, friendship and solidarity. Most crucially, though, as in Kgalagadi and in Nepal, the dominant form of mutual support is the share-rearing of livestock.

> The most common arrangement is that a household will raise a female goat, duck or chicken given to them by another, usually richer, household. After the animal has given birth twice, the first-born and the mother are returned to the owner, and the rearer keeps the second born. In the case of a male animal, the proceeds after sale are divided equally between owner and rearer. (Beck 1989: 27)

Beck complains that the vital importance of share-rearing in sustaining poor households during crisis has been overlooked by researchers, even though the system has been in operation in Bengal since the 1930s. The upshot is that policy-makers have yet to learn to recognize sharing strategies and to appreciate the benefits to both owner and rearer (Beck 1989: 27).

The threat to livestock share-rearing, a practice most Fonogram villagers now find 'increasingly difficult' to arrange, comes from the government's Integrated Rural Development Progamme (IRDP), a programme for poverty alleviation which provides subsidy and loans to the poor to enable them to buy assets, mostly livestock (Beck 1989: 29–30). A top-down planning approach, IDRP identifies beneficiaries for loans and subsidies to stimulate a central meat market. The effect, as in Botswana, is that cattle are taken out of local exchange arrangements. Beck therefore recommends that livestock owners should be encouraged to keep their cattle in the locality, which could be done through ensuring that the poor who borrow livestock to share-rear have access to loans to buy good-quality feed. Local share-rearing practices could then continue: 'As share-rearing can benefit both (richer) loaners and (poor) borrowers, it presents a "gap" where reformist policy can feasibly build upon strategies used by the poor' (Beck 1989: 30).

Despite the parallels between West Bengal and Kgalagadi, and between their respective analyses, Beck and Solway do seem to part company when the (potential) role of government is considered; Beck believing firmly that 'good' can come from assisted development, Solway equally firm in her scepticism about the idea of intervention. This does not mean, however, that the Botswana government has lost academic support for its endeavours. Richard Morgan, for instance, believes that the 'lack of security of rural incomes is caused primarily by the extremely risky nature of the rain-fed arable farming systems on which many rural people will depend, and by the lack of seasonal or permanent job opportunities' (Morgan 1988: 119). Considering the underlying causes of vulnerability to be apolitical, Morgan calls upon the Botswana government to ensure that recovery programmes should aim to diversify economic activities and farming systems. This entails, he comments, 'the regaining by many households of their positions in the livestock-farming economy, where greater economic returns are available; some form of state-assisted restocking is required for this' (Morgan 1988: 120). In view of Solway's argument that it is precisely because of government policy that the livestock-farming economy has been eroded, it is ironic to think that government could be the appropriate instrument for enabling the poor to regain control.

There is a rider to this: before we wholeheartedly agree that 'local' is best, let us recall the earlier local–global debate (chapter 1) in which this kind of dichotomy was revealed to be highly artificial. So-called local solutions may be far more global than first meets the eye – and hence not as controllable 'from within' as first imagined. The 'global' exists in the 'local', so strategies are not immune to change. A community may at one point successfully combine local and supra-local strategies, but without the guarantee that its successful formula will continue. The Zaghawa people of Darfur, a celebrated example in the anthropological literature, experienced this at their peril.

Is Better State Intervention Possible?

Before we answer this question, let us reflect on what happened to the Zaghawa people of Darfur, who in the anthropological literature gained fame for the expertise with which they could ride out drought through their market engagements. Their story warns that so-called local coping strategies, which are always in flux, cannot be bolstered through reliance on a deregulated private market.

Case Study 7.5: Famine and the Zaghawa of Darfur

Central to survival during famine is the ability to use cash in a non-inflationary environment. When essential necessities and food/grain can be bought without the usual dramatic drop in the value of those assets vulnerable people own and sell (especially livestock and land), their survival chances and livelihood prospects are optimized. An African society reputed for its ability to ride out drought through a strategy which combines economic diversification and engagement in markets are the Zaghawa people of Darfur. Zaghawa 'pursue a strategy of six months of cultivation on rainfed plots and six months of dispersal to practise craft activities . . . at distant market centres' (Fleuret 1986: 228). On the basis of a literature review in which the Zaghawa strategy is duly acknowledged, Anne Fleuret concluded that 'the integration of small-holder farming and pastoral households in the contemporary world market economy [has become] an essential component of their ability to withstand food shortages precipitated by drought' (Fleuret 1986: 228). By the time Fleuret's article was published, however, it was already clear that the celebrated 'mixed economy' the Zaghawa pursued was collapsing, possibly without any chance of an early recovery. Their 'integration' in the world market economy, tightly interwoven with local political affairs, was not the panacea it had seemed.

What, then, is the Zaghawa story? Throughout the 1970s and early 1980s, Zaghawa potters (female) and blacksmiths (male) generated enough cash for their communities back home to easily buy the supplementary grain and other goods required to help everyone through the drought (see Tobert 1985: 214). After fifteen years of successful diversification, however – years during which 'excess cash was spent on enlarging the herds' (Tobert 1985: 214) – the accumulated wealth became insufficient to see the Zaghawa through the 1984–5 drought. Their reputed mobility, cash earnings and investments notwithstanding, October 1984 saw 'several [Zaghawa] potters . . . begging for money against the sale of *future pots*'; their diversified, partly cash-based survival strategy in tatters (Tobert 1985: 218; emphasis added).

El Sammani (1990) confirms that the Zaghawa migrations and 'mixed economy' strategy proved ineffective in 1984–5, and that many Zaghawa (and other groups) became tied to permanent camps. But El Sammani believes that the demise of the migration strategy did not happen all that suddenly; it set in back in 1968–73 when 'a high proportion of migrants from northern Darfur, Kordofan and eastern regions resettled permanently in irrigation schemes in central Sudan', among them sizeable groups of Zaghawa (El Sammani 1990: 186–7).

While cash and migration can be very effective coping strategies, they do exist within volatile markets for goods and labour. This means their long-term effectiveness must not be assumed. In the same way that long-term 'spontaneous resettlement' may cease to be an option when land values rise (see e.g. Pottier and Fairhead 1991: 455), so well-functioning markets for goods may cease to operate. Besides not being able to offer pots for sale in 1984–5, Zaghawa traders, it is now clear, had fallen victim to some fundamental changes in the regional fabric of economic and political relations. (This again demonstrates how important it is that 'real markets' should be understood.) Early on in the 1980s, the wealthier nomadic pastoralists in the region disengaged, slowly but decisively, from long-standing alignments and survival structures. Essentially, wealthy herd owners lost interest in building up political clientage through share-rearing on the 'customary' scale, after becoming more interested in livestock commerce. The result was that a share-rearing system involving livestock – a safetynet very similar to the ones found in Botswana and West Bengal – disappeared. As 'many herd owners broke away from [their] networks of supporters and affiliates, severing long-term relationships and altering social duties and expectations' (El Sammani 1990: 189–90), the Zaghawa suffered a knock-on effect. It was indeed on these same 'supporters and affiliates' that Zaghawa potters and blacksmiths relied when they so successfully traded their wares to ensure survival. After losing the generosity of their patrons, these groups began to compete for scarce resources amidst unprecedented inter-tribal hostility, and forgot about their own clients. Many became destitute.

Whatever the reason why Zaghawa potters were unable to provide pots in 1984–5, their usual customers had lost much of their own livelihood security and purchasing power after their own patrons switched from an interest in local politics to an interest in commerce and national politics.

If famine prevention is about political alignment and patronage, rather than the workings of the so-called free-market economy, does it still make sense to expect that vulnerability to famine can be lessened through better state intervention? Can states be relied upon to bolster coping mechanisms and make them durable?

Despite the clear signal (by Solway, Beck, El Sammani) that central state planning and livestock commerce easily combine to impair local mechanisms for patronage and survival, Drèze and Sen (1989), like

Morgan, call upon states to continue with their central-planning approach to drought mitigation. Drèze and Sen take the view that rural-based coping mechanisms are simply inadequate (fragile, 'evil'. . .) to do the job properly. Salvation, they claim, can only come from more and better state intervention, since the design of 'famine prevention systems that do not leave the rural community to its own fragile devices is inescapable' (Drèze and Sen 1989: 75). They also call for an advanced watchdog role for the free press.

Drèze and Sen regard the absence of a (relatively) free press and political opposition in China to have been a chief cause of the disastrous famine that occurred there in 1959–60 (Drèze and Sen 1989: 212–13). Notwithstanding this famine, Drèze and Sen argue that China, at least prior to the 1979 reforms, managed to develop a comparatively superior, broad-based social security system. It may have had a famine at a time when India knew how to avoid such disasters, yet China's attack on poverty was much more advanced.

On the other hand, the authors express concern regarding China's ability to sustain its social security system, given the post-1979 transfer of responsibilities away from communes and onto households. Despite the gigantic 'leap forward' in agricultural production, which doubled between 1979 and 1986, and despite the noticeable reduction in poverty (due to personal incomes being more secure), the authors are concerned about the gradual erosion of what used to be guaranteed rights for all, for example access to health (Drèze and Sen 1989: 215–16). China is still 'considerably ahead of India' in terms of the provision of communal health facilities, but 'the recent economic reforms, with their negative effects on public support (especially at the local level in the rural areas), have moved China a little bit in the direction of India, and that . . . is not a particularly helpful development' (Drèze and Sen 1989: 220). It now remains to be seen whether the more recent, partial return to a more collective village-based system (Croll 1994) can reverse the feared erosion of public services.

The Indian state of Kerala provides Drèze and Sen with the ideal model for action, for it has fought poverty, hunger and deprivation with some success (Drèze and Sen 1989: 212). The reasons for Kerala's success are multiple, as seen in chapter 3, and include the implementation of thorough land reforms, a high adult literacy rate (the highest in India), and a high level of female education. Kerala's success with land reform must also be attributed, and in no small measure, to 'the partially matrilineal system of inheritance in parts of Kerala and the relatively long history of its left-wing activist politics' (Drèze and Sen 1989: 224). Maharashtra, another Indian state renowned for its ability to cope with drought, especially in 1973, did not reform to the same extent but operates an effective famine prevention policy anchored in a large-scale, cash-based strategy of employment provision (Drèze and Sen 1989: 132). The strategy is 'supplemented by "gratuitous relief" for those unable to work and without able-bodied relatives' (Drèze and Sen 1989: 129). Guaranteed access to income during the 1970–3 drought prevented food entitlements from collapsing.[1]

Importantly, Maharashtra's 'Employment for all who wanted it' policy emphasized the need to carry out essential food production tasks during the drought itself. People were paid for 'bunding fields, constructing percolation tanks, well construction, clearing existing tanks of silt, terracing land and building roads' (McAlpin 1987: 396). Carrying out these essential tasks ensured not only the survival of those at risk, but also the speedy recovery of the agricultural sector. Thus, in '1973–74, the first post-drought year in Maharashtra, the production of foodgrains rebounded to 106% of the average production of the 2 years immediately preceding the drought' (McAlpin 1987: 396).

Lest Maharashtra's recipe for successful prevention is thought of as simple and straightforward, we must ask a further question: where did the relief grain come from? Answer: it was imported; production shortfalls were mitigated because the cash encouraged 'the normal market process [whereby] grain [moved] from where it is cheap to where it is costly' (McAlpin 1987: 402). This interesting statement hints that there is something 'unreal' about Maharashtra's success: if famine is caused by normal free-market processes (Sen 1981), how can the cause also become the remedy? The absurdity of the suggestion is exposed when it is realized that the import of large amounts of foodgrains into Maharashtra was illegal; the import flouted the ban on inter-state movements of food within India. The acknowledgement that illegal imports through private trade constituted 'an essential mechanism of famine prevention' (Drèze and Sen 1989: 129–30) raises questions about costs and victims in neighbouring states; questions that throw doubt on the replicability of the approach in the event of a more widespread drought. The ultimate irony is that prevention in Maharashtra in (1970–3) illustrated 'the importance of demand failure as an explanation of famine, and the vulnerability of the poor to food price rises' (Devereux 1993: 74), while demonstrating too that its own successful response was nothing short of an invitation to famine elsewhere.

Misgivings about India's claim to possessing the key to famine prevention has also come from another quarter: chronic malnutrition. Despite occasional successes with famine prevention in Indian states, no progress has been made with eradicating hunger and poverty. The lack of progress makes it very doubtful that India would have any 'transferable lessons' for implementation elsewhere: '. . . India may have averted large-scale famine, but she certainly has not made an impression on the problem of malnutrition. Nearly half of the entire world's malnutrition is said to be in this one country' (Harriss 1988: 162). Da Corta and Devereux (1991) make the same point: famines have been eliminated by allowing mass poverty, vulnerability and hunger to persist. Recurrent famines 'have been replaced by recurrent near famines and recurrent famine relief or, at best, by institutional-ised dependence on relief in normal times' (Da Corta and Deveureux 1991: 11).

The most impressive gain is that India by the late 1980s had built up a formidable grain reserve through which it had become 'less vulner-able than it used to be to external political pressure using food as a lever' (Harriss 1988: 159). Despite the achievement, India's failure to eradicate chronic malnutrition and poverty remains disturbingly in evidence, while the 'free press', qualified by Drèze and Sen as 'a polit-ical "triggering mechanism" which brings the protection system into play and . . . keeps the public support system in a state of prepared-ness' (Drèze and Sen 1989: 212), has remained silent on the issue.

The chief explanation for the failure to eradicate poverty and mal-nutrition, Harriss writes, is that land reforms have been implemented in only a few states (Harriss 1988: 162; see also chapter 2 above). She cautions that improved technology 'has to date been concentrated on a few crops and a few regions – wheat particularly, in the north (west) of India' (Harriss 1988: 163). Although it can be said that the adop-tion of such technology has involved almost all classes, it is also the case that 'poor producers may be the last to adopt and be compelled by debt rather than entrepeneurial zeal to "modernize" their agricult-ure' (Harriss 1988: 163). The massive urban bias towards grain pro-curement must not go unnoticed here: states buy up 'elite' grains (especially wheat) but show no interest in opening up attractive mar-kets for sorghum and millet, crops more appropriate to the needs of the poor (Harriss 1988: 164).

In contrast to Drèze and Sen, Harriss concludes firmly that there is little point telling anyone, and certainly not African states, that India has 'transferable lessons' for them. Simply 'there are so many differ-ences that affect the capacity of individuals and governments to avert famine that India's experience, even the most appropriate elements of it, is untransferable' (Harriss 1988: 166).

Drèze and Sen think differently, and even believe they know of 'some African successes' (Botswana, Cape Verde, Kenya to some extent, Zim-babwe), where prevention attempts have been based on the very prin-ciples established for India. 'Lessons' include: the importance of entitlement protection systems involving direct public interventions; the importance of a strong political leadership role for central govern-ment, needed for the purpose of coordination; the importance of combining strong leadership with private trade; the importance of diversification of economic activities, notably through wage employment; early warning and early response (Drèze and Sen 1989: 158–61).

It is hard to share such optimism. Zimbabwe's delays over land reform (see chapter 3 above), coupled with the 1991–2 drought experience, shows indeed that effective famine prevention can occur without there being much progress in poverty alleviation (see also de Waal 1997: 57–64). Equally, in Botswana's Kgalagadi district, where famine is again effectively eradicated, there is little hope of seeing an end to poverty. In promoting livestock commerce and new forms of land use, the state has here, too, taken away a number of flexible local protection mechanisms. Once again, a national strategy for famine eradication carries the cost of continued poverty, vulnerability and hunger.

Conclusions

Sound famine relief and prevention require sound theory about how famines develop. While famine theory as such has been only briefly discussed here (but see Devereux 1993), the increase in empirical studies of famine has led to two major corrections in how relief and prevention should be understood. The first correction is that food itself is rarely the key to reducing vulnerability. As empirical studies make clear, food security and the ability to withstand famine are best understood as components of livelihood security. Second, it is now widely accepted that interventions that occur early on in the development of a famine and build upon existing coping strategies stand a better chance of being effective, but there are conditions to be fulfilled. Above all, interventions must aim to support local initiatives. They will then both save lives and preserve a way of life.

It would be naive, however, to imagine that the move from better theory to better practice is an easy one. First of all, political constraints exist and they will continue on a number of levels. Alliance-building and principles of 'selectivity' exist within international circles, just as they do within nations, districts, villages and households. The 'culture of disempowerment' is very pervasive, and an undermining of that culture is unlikely as long as the agencies involved in relief and prevention remain reluctant to tackle the issue of accountability head-on.[2]

Even should it prove possible to remove the political agendas that drive relief options, there still remains the logistical problem of predicting which *specific* localities, groups and individuals are most at risk in the face of *generalized* uncertainty (such as the threat of drought). A straightforward analysis of structural vulnerability may not be enough, since vulnerability is also being determined (at least in eco-logically varied situations) by altitude and agricultural cycles. More-over, every famine impacts on the next, hence no two famines are ever alike; nor do proven coping strategies necessarily continue (cf. the Zaghawa study above). Markets may cease to be reliable, migration options may be closed off. The implication is that any commitment to bolstering existing coping mechanisms requires up-to-date knowledge on rural economy and society, as well as political commitment.

Given the diversity of famine situations, given also the ongoing (but under-researched) controversy about whether local patronage or state patronage should be prioritized (and is the divide always clear?), the more reasonable solution is to examine the merits and drawbacks of either option within highly specific situations and to ensure that po-tential famine victims have some choice regarding the kind of patron-age system they wish to have. The ethnographic literature is still limited, but the conclusions which Beck (1989), Solway (1994) and El Sammani (1990) reached independent of one another are important. State-controlled programmes for commercializing the rural sector, these re-searchers show, undermine local social safety-nets which, despite their built-in penchant for inequality, nonetheless offer a local and speedy response mechanism when hardship strikes. Where local patronage is replaced with national patronage, the new patrons are able to avert national disaster, but they show little interest in sharing power and privilege. Poverty eradication is not on the agenda. In this respect, Drèze and Sen (1989) have been over-anxious to bring some good news from Africa.

The patronage question, however, is closely linked to that of how markets are structured. Where the markets for land, labour, credit and goods are tightly interlocked, local patronage is unlikely to offer much protection, while state patronage may offer welcome alterna-tives (see e.g. Jodha 1988). And vice versa, where markets are only moderately interlocked, local patronage may be the option vulnerable groups and individuals prefer. Reality often being somewhere in be-tween, it is imperative that in-depth, continuous research into local people's perspectives and struggles is intensified. Many situations may well reveal a mixture of (maybe declining) dependence on local redistributive mechanisms and (maybe increasing) dependence on state or other supra-local institutions. Martha Chen showed this to be the case for the Gujarat village she researched (Chen 1991: 213–14; see also Swift 1993: 9).

If policy analysts and planners could start from the position that survival mechanisms are potentially local-and-global (cf. chapter 1 above), then we may be one step closer to designing prevention pro-grammes that offer choice between a diversity of strategies; strategies that could then also be combined in a variety of ways. But relief and prevention work, like development aid generally, can only be truly effective if potential recipients have the power to determine what is used and how (see de Waal 1989: 32). Such a dialogue must never be considered a luxury.

Vulnerable communities should not have to watch the destruction of their local, somewhat controllable patronage systems for the sake of distant safety-nets over which they have no control and which are not bound by local commitment. Enabling food-insecure groups to exercise choice in this matter, enabling them to choose between and possibly combine (more) local and (better) state-led forms of protection, may be a step towards real progress. External support to local share-rearing arrangements, provided this can be done realistically, might enhance the resilience of autonomous rural economies and open up new possibilities. In addition, historically derived imbalances in terms of access to resources must be redressed if poverty is to be eradicated. There appears to be no alternatives to the *implementation* of thorough programmes for land reform in regions where they are needed.

To keep choices open and plan for better choices/policies will also require that analysts pay attention to the structure of household relations. These relations were not made an issue in this chapter, but the conclusion that relief and prevention need to be understood and tackled in highly localized settings means that all the domestic issues discussed above apply and must be addressed.

8

Attractive Simplicity?
The Shape of Modern Agricultural Research and Policy

'Ask me about my life and I will tell you about cassava'.

farmer Virgilio, late 1980s, Dominican Republic,
quoted in Box, 'Virgilio's Theorem'

In this chapter we examine the orientation and impact of modern agricultural research and policy as set by International Agricultural Research Centres (IARCs). We ask which agricultural research and policies are favoured, why, and what is their transformative power. A set of related themes will surface: the link between agricultural research and food security; agricultural policy and the power of environmental crisis narratives; the value of non-western approaches to food cropping; how to bridge the gap between small-scale farmers and western-trained technical experts. Erroneous policy assumptions will be exposed; they must be put right if the gap between farmers and policy-makers is to narrow. The chapter deals with critiques, external and internal, of how (selected) IARCs operate. We ask: What kinds of knowledge do IARCs promote and for the benefit of whom? What is being done to enable 'invisible' peasant farmers to once again work on their own account? And are programmes gender-sensitive?

Modern Farming and Food Security: A Troubled Relationship

Developers still conceptualize their interventions in terms of unilinear progressions (see chapter 6 above), as they have done ever since colonial administrators assumed that their 'subjects' wanted to progress and develop as they themselves had. In colonial times, local approaches to economy and farming were labelled backward, primitive and unscientific; administrators aimed to facilitate the linear progression to modern, 'rational' forms of economy and production. Cultural context was hardly relevant, except as a potential source of opposition to official projects (see Cochrane 1979). Administrators adopted a blanket approach to agriculture and indeed to other sectors of policy intervention, most notably health. Few questions were asked regarding the desirability and appropriateness of the Western interventions themselves.

Central to the administrators' evolutionary thinking was the assumption that rural communities suffered from economic stagnation and decline, often in conjunction with social and moral breakdown. The assumed link between economic and social stagnation could be strong, as we saw for colonial and post-colonial policy in Zambia and Peru (Moore and Vaughan 1994; Salas 1994; van der Ploeg 1990). As a self-fulfilling prophecy, the discourse of stagnation and breakdown ensured that guardianship in farming would move from the farms to the research stations, where a different world-view prevailed. A further assumption was to believe that the benefits of higher crop yields would 'trickle down' to those who worked the land. This assumption turned into one of the more powerful myths of the twentieth century. It may be useful also to recall, at this point, two issues raised in previous chapters. First, governments declaring an interest in scientific agricultural research often did so for political reasons; they perceived that 'improved' agriculture could be an effective instrument in fighting insurgency (see chapter 4). Second, when IARCs began operating, policy-makers understood food security to be a national issue – not a household concern (see chapter 2); and 'national issues' tend to be those that elites recognize.

Given these circumstances, it makes sense to ask what implications 'scientific' agriculture has for the nutritional status and health of those who take part. Having previously used Zambia as an illustration of how narratives combine to produce discourses in support of modern agriculture, let us continue with this example and reflect on the implications of the hybrid maize campaign for nutrition and health. The story of Zambia is representative of developing countries.

Modern Farming in Zambia: Lessons for Food Security

Following independence, Zambia strove to secure a steady and cheap urban food supply in hybrid maize (SR-52), and to end economic dependence on the 'White South' (Rhodesia and South Africa). The government of Zambia used national resources lavishly – the copper economy was strong – to fully subsidize the project. Subsidies went on 'fertilizer, an expansion of the network of input supply and crop collection depots, and a range of other institutional support services to farmers, such as extension advice, farmer training, credit provision and subsidized land preparation by government mechanization units' (Wood 1985: 140). After the copper industry collapsed in the mid-1970s, Zambia came to depend on international assistance and loans and, in the 1980s, phased out the subsidies under IMF pressure. By then it was already clear that the drive for national food security through SR-52 had left many participating farmers and their households short of a balanced diet.

The most powerful single explanation for what went wrong is that the country's agricultural policy had been premised on several assumptions that would later prove erroneous. First, hybrid maize had been promoted according to the colonial mentality that progress in farming required a drastic, nationwide overhaul of existing practices. The objective had been to move from shifting agriculture to semi-permanent cropping, everywhere (Sharpe 1990). In their zeal to modernize and standardize farming, politicians and policy-makers ignored the contribution to food intake which existing production systems could and did make (Hansen 1991; Moore and Vaughan 1994). Like their colonial predecessors they failed to appreciate that low-yielding food systems were diverse and capable of sustaining balanced livelihoods and diets. In the case of Zambia's Northern and Eastern Province, they undervalued, for example, the semi-permanent intercropping systems and women's crops that existed alongside *citemene*. They also overlooked the contribution of bush products and the role of local exchange networks in securing foodstuffs essential to a balanced diet (Sharpe 1990: 586).

Art Hansen (1994) confirmed this policy 'blindness' for Zambia's North-Western Province, which in 1989 suffered an invasion of cassava mealy-bug. The threat of famine, which followed, was due to the imposition of national agro-economic policies over which villagers had no control (Hansen 1994: 12). Being incorporated into the national maize economy, North-Western Province had lost the diversity it knew in the 1930s when its various agricultural systems, centred on cassava, included major bush gardens and secondary gardens near homesteads.

The second error in national policy had been to assume that hybrid maize would grow well everywhere. From the vantage point of North-Western Province, Hansen comments: 'Maize is promoted by many governments and nutritionists as a better crop and food than cassava, so the change might appear to have been for the better. Maize, however, requires more fertile soils than does cassava and, unlike cassava, cannot simply be left in the fields longer to grow' (Hansen1994: 16). Soils were also poorly suited in other parts of the country (Pottier 1988: 21), but Government stuck to its hybrid maize campaign, showing little interest in diversification. After the mealy-bug problem had been solved in North-Western Province and people wanted to resume cassava cultivation, they found there were 'no parental stems to cut and use. Although the Zambian government [had] had programs for many years to produce and upgrade maize, there was no major program to produce cassava for replanting' (Hansen 1994: 16). This blinkered policy proved costly; what was good for economic independence was not so good for the diet and health of the nation's industrious smallholders.

Barry Sharpe demonstrates the cost on the basis of household data collected by the Integrated Rural Development Programme (IRDP) in Serenje, Mpika and Chinsali in 1985–6. Hybrid maize was popular in those districts. Sharpe's central finding was that surveyed households showed no improvement over the situation that had existed there as far back as 1933 (Sharpe 1990: 585). The basic problem was that the money farmers made from hybrid maize was insufficient to make up shortfalls in other crops, shortfalls caused by the diversion of land and labour. Children's diet and health suffered greatly. For Northern and Eastern Province, the longitudinal IRDP data indicated that nutrition might in fact have worsened compared with the crisis decade of the 1930s (Sharpe 1990: 589). Significantly, the smallholders who had contributed the most to 'feeding the nation', and who were considered to be better off, suffered just as badly as resource-poor producers, if not more (Sharpe 1990: 599–600; and the discussion of ARPT below). This situation had come about partly because of the reduced availability of household food supplies (maize having displaced several home-grown crops), partly because the cash reward for maize cropping was too low, and partly because the additional burden of hybrid-maize processing (shelling and bagging) had fallen disproportionately on women (Sharpe 1990: 595). The IRDP data also revealed a substantial reduction in the hectarages of finger-millet, local maize, and other crops grown on semi-permanent plots: cassava, groundnuts, beans, sweet potato, pumpkin, and vegetables.

Crisis point was reached with the collapse of copper on the world market; rural areas reacted to the recession by exporting more than they could afford. As a result, the supply of foodstuffs that used to circulate in local markets to bridge seasonal food gaps started to dry up (Sharpe 1990: 590). Such foodstuffs were now sold to the towns, because the money that could be earned from maize itself was too little. And for those who did make money from maize, much of it stayed locked up in the loan system that secured the inputs for the next growing season. The outcome was 'a movement from subsistence to poverty, from complex and varied farming systems to an impoverished pseudo-traditional agriculture that [failed] to meet consumption needs' (Sharpe 1990: 588).

Although it is important to recall that the impact of an imposed national policy is never totally uniform, small-scale commercialized maize farming in Zambia can be portrayed as an example of growth with impoverishment; a case which shows beyond doubt that nutrition must be put back into agricultural policy (cf. DeWalt 1991). After confirming that 'progressive farmers' were indeed often severely affected in terms of nutritional status, Zambia's ARPTs (Adaptive Research and Planning Teams) made it their objective to reverse the situation.

Since the diagnostic approach by ARPTs shows how policy decisions can be made differently, that is, in more decentralized ways (cf. Maxwell 1992), let me present the situation ARPT-Copperbelt encountered in two of its locations: St Anthonys and Ibenga. In St Anthonys, which has good access to the market town of Luanshya, soils are good and farmers specialize in hybrid maize. It has a maize depot for buying inputs and selling maize. Ibenga, by contrast, has very poor soils and low crop yields; its prospects of producing hybrid maize never looked good. Ibenga farmers thus grow more sorghum and sweet potatoes, and tend large vegetable gardens. The nearest maize depot, which farmers ignore, is 15 km. away, but there is a nearby outlet for vegetables, which Copperbelt traders frequent (Mwape and Russell 1992).

Despite its 'progressive' outlook, St Anthonys in the early 1990s experienced the greater shortage of food. Its 'progressive' farmers ran out of stored food before the hungry season began, and then faced the problem that money made from maize could not make up the shortfalls. St Anthonys illustrated how dependence on outside institutions and monocrop programmes could adversely affect nutrition security. Ibenga farmers, on the other hand, were able to make their food stocks last longer. Ibenga's food strategy, irrespective of farmers' socioeconomic means, was to grow maize and sorghum for the purpose of subsistence, and to obtain income from vegetables grown as a dry-season crop. Other produce such as sweet potatoes, charcoal, honey, fruit and mushrooms were also sold locally. Ibenga's was the more diversified strategy; it made full use of local markets. (The contrast between the two locations parallels the earlier observation that people affected by famine may have their long-term survival chances reduced by inappropriate interventions.) Because of the wider range of locally marketable crops, Ibenga knew a comparatively short hungry season. Farmers stored their own maize and sorghum for use in the first quarter of the calendar year and bought additional foods, maize for example, with money made from the dry-season sales. I shall return to these two villages to highlight how ARPT intervened.

To sum up, Zambia's transition to hybrid maize farming was accompanied by different types of impoverishment: reduced crop diversity; an inability to procure foods to supplement the diet; a decline in local market activity; and a loss of control over labour allocations and their rewards. The attractive assumption of the early 1970s, that national food security would bring prosperity and health for all, proved too simplistic.

The Power of Attractive Simplicity

Zambia's experience with scientific agriculture is not unique to Africa, nor are African experiences unique in the world. It is therefore unsurprising that replicas of Zambia's misadventure with scientific farming can be found elsewhere. Andean Peru, as already seen, suffered a comparable fate when the 'scientific potato' displaced the (under-researched) bitter varieties which the region grew in abundance. Bitter potato varieties could be made 'into potato-starch which is the best form of storage' (Salas 1994: 66). Here, as in Zambia, regional markets declined, especially since the 'scientific potato' demanded that local peasant farmers give up ways of farming that had been regulated through 'local and relatively autonomous markets' (van der Ploeg 1990: 162). These local markets valued 'mutual dependency structured by a socially controlled reciprocity' (van der Ploeg 1990: 160). The transition left farmers with 'no assurance that there [would] be increased returns of labor commensurate with the costs involved' (Bernstein 1977, quoted in van der Ploeg 1990: 170). Their dependency on external markets also undermined the ability to cope with uncertainty. Van der Ploeg sums up: 'The pattern of relatively autonomous, historically guaranteed reproduction, described simply but graphically by the farmers in Chacán as "*trabajar por cuenta propria*," ("working for one's own account," for oneself), not only implies specific dynamics but [also the ability to cope with] specific vulnerabilities' (1990: 169–70).

It was not that Andean farmers did not from time to time attempt to pull away from the new markets and credit institutions, but opting out created its own difficulties. Since not all farmers would pull out at the same time, those who did found the way back to community-based labour arrangements blocked (van der Ploeg 1989: 161). Trapped, such farmers could see no alternative to playing the 'development game' on other people's terms. Despite the questions raised in the previous chapter about van der Ploeg's analysis, we may accept that a broad transformation did take place. Above all, between 1950 and 1981, highland agriculture showed signs of extensification as land acquired a purely commercial value (van der Ploeg 1990: 156). The 'scientific potato' would have been worth it, argues van der Ploeg, had the *intensification* of Andean agriculture been promoted, but this did not happen.

These examples from Zambia and Andean Peru show how complexity and variability are systematically reduced under the impact of modern agricultural policy. The reason for this reduction, research increasingly shows, is an 'anxiety to generalize and systematize', an anxiety nurtured by the underlying belief that policy-makers are regularly up against remnants of ancient practices unsuited to modern conditions (Moore and Vaughan 1994: 43). Significantly too, this anxiety lives on. After Zambia gained independence, the narrative emphasizing non-sustainability and fragility continued in two ways. First, the Kaunda government continued to prioritize resettlement (Moore and Vaughan 1994: 137–9); second, it kept alive the gender-blind colonial notion that farmers would be men:

> A progressive farmer would be a man who wished to separate himself from the network of kin relations that dominated most people's lives; he would build himself a decent brick-built house, and he would be modern without being too urbanized; he would be keen to educate his children, and his wife would be keen to learn the rudiments of 'domestic science'. (Moore and Vaughan 1994: 115)

Such policy narratives persisted because those in charge of economic and food security, including of course their own security, were fascinated by the *attractive simplicity* found in straightforward ethnic and evolutionary paradigms (Moore and Vaughan 1994: 25). This simplicity held that centuries-old, primitive practices were *suddenly* confronted with the modern twentieth century, so something had to be done.

Development narratives and discourses thrive on explanations marked by attractive simplicity. In a comment on Ethiopia's environmental reclamation programme of the mid-1980s, Allan Hoben (1995) repeats the point, stressing that the Ethiopian programme was underpinned by a narrative that had two basic characteristics. First, it was simple yet explained everything: the people of Ethiopia were helpless and ignorant, so how could the civilized world just stand and watch? Such a narrative sufficed to justify intervention. Second, the narrative responded fittingly to a range of 'understandings and sentiments', and steered clear of politics. It thus appealed to a wide audience, both inside and outside Ethiopia.

Some commentators, however, argue that the need for attractive simplicity in rural planning is unavoidable. Roe puts it thus:

> Rural development is a genuinely uncertain activity, and one of the principal ways practitioners, bureaucrats and policy makers articulate and make sense of this uncertainty is to tell stories or scenarios that simplify the ambiguity. . . . The more uncertain things seem at the microlevel, the greater the tendency to see the scale of uncertainty at the macrolevel to be so enormous as to require broad explanatory narratives that can be operationalized into standard approaches with widespread applicability. (Roe 1991: 288)

Whether development practice must inevitably be grounded in standard (meaning: technical) approaches with widespread applicability is questionable, though. Such a view may itself be part and parcel of the culture of disempowerment on which development narratives feed.

Asking how ARPTs (Zambia) and CIP (Peru) have responded to the uncertainties they faced can throw light on how unavoidable simplification and standardization really are. Let us compare responses before moving on to other IARCs.

Recent Trends in Agricultural Research and Food Policy in Zambia and Andean Peru: A Contrast

Zambia's ARPTs

Zambia's ARPTs strive to shorten the hungry season (or 'food-insecure gap') through exploring conditions, strategies and possible interventions with Farmer Research Groups formed at the village level. ARPT interventions are therefore tailor-made to specific circumstances and needs, wide-ranging, and agreed *before* they take place. Interventions agreed by the Farmer Research Groups in St. Anthonys and Ibenga, for instance, included the privatization of agricultural inputs and credit services (for the larger landowners in St. Anthonys); the introduction of varieties of maize, sorghum, groundnuts and cowpeas that mature during the January–March hungry season (both villages); the

introduction of mole-resistant root crops (St Anthonys); the introduction of velvet beans as a green manure intercrop in maize (Ibenga);
the introduction of high-value crops that do not coincide with the
main maize/sorghum planting season, for example Irish potatoes, climb-
ing beans, garlic (both locations); improvements in the marketing of
off-farm activities (mushrooms, honey, locally made beer, craft work)
essential for raising money to procure food/grain during deficit periods (both locations) (Mwape and Russell 1992). There was, in other
words, something for everyone to choose from.

These bundles of possible strategies, Mwape and Russell make clear,
reflect a significant policy shift. Not only are strategies pursued with
reference to location-specific circumstances, there is also a shift away
from the selection of improved technologies for main-season crops
(for example hybrid maize, groundnuts and sweet potatoes) towards
'the development of low input soil fertility maintenance systems'. The
latter focus on 'the selection of earlier maturing varieties and techniques for increasing the use of Dambos [seasonally flooded marshes]
for dry season food production' (Mwape and Russell 1992: 167). If
we can talk of a standard approach within the ARPTs, it is one which
honours diversity: crop diversity along with a more even spread of
workloads, food availability and income. The spreading of workloads
and incomes also addresses gender imbalances and aims especially
to reduce poor women's dependence on expensive informal credit
arrangements (Sikana and Simpungwe 1995, writing about ARPT-
Northern Province). The 'standard' approach thus requires a lot of
site-specific attention and urges extensionists to rethink their blind
faith in the beauty of diagnostic simplicity.

ARPT's approach and belief in the necessity for maximum diversification contrasts sharply with the approach taken by CIP in the
Peruvian Andes.

The International Potato Centre (CIP), Lima, Peru

Faced with labour bottlenecks and low farmer morale, scientific researchers at CIP reconsidered their approach in the early 1990s. They
went in search of, and found, the 'friendly potato' (*la papa simpática*);
a cluster of out-of-season varieties which would catch the higher market prices (Prain et al. 1992: 61). The 'friendliness' of these varieties
was also linked to their uniform shapes and stolon lengths, which meant
harvesting could be quicker, less dependent on manual labour and
therefore less costly. Releasing labour, Prain stresses, is 'very important', as the region is known for its 'constant labor shortage' (1992:
61). This reference to the problem of labour makes good sense in view

of van der Ploeg's analysis of how agricultural labour had been re-structured. (Other desirable characteristics – such as colour, fast cooking time and good taste/texture – were also experimented with.)[1]

Although the search for the 'friendly potato' pays attention to what Gordon Prain and colleagues call 'food systems evaluation', one cannot fail to note that the main advantages of this new potato – reduced labour input and cost – respond to household needs that did not exist before commoditization began. Indeed, before modern varieties and credit became available, labour was mobilized from within the household and through extra-household reciprocal arrangements (*ayni, compania*), while monetary costs were virtually non-existent. In short, although CIP's new approach was concerned with a 'broad farmer perspective' and with farmer 'preferences', it addressed conditions that had arisen in the wake of commoditization, a process which disrupted access to existing production factors – and to which CIP had contributed. Viewed within the socio-historical context of Andean farming, the so-called farmer preferences are preferences on breeders' terms. Prain et al. do not detail how the heralded savings on labour fit within the overall framework of *restructured* labour relations.

The absence of a historically situated analysis becomes understandable when CIP's philosophy is put under the magnifying glass. Like other IARCs, CIP sustains a 'Western knowledge enclave' which produces transnational knowledge not owned by local communities (Salas 1994: 59). Institutional claims regarding an improved breeder–farmer partnership must therefore be treated with scepticism. What CIP is in search of, argues Salas, is not so much a farmer-friendly potato as an easy to produce and process 'ideal potato'. While acknowledging that CIP has been innovative in terms of its social science methodologies (see Rhoades 1982, 1984, 1986), Salas remarks that

> CIP, by and large, strives to create [an] 'ideal potato' . . . free of nematodes, insects, fungi, bacteria and viruses; resistant to environmental stresses such as frost, heat, hail or drought; and adapted to the lowland tropic. The ideal potato can be created only in the laboratory, under artificial conditions and through the control of senior scientists. (Salas 1994: 59)

Despite its commitment to 'working with farmers', and some successes with methodology, CIP is still in the business of creating 'scientific potatoes' that only laboratories can produce and reproduce. In fact, Prain comes close to agreeing with Salas in an article on the 'radical transformation of current practice' regarding CIP's work with sweet potato farmers in Mindanao, the Philippines. Looking back on CIP's research in Peru, Prain acknowledges that its research programmes put *scientists before farmers* : 'So far we are still talking of *integrating* the user's perspective into genetic resources research, of farmers participating briefly in our show' (Prain 1993: 108). With this *mea culpa* as opener, Prain then asks of CIP's work in Mindanao what the chances are of 'going one step further, of us participating in an on-going, local R&D [Research and Development] process?' (Prain 1993: 108).

One Step Forward, Two Steps Backwards? The New Farmer–Scientist Partnership Within the IARCs

Concern over stark imbalances in the farmer–scientist relationship exist not only within CIP, but also in other IARCs. Here is a selection of responses to the concern – a concern which, I should add, received much attention in the wake of the 'bad press' disclosure that international guardianship of germplasm collections had been abused for profit (Mooney 1993). The responses under review here have all benefited from considerable input by agricultural anthropologists: Fujisaka (IRRI), Prain (CIP), Rhoades (CIP), Sperling (CIAT) and Voss (CIAT).

CIP and Mindanao's Sweet Potato Farmers

Prain's answer to the challenge that a more balanced farmer–scientist relationship must be created is to suggest that a 'possible entry point . . . can be found in the ideas surrounding *in situ* or communal germplasm conservation' (Prain 1993: 108). This 'radical transformation' is two-pronged: first, farmers' expertise in biodiversity conservation must be acknowledged and backed with support from governments and NGOs (Prain 1993: 108); second, community-based genebanks will take care of the problem of erosion which exists in *ex situ* germplasm collections (cf. Fowler and Mooney 1990).

Convinced that the concept of community genebanking has already taken firm root on Mindanao, Prain looks to the future with hope:

> The hope is that the local curators of the genebank will become the local evaluation specialists, a role which would take on more institutional significance and hence offer more prestige . . . than in the past. . . . [It] will be important to support the notion that possessing a large number of different tasting, different performing varieties is a source of prestige within the community and is an important resource in times of calamity and for future generations. (Prain 1993: 109–10)

The next goal is to ensure 'fuller recognition and performance of local R&D as a legitimate research mode. . . . Instead of inviting users to participate in a schedule which is essentially researcher-determined, social and botanical scientists [must take] the chance to participate in a process which is genuinely driven from the local point of view' (Prain 1993: 110).

Prepared to accept that such role reversals would constitute a significant step forward, I regard them to be no more than *a first step*. A further, equally essential but more difficult step is to move towards ·the full recognition of – and remuneration for – the contribution which farmers in 'the South' *have already made* to farming and farming profits in 'the North'. Exciting though the 'community genebanks' approach is, it is clear that the idea can easily become an exercise in window-dressing; a smokescreen to shield the deeper commercial and political interests (money; the use of agricultural 'progress' for political control) that lie behind the way scientific agricultural research works in practice. Moreover, and of the utmost importance, we need to ask how 'prestigious' participation by farmers relates to local-level politics. This is potentially an awkward issue, as highlighted during CIAT's work in Rwanda just before the genocide (see below).

The issue of compensation, more than that of local politics, is now coming into the open, and progress can be reported. One suggestion has come from Trygve Berg (1993). Referring to local community seed banks in Tigray, Berg suggests that 'The dissemination of genetic materials in the form of enhanced germplasm for local selection could be a way of compensating traditional seed selectors for their contributions to the genebanks of the world' (Berg 1993: 75). The question of farmer recognition and reward has also been addressed as a matter of urgency in CIAT's Central Africa programme. But the challenge is huge and must be fought on many levels, as the previous chapter made clear.

The International Rice Research Institute (IRRI)

The search for labour-saving technologies in a drastically restructured labour market is a priority also within the International Rice Research Institute (Fujisaka 1992, 1994), based in Los Baños, the Philippines, where farmers and researchers are again not collaborating on an equal footing. This became apparent early on in the Green Revolution when IRRI bred rice varieties for yield, but not taste. This suggested that 'IRRI plant breeders were less holistic in their perceptions of rice breeding than were Asian villagers, who considered taste important, along with yield, pest-resistance and lodging-susceptibility' (Colletta 1990:

101). Results were poor overall. According to Sam Fujisaka, the widespread adoption in Asia of high-yielding rice varieties in the late 1960s and 1970s resulted in 'a slowing of the rate of growth of farm yields, high input-use intensity, and an apparent decreasing efficiency of inputs' (Fujisaka 1992: 69). These problematic changes, which to some extent have now been overcome (Gerke 1992), are very similar to those van der Ploeg and Salas noted for Andean potato growers in Peru.

For far too long, the research orientation at IRRI remained purely extractive, with rice researchers failing to publicly acknowledge techniques 'borrowed' from smallholder farmers (Fujisaka 1992: 70). Fujisaka lists several reasons why agricultural scientists do not acknowledge that their advances are built upon farmer experimentation:

> scientists are under pressure to come up with their own innovations and tend to 'forget' farmer origins of technologies; borrowing from farmers is considered 'unscientific' (R.E. Rhoades, per. comm.); or researchers accept the idea that little can be gained through the study of traditional agriculture because even sustainable traditional systems have not been able to increase production at rates matching increased demand. (Fujisaka 1992: 72).

But, writes Fujisaka, this is the past. In more recent times at IRRI, during the third research phase, a new dawn has broken whereby indigenous innovation and science have merged in better partnership. Fujisaka's examples speak of reversals in research practice much along the lines Prain suggested for CIP. IRRI now aims first and foremost to improve 'traditional systems' through farmer-to-farmer technology transfers. To this end, IRRI organized visits by farmers to neighbouring regions to initiate them in alternative local-technology approaches. Thus farmers from Claveria (Philippines), an area known to have limited methods for controlling soil erosion, have visited Cebu, where control methods are more advanced, to learn directly from other farmers. The practice of direct learning is long overdue (Keesing 1990: 72). Farmers from Claveria also visited Tupi in south Cotabato, where upland rice farmers use a home-improved steel lithao (*panudling*), a harrowlike implement normally made of wood. This latter visit was organized in the hope 'that the Tupi *panudling* might be an appropriate labor-saving technology for farmers in Claveria. [It worked.] . . . Claveria farmers modified the *panudling* by angling the blades forward to achieve better penetration in the heavier soils, and about sixty interested farmers tested the system' (Fujisaka 1992: 76). The new emphasis on farmer-to-farmer training at IRRI, clearly an improvement on the previously extractive research, should not detract, however, from the need to ask why Claveria farmers have labour-related problems in the first place. (I do not have the answer, but the question must be asked.)

Even more recently, IRRI implemented certain upstream shifts in its 'mandate' (Fujisaka 1994: 231), which included networking with university research centres and NGOs. This collaboration, however, may signal the beginning of a disengagement from social science research, the 'return to more basic rice germplasm improvement' research. The new partner 'centres and national programmes [would thus be] given the responsibility to conduct more of the needed on-farm, systems and participatory research' (Fujisaka 1994: 231). How welcome the news is is uncertain, since the new partners may or may not formulate their social research interests within the context of a political economy which highlights *farmers' restructured access to scarce production factors.* Given the post-Cold War climate within which NGOs and universities now work and compete (Hulme and Edwards 1997), agendas for politically informed social research may not be as thorough as they should be. And yet, as recent lessons by CIAT researchers in Rwanda have established, fostering a research interest in local politics is crucial to programme success.

International Centre for Tropical Agriculture (CIAT), Great Lakes, Central Africa

CIAT research on bean cropping in Africa's Great Lakes Region has also shifted its 'mandate'. When it started up in 1983, the CIAT programme aimed to enhance stability and productivity in *existing* bean mixtures through the addition of new varieties that incorporated desirable characteristics (Voss 1992: 36). The objective was a first step in the creation of non-extractive partnerships. With time, the plant breeders involved came to appreciate not just a fuller range of local evaluative criteria, but also some important gender concerns (Sperling 1992). The research phase (1988–93) prior to the Rwandan genocide saw further progress in terms of farmer–researcher interaction.

Early on in the programme, however, CIAT's resident anthropologist had voiced concern over the economic and social context in which the 'improved' bean varieties were introduced. The specific concern was that the promotion of improved lines could be detrimental to conserving or increasing biological diversity. The danger had two sources: the market preference for beans of uniform colour and the opinion of government workers who held that pure, improved lines were modern and more productive. Unless countered, these biases were likely to impair farmers' ability to improve mixtures (Voss 1992: 34). At the centre of the concern was the performance of extension workers. Despite CIAT's clearly stated primary aim – which was to enhance stability and productivity in existing bean mixtures – Voss found that the programme's technicians and extensionists often extolled the virtues of planting improved varieties separately rather than adding them to the mixtures (Voss 1992: 36, 47). The advice farmers received thus went against the programme's chief objective. Voss concluded that 'Research goals must be carefully explained to the people who provide the direct link with farmers so that messages will be passed on accurately' (1992: 47).

It is conceivable that these messages were correctly transmitted and received, but that bias crept in regardless. This may well have happened because of the extension workers' (and the government's) faith in the absolute superiority of science over local knowledges and practices; a conviction on which the authority of Rwandan extension workers rests (Pottier 1989a). The distorted messages by technicians and extensionists were a neat reminder that intervention programmes and their results must always be situated and evaluated in the context of local economic, social and political realities.

In an attempt to take such broader realities on board, the CIAT-Rwanda programme then moved through a number of progressive stages, much like IRRI did, and achieved significant advances in farmer–scientist participation during 1988–93 (Sperling and Scheidegger 1995). Over the period, and to the credit of CIAT's agricultural anthropologist, Rwandan farmers became more involved in on-station bean selection, while a countrywide programme was also launched to decentralize seed selection. The programme achieved a major breakthrough when senior women farmers and research scientists involved themselves in community-based screening. The move towards 'devolution', Sperling and Scheidegger reflect, 'was a healthy mixture of empowerment and economics. Communities should have the right to select their own delegates to screen on-station' (1995: 5).

The social benefits were unmistakable. First, farmers received recognition for their role as innovative technical experts. Encouragingly, '[the] participatory experiment . . . proposed that varieties selected by communities and which later showed wider adoption, should be brought back into the formal system and baptised as farmer-breeder varieties' (Sperling and Scheidegger 1995: 6–7). Second, CIAT/ISAR plant breeders came formally to appreciate women's skills in seed selection.

Despite these significant advances, however, some serious disquiet arose over the *actual* selection of farmer representatives and the effect on the process of 'empowerment': rather than challenge power structures and male hierarchies, the programme achieved the opposite effect (Sperling and Scheidegger 1995: 7). CIAT/ISAR researchers developed

> the sense that some of the so-called community-selected experts were neither very informed, nor very representative of community interests. For instance, one community was represented by the government agronomist's sister, and the sector head's wife. The male authorities in charge linked power with knowledge, and imputed male knowledge to their female sidekicks. If he was an important official, *she* must be a farmer expert. (Sperling and Scheidegger 1995: 7–8)

While there were many advantages in working through Rwanda's community structures (for example they exist countrywide and control land), there was the formidable drawback that community leaders used the project for the purpose of control. This was revealed in the way 'key figures in charge sometimes fell short of their obligations to community participants', as when rewards (for example selected seeds) were not distributed to deserving evaluators (Sperling and Scheidegger 1995: 8). In short, despite the advantages of working through existing administrative structures, the programme risked being an instrument of 'control' (for the administration) rather than of 'service' (1995: 8).

That agricultural programmes are regularly 'hijacked' for political purposes is increasingly understood (see e.g. Gatter 1993: 181). This is where anthropology has a special contribution to make to the research agendas of IARCs. These agendas must concern themselves not just, as already argued, with the analysis of society and history in the target area, but also with the implications the programmes introduced will have for the future development of social and political relations within and between communities. In principle, the move towards community-managed genebanking is most positive; in practice, its evaluation requires insight into the workings of local society and politics if benefits are to be equitably shared among deserving participants. Contextualization is particularly important since local genebank curators are likely to achieve (even) higher prestige *because of* their involvement (see Prain 1993, discussed above).

Social scientists involved in the research programmes of IARCs need to ask some hard questions, including questions about the role of IARCs in international politics and finance. I have made this argument in the context of agricultural rehabilitation in post-war, post-genocide Rwanda (Pottier 1996), where the 'Seeds of Hope' programme went ahead without the benefit of a proper 'needs assessment' exercise. Such an exercise should have been undertaken immediately following the war, when it was easy to establish that the needs for seed were less than feared. The 'oversight' made me suggest that 'Seeds of Hope' helped itself before it helped Rwanda. Specifically, I argued that this international rescue package – as it unfolded, but not in its initial conception – aimed to validate the existence of the IARCs at a time when they were hit by shrinking budgets and worldwide scepticism (see ODI 1994). Had a 'needs assessment' been carried out immediately following the end of military hostility, the claim that Rwandan farmers had virtually depleted their crop genetic resources, and were thus in need of a large-scale intervention, would have had to be withdrawn.

Beyond Token Partnership: Mission Still Possible?

It is time to be more aware of social and political contexts. Social science research within IARCs has undoubtedly made progress in the search for more farmer-friendly methodologies, yet these methodologies need to be grounded in a full-fledged analysis of the politics of intervention. Social scientists within the IARC system do not normally ask questions about the (imagined) 'zone of effective neutrality' (Parsons 1970: 338) in which they work. The above reflections by Sperling and Scheidegger, however, should be an incentive to develop a stronger interest in how programmes are relocalized politically.

Which questions then need to be asked? In 'Taking the Part of Peasants', Bernstein argues that it does not do for interventionists to say that they champion the cause of the small-scale farmer:

> As peasants are not a uniform social category or 'class', we have to ask: taking the part of *which* peasants? in what circumstances? for what reasons? by what means? This is more demanding of both theory and practice than awarding the 'freedom of the market' to all peasants on the assumption that they share the same conditions, aspirations, goals and interests. (Bernstein 1990: 76–7)

The IARCs do not at this stage ask too many questions about 'which peasants?' they serve. The evidence available rather suggests that they tend to champion 'middle peasants' who represent the 'natural' condition of the peasantry, in the same way agricultural populists tend to understand the world (Bernstein 1990: 72). This succumbing to 'blanket advocacy of "the peasant way"', however, is outright dangerous. As the civil disturbances and genocide in Rwanda so poignantly showed, what gave rise to the onslaught was not some primordial ethnic hatred, but class formation, class contradictions and *specific* local circumstances (Longman 1995). Agricultural researchers every-where must guard against the populist imagery of 'the peasant way' and become more committed to 'a political project of changing social relations and practices' (Bernstein 1990: 77). This will include the crit-ical analysis of the performance of individual researchers and of the general functioning and ethos of the agencies for whom they work. The analysis will also address questions about the trusteeship role of IARCs, particularly regarding the continuing imbalance in profits between North and South (Mooney 1993: 175–8).[2]

Profits aside, Mooney's specific concern is that 'genetic resources are often incorrectly described as the "raw materials" for biotechnol-ogy' (1993: 173). This incorrect representation enables the IARCs to use farmers' genetic materials as 'bargaining chips in negotiations which are resulting in the extension of patents' (Mooney 1993: 174). Mooney draws attention to five such instances, three of which are examples of biotechnology corporations that obtained germplasm from CIP for development into patentable materials. These examples starkly expose the ultimate danger that the IARCs, in their self-appointed roles as international trustees, abuse the 'informal' trust agreements with farm-ers and expropriate both farmers' resources and their knowledge about them (Mooney 1993: 174).

Once again, the problem of 'which farmers?' arises: who are the community representatives, and how do they relate to what is so loosely called 'community knowledge'? Natural/biological and so-cial scientists need to develop an approach to indigenous technical knowledge (ITK) which goes beyond the assumption that there is 'fixed knowledge' out there to be captured (see Fairhead 1992b; Scoones and Thompson 1994). They need to adopt an approach which asks how local farming concepts make sense in their specific socio-cultural, political, economic and ecological milieux; they need to develop an awareness of how farmers flexibly alter practices to suit diverse social and ecological circumstances (Fairhead 1990, 1992b). At the most basic level, social and agricultural scientists need better to appreciate that farming decisions are compromises, that 'the farmer continues to balance everything he or she wishes to accomplish against valuable resources and time' (Hansen 1991: 42). It is this real world of compromises, which includes class and gender concerns, that future researchers and community/extension workers must explore.

In *Beyond Farmer First*, Scoones and Thompson (1994) urged that development practitioners drop the idea that ITK is a tangible resource to be tapped, extracted and documented. Instead they proposed an approach which recognizes that knowledge is situated practice. The proposal followed a similar request by Last and Chavunduka (1986) in the context of a debate on 'traditional' medicine; a request acknow-ledged at the original *Farmer First* conference. Last and Chavunduka had argued:

> There is an inherent danger that traditional medical knowledge will be defined simply in terms of its technical herbal expertise, that this exper-tise will in turn be recognised only for its empirical pharmacognosy, without reference to the symbolic and ritual matrix within which it is used – still less *the social matrix in which those rituals and symbols have meaning*. (Last and Chavunduka 1986: 267, cited in Chambers et al. 1989: 38; emphasis added)

To appreciate how knowledges and practices in smallholder farming emerge out of complex social processes involving situational, cultural and institutional factors (Long 1992: 27), researchers will need to get used to asking the following kinds of questions:

- Which farmer knows what? Who talks to whom about what? Do people 'know', 'think', 'believe' or 'suppose'? (And how useful are these Western categories?) How much disagreement is there? Is variation expressed, disputed, and how is this done? How do farm-ers come to 'know'? How confident are they in what they know?
- What is the relationship between farming knowledge and farming practice? How do technical options relate to the socio-political environment?
- How useful are categories derived from Western science (for ex-ample disease, fertility, erosion, intercropping) for eliciting local agro-ecological knowledge? (Fairhead 1992b: 3–4, 14–15, 21; see also Fairhead 1991, 1994).

The gap between agricultural scientists and policy-makers on the one hand, and peasant farmers on the other, resembles the gap which ex-ists between patient and doctor. Parsons perceived the encounter be-tween patients and doctors as a functional procedure in which the two parties worked harmoniously towards the same goal, with the doctor acting in a 'zone of effective neutrality' (Parsons 1970: 338). This is now outdated. The more correct view, as Anderson and Helm (1979) argue, is to see the encounter between patient and doctor as a process of 'reality negotiation between participants with competing conceptualizations'; it is a negotiation which is inherently conflictual (Anderson and Helm 1979: 268–9). During the encounter, the doctor has the advantage of scientific 'rationality' and 'objective' knowledge, while the patient's notions of illness are reduced to folklore or old wives' tales.

Conclusion

Agricultural policy-makers, researchers and extensionists do not work in 'zones of effective neutrality'. They must therefore become better aware of (or express their awareness of) the political economy of the regions and cultures they work in. They need also sharpen their awareness of how they themselves are perceived by the farmers who benefit; 'farmers' being a highly diverse category. In going beyond token partnerships, agricultural policy-makers and scientists must ask some searching questions about their own identities and roles, and their relationship to the social matrix in which the knowledges they claim to champion have evolved. How important this social matrix is was superbly expressed by one farmer, Virgilio, from the Dominican Republic, when he conversed with Lucas, a Dutch research scientist:

> 'Lucas, I understand you want to know. You are a scientist and you want to know. But there is only one way to know what I know about cassava. Speak with me; don't speak to me like others did. *Ask me about my life* and I will tell you about cassava.' (farmer Virgilio, Dominican Republic, speaking with Louk Box, in Chambers et al. 1989: 61; emphasis added)

Just as there is a need for doctors to learn about how they relate to patients, seeing them as individuals rather than as 'cases', so there is a need for those involved in agricultural research and crop development to situate farming practices and associated knowledges in the context of *life itself*. And that, as the ARPT agenda in Zambia suggests, involves stepping up the ability to recognize and respond to diverse, localized needs.

9

State of Play
Anthropology, Food Security, and New Directions in Research

An article on the patenting of Himalayan basmati rice and Andean quinoa, a staple grain, caught my eye just as I thought it safe to wrap up. 'Against the Grain' *(Guardian Weekend*, 25 April 1998) immediately reminded me of how uncomfortable anthropology can be (see Firth 1981). In chapter 6 of this book, on scrutinizing the argum-ent that 'Third World' peasant farmers become confused, degraded selves when faced with the spectre of biotechnology, I had voiced scepticism: the concept seemed an exaggerated reaction in which 'crisis talk' over-shadowed the diversity and complexity which exist within the developing world; a world where farmers use human agency to overcome structural constraints. Would 'Against the Grain' unsettle me, make me reconsider?

On quinoa, recently patented, the article stated: 'Put crudely, [Andean] quinoa farmers are now expected to pay the [US-based] patent holders for the end-product of their own centuries-old knowledge' each time their quinoa enters the United States of America. Himalayan basmati rice, it followed, might soon be subjected to a similar levy now that Rice Tec Inc., a Texas-based breeding company, had obtained 'a patent allowing it to call strains of rice it has developed "basmati", even though they will be grown outside India'. The article made no comment on the effects of patenting on Himalayan or Andean farm-ers' confidence or self-perception, but quoted Vandana Shiva who, in conversation with the *Guardian*, spoke of bio-piracy: 'The [basmati] patent represents an attempt to steal both from nature and the farmers who have nurtured basmati for centuries, as well as to sell counterfeit food to the consumer.' Despite having argued that the new biotechnologies are not inherently evil, because they enable biodiversity to be used in ways not used before, I found it impossible to disagree with the view that patents on life-forms, and their current applications, represent acts of bio-piracy. I felt in strong agreement with Shiva.

The agreement, however, did not mean I could accept that bio-piracy and, more generally, dependence on difficult-to-control markets for 'improved' agriculture would be *the overriding factor* in how farmers constitute their 'selves'. Sympathy with the unequal struggle of Andean and Himalayan smallholders did not mean I was prepared to make inferences about their state of mind. Smallholder wheat-farmers in Punjab (Leaf 1983) and rice-growers in Bangladesh (White 1992) were also up against tightly structured inequalities, yet they accepted being part of an interdependent world from which some benefit is derived. Likewise, Long had referred to Oaxaca migrant workers on Californian farms as possessing a truly transnational sense of self (Long 1996). 'Against the Grain', then, did not kindle doubt: although they certainly faced formidable legal battles, Himalayan and Andean farmers, through their legal representatives, would not take things lying down; the patents would cause hardship, perhaps a great deal, but would this destroy every form of pride and determination? I could not bring myself to believe self-effacement was on the cards. (The struggles Thakurs had won in Pariawan, Uttar Pradesh, described by Lerche, also came to mind.) Surely, struggles for justice are ongoing, and identity construction is a more elaborate, multifaceted process.

My reaction to 'Against the Grain', however, was not an attempt to belittle the struggle of basmati and quinoa growers, far from it. In actual fact, the effect of the article was to awaken a stronger interest in the legal battles surrounding patenting, and this from two points of view, compensation and representation, both of which I consider to be compelling research issues. Three questions immediately sprang to mind: How is the crisis over patenting talked about in situated everyday languages? How is compensation talked about? And who represents the interests of the peasant farmers in court, or better perhaps, *whose interests* are represented? It also dawned on me that a framework for action which aims to foster 'a culture of mutual understanding' between plant breeders and farmers (IDRC 1994) needs to recognize that the challenge involves more than two parties; it is not a question of nation-states versus multinationals, although resolving their differences would be a starting-point. One day 'India' may score a victory in the basmati court battle, but would this mean basmati rice growers had won? (Why does Bhopal come to mind here?) Who is representing 'the farmers'? And *which farmers* (Bernstein 1990) are represented? The point is this: legal battles and law courts form one site of interest for the fieldworker anthropologist, but so do the Himalayas and the structures of inequality under which basmati farmers labour. So I asked myself: what are the relationships between these two complex worlds? How do they affect peasant farmers' morale? What loopholes do peasant farmers explore? Are women and men equally affected? Clearly, the two sites – the rice fields and the courts – need to be bridged conceptually, and researched. In truth, neither site/ level has so far been much researched: the enquiry into how smallholder farmers constitute their 'selves' in the fast-changing world of hi-tech farming and commoditization has only just begun; as for anthropology's interest in researching legal battles, that interest too awaits expansion.

The quandary which has gradually surfaced with every chapter in this book is now fully exposed: will social scientists investigating aspects of food (in)security ever reach the point where they manage to combine a full analysis of the structured impediments to food security (various types of inequality in production, distribution and consumption) with an equally full analysis of the differential experiences of that insecurity and of the myriad ways in which food-insecure people attempt to overcome constraints? The need for such a dual focus has been particularly evident in the way exaggerated claims about on-farm biodiversity decline in West Africa have been countered in new research. This research shows, on the one hand, that human strategies for the maintenance of biodiversity are multi-stranded and not too greatly affected (if at all) by commoditization, yet, on the other hand, researchers concede that biodiversity maintenance, which sometimes occurs at the community rather than at the household level, does not necessarily guarantee the maintenance of an adequate diet. Markets can indeed be greedy, taking more than they give back (Guyer 1996; Guyer and Richards 1996).

The necessity of focusing simultaneously on broad structural variables and on human agency is manifest, too, in the ways in which access to land and labour have become restructured in the course of the twentieth century. On several occasions we have learned that food and economic security require secure access to land. It is a factor, for example, in the maintenance of agro-diversity in Kofyar households (Netting and Stone 1996), in the way Sagadans can use 'improved' seeds to boost their agricultural performance (Voss 1987), and again in Kerala's successful attempt to make the greater majority of its people more food-secure and healthy. Secure access to land remains a chief guarantor in keeping households and individuals food-secure.

And yet, and here lies the dilemma, loss of land, it also transpires, does not invariably result in destitution. Once again, the temptation of 'disaster talk' has to be resisted. In the same way that researchers in West Africa now argue against the idea of a single negative correlation between commoditization and on-farm biodiversity, so anthropologists researching in South-East Asia inform us that landlessness does not necessarily mean an irreversible cut in the quality of life. Gerke (1992) and White (1992) offer powerful arguments in this respect. Both accept that the 'modernization' of agriculture, in Java and Bangladesh respectively, has exacted a heavy toll – in terms of lands lost, livelihood strategies lost, and environmental damage – yet neither is prepared to end the analysis on (the expected?) disaster note. On the contrary, overridingly positive results are reported, for there is now more agricultural wage work available, and women (and some men) are moving into new economic fields with some success. The role of human agency is well highlighted, too, in Ben White's argument that polarizing tendencies and personalized (moral) relations can and do coexist (chapter 3), as it is when Berry explains for sub-Saharan Africa why commoditization has not resulted in the large-scale alienation of land.

At the heart of these delicately balanced analyses lies the insight, derived from detailed ethnographic study, that commoditization and 'modern agriculture' are not monolithic phenomena. Modern agriculture, for instance, comes in many guises, each time with a life history. In Java, this implies that recent technical improvements have wiped out some of the social costs incurred in the early stages of the Green Revolution. While job losses and the threat to livelihood security were very serious in those early days, and continue to hurt, there is today more work available both on and off the farm. This compensates, somewhat. Gerke's optimism regarding recent developments in 'improved agriculture' is shared by White, whose research in Bangladesh concluded in much the same fashion: Green Revolution agriculture imposed heavy initial costs, yet households dependent on agricultural wage labour have become better off. Such findings reinforce Leaf's (early) plea for a broad, multifaceted assessment of the Green Revolution phenomenon and its impact on farmers' livelihoods; the enquiry must not boil down to a commentary on the single issue of displacement.

Broadening the debate, however, also means taking seriously the perspective that 'scientific agriculture' can be an instrument of governmentality. Agriculture generally, it is increasingly understood, functions as an idiom of social expression (Gatter 1993; Hansen 1991; Richards 1989). Several of the case studies in this book illustrate this. Yet it equally needs emphasizing that 'scientific agriculture' is often used strategically for political ends. As a political project, 'improved' agriculture may be used by governments to fight insurgency (Hart et al. 1989; Hirsch 1990); it can also be a vehicle for personal gain at the community level (Sperling and Scheidegger 1995). The interlinkages between scientific agricultural research programmes and governmentality, which are multiple and varied, present anthropology with a research field ready to be explored further.

A further comment on the (possible) social benefits of 'improved agriculture' is also in order. (As with the findings on biodiversity in West Africa, there is again a need for caution.) While the longer-term effects of the Green Revolution may not be as negative as initially assumed, there are limits to how creative resource-poor people can be. True, thousands of Javanese women moved successfully into petty trade in the 1980s and early 1990s to offset the loss of their peasant farmer status. Yet to flourish within these new-found trade avenues women, as Gerke stresses, need to manage their time differently. This is prompted by the fact that 'running a small trade business or looking for so far unexploited working opportunities [require] more initiative [and time] than harvesting and pounding in agriculture' (Gerke 1992: 96). Now what does it *mean* to Javanese women that they must manage their time differently, and better? It is not a question of 'if only they knew how to' (cf. Wheeler 1986), but rather a question of how *the meanings of time and associated meanings related to propriety* will be negotiated within households and communities. What Javanese women are going through, what women everywhere go through when they need extra time to explore new options to keep households food-secure, is not simply a struggle over resources (time, money, access to goods, and so on), but a 'struggle over meanings' (Agarwal 1994a). Agarwal has made clear what this struggle has entailed in South Asia, and we have added case studies from Africa (Ma Cousine in Kinshasa; Mandinka women on the Jahaly Pacharr project). All have shown how resource management provokes continuous discussion over meanings. One important aspect of the research challenge here is to gauge the extent to which these struggles over meaning are personal, collective or a mixture of both; another is to better understand how economics and morality entwine during such negotiations (Fairhead 1990; Kabeer 1990; Schoepf and Walu 1991). And of course, these processes take place at multiple levels: household, lineage, community, bureaucratic worlds, national governments, transnational companies, and so on. Our understanding of how access to household resources is negotiated and renegotiated, sometimes under volatile economic conditions, is still at an early stage of development. Much remains to be learned.

Meanings are also produced through the encounter with international and national programmes for drought mitigation and the prevention of famine. Here, the signs are that governments may use programmes to bring vulnerable communities in line with 'modern' conceptualizations of what kinds of people there ought to be. Evidence suggests that certain top-down economic interventions do have the power to destroy existing community-based strategies for coping with hardship (Beck 1989; El Sammani 1990; Solway 1994), directly or indirectly, yet information on how resource-poor groups and individuals react to these programmes remains scant. That there is likely to be reaction, however, becomes clear in those instances where valued farmer–trader links are tampered with 'from above' (by government or NGOs) and where a backlash has occurred to reinstate 'local ways' (Babb 1987; Tierney 1997).

The theme of how meanings are negotiated ties in nicely with the study of how peasant farmers – a category always in need of deconstruction – use initiative when 'modern agriculture' imposes conditions that become unacceptable. How much leeway there is, and how the scope for manoeuvre is structured, warrants further investigation. That experiences are diverse is beyond doubt: in central Luzon, Philippine farmers pulled out or modified their farming practices when 'improved' rice technologies became too expensive (Banzon-Bautista 1989); in India, where markets (for goods, inputs, credit, land) are firmly interlocked, resource-poor farmers may need to keep going because of coercion (Harriss-White 1996); opting out also proved impossible for Andean peasant farmers (van der Ploeg 1990). The ability to opt out of the engagement with modern production processes, or to modify it, appears closely linked to how markets are structured. This, then, is one of many reasons why food domains must never be studied in isolation.

Acknowledgement of how food domains interconnect is vital if policy-makers are ever going to write *integrated food policies*, as opposed to *agricultural* policies (DeWalt 1991; McMillan 1991). In this respect, Croll's data on how intra-household labour relations in China evolved to reproduce familiar inequalities makes an illuminating contrast with the question of land, on which policy-makers had achieved success through the allocation of land rights to women (Croll 1994). The gains achieved, however, seemed to be offset once the 'double day' women continue to work was taken into account. The lesson for policy-makers could not be more straightforward: land and labour, so strongly integrated in people's everyday lives, must not be divorced in policy work. The message relates closely to another observation, again coming from anthropology, namely, that 'real' strategies for livelihood security and environmental management are inseparable (Davies and Leach 1991). If policy-makers aim to intervene *meaning*fully, they must end the practice of compartmentalizing the food question into what they deem to be manageable sectors.

A similar concern over misguided preconceptions has spurred many an anthropologist to challenge deterministic models of agrarian change and development (for an overview, see Long 1992). Glimpses of this 'war' have been plentiful in the present book. The notion of strict polarization, for instance, shows up as untenable, since personal (moral) relations can persist in conjunction with impersonal relations. Untenable, too, is the broad cultural–regional divide between more corporate and less corporate household systems (cf. Kabeer 1994), which has proved to hide more than it reveals. What is intriguing, however, and a crucial pointer for future research agendas, is that arguments never seem entirely won or lost. Critiques and counter-critiques in this book all suggest that researchers must be prepared to reposition themselves and rethink if necessary.

It is instructive quickly to recall some of the other 'disagreements'. The technicist approach to agrarian change (Bray 1991), for instance, was challenged for overlooking aspects of political economy (Hart et al. 1989), yet proved very useful in making sense of certain differences between India's advanced wheat- and advanced rice-growing regions. Similarly, the argument in defence of a 'functional perspective' on intra-household food sharing (Wheeler and Abdullah 1988) was judged too lightweight to dispose of the insights that can be gained from a 'resource control' perspective, yet it raised questions about seasonality and physiological processes that anthropologists can ill afford to ignore in future. The same can be argued of the gloom-and-doom portrayals of how 'scientific agriculture' impacts on resource-poor communities and individuals (Shiva 1992; van der Ploeg 1989, 1993). Criticized for their narrow approach to how 'selves' are constructed, these analyses nonetheless provide excellent frameworks within which to think. And to add one further 'disagreement', while claims about community benefits and positive experiences of interdependence (Leaf 1983) fail to be fully persuasive in the absence of a clear focus on intra-household relations and language use, not to mention problems connected with using the concepts of 'community' and 'society' in the first place (see Ingold 1996: 55–98), there is much merit in Leaf's argument against the overemphasis on displacement. What is refreshing about all these arguments and counter-arguments is that they raise issues and perspectives that may well apply on the ground the next time a fieldworker, even a seasoned one, embarks on a new piece of research.

Openness to 'other' perspectives does not mean, however, that research should become apolitical. On the contrary, I would strongly argue the opposite: that receptivity to 'other' viewpoints implies judgement and, consequently, demands that extra attention be paid to the conditions and structures that produce poverty. The following issues, many addressing aspects of the development industry itself, must go on the agenda of anyone wishing to research the 'real' world of food (in)security:

- Do agricultural research scientists and extension workers treat farmer knowledge – correction: farmer knowledges – as fixed, or as evolving and contestable?
- What is the political backdrop against which advances in scientifically improved farming are divulged to nations and communities? How are interventions locally interpreted and reinterpreted, by farmers and by officials? Is community-managed genebanking a neutral activity?
- To what extent have farmers – and which farmers? – lost control over their food production capacities? What exactly is the nature of the 'farmer preferences' that IARCs identify and respond to? How do such preferences relate to the (often very dramatic) restructuring of production factors and relationships caused by commoditization and the facilities for 'improved' farming? Are 'farmer preferences' merely preferences on plant breeders' terms?
- How much do developers (and academic researchers) know about the capabilities and drawbacks of community-based mechanisms for drought mitigation? What happens when local safety-networks are eroded by state programmes (for example for the commercialization of livestock)? Is state patronage (and which type of state patronage?) always the better alternative?
- What do answers to the above reveal about the quality of farmer–researcher partnerships?

Policy-makers may choose to ignore these questions, perhaps seeking an excuse in the 'urgency' with which programmes 'need' to be implemented. Yet, as the structural adjustment debacle so convincingly shows, little is to be gained from not taking the trouble and time to understand the inner workings of 'real' markets or 'real' households. One challenge for those who took part in the World Food Summit in Rome, November 1996, will be to explore how a commitment to food 'preferences' can be broadened into a commitment better to understand 'cultural perspectives' on food. The step is by no means small, but, as I hope the chapters in this book have made clear, there is at least one basic step which every policy-maker committed to good professional practice can and must make. It comes down to asking two simple questions habitually omitted, as seen for example in the Indian food security projects Greeley (1991) analysed (see chapter 2): first, what is the political context in which interventions take place?; second, how do interventions affect that same context?

It would be unfair, of course, to insinuate that only development practitioners need to come to terms with 'real' worlds. Academics, too, for too long, have fallen into camps that seemed irreconcilable: crudely, one camp with Marxist dependency theorists who believe capitalism is transforming all social and economic relations into impersonal ones; a second camp peopled with liberal thinkers oblivious to the often hugely disastrous impact of capitalist penetration, and having eyes only for the (mostly invented) propensity of people everywhere to strategize and maximize. Such one-sided approaches are unhelpful – unless carefully combined. Researchers must take responsibility and acknowledge both the strengths and the shortcomings of the theoretical frameworks they favour, and appreciate the insights to be gained from theories habitually discarded. As the ethnographic materials brought together in this book make quite explicit, economic and food insecurity is firmly grounded in structured conditions and relations, yet human agency is also at work – admittedly mostly within the realm of the 'permissible' – to overcome constraining conditions, and change them if possible. Put differently, talk of 'passive victims' must be avoided, but not at the expense of encouraging blindness to the structural parameters that constrain life chances and options. Gerke's appreciation of Stoler's research on Java in the early days of the Green Revolution (Stoler 1977) is a fine demonstration of how seemingly opposed perspectives can be integrated, as is Ben White's (1989) argument against polarization.

For theoretical integration to develop further, anthropological fieldwork must become fully multi-sited. Della McMillan already made this clear in her introduction to the edited volume *Anthropology and Food Policy*. She wrote:

> starting from a base of extensive anthropological fieldwork . . . an anthropologist can talk about food preferences and how malnourishment occurs within a family or community context and can raise questions from this base about the nature of national and international food policies which, unknown to local consumers, directly affect their well-being and, indeed, their social and political lives. (McMillan 1991: 2–3)

Paul Doughty similarly called upon fellow anthropologists to be more aware of how 'macro-level' food policies (and forms of assistance) can have far-reaching implications even for geographically remote communities (Doughty 1986: 48).

In view of the arguments made in this book, two further points should be added to the request for more multi-sited study. First, studying food issues, whether within households or in the offices of policy-makers, must not be 'just academic'. The aim of such research must be to understand and to transform. Specifically, it is time to end the 'impressive' fact that the people who are continually affected by experimental policies 'have virtually no participation in the policy making process that determines market prices and products' (McMillan 1991: 2–3). Bluntly put, academics must be lobbyists. Effective lobbying, and this is the second point, will have the advantage that anthropologists can position themselves to tackle the new research challenge, which is to understand how so-called global structures and processes are infiltrated and shaped by so-called local ones (see chapter 1). International Agricultural Research Centres may claim that bottom-up influence is precisely what their new 'mandates' now encourage, but the issue of how empirical knowledge(s) is (are) understood, absorbed and used by 'global' structures remains unclear, even murky, for there is a lot of 'selective visibility' going on, along with lucrative financial deals. As a promising research area, the 'splintering of hegemony' (Kandiyoti 1999) deserves our fullest attention, not just for the sake of knowledge itself, but for the contribution such study can make to the creation of policy worlds more transparent and capable of better regulation.

Notes

Chapter 3   Land and Livelihood: Land Ownership, Access, Reform and Research Responsibilities

1   A recent example of the technicist view of agrarian change is Francesca Bray's (1991) argument that China's commune approach to wet-rice farming became unsustainable not because of politics but because of its scale. Efficient farming demands an intensive, small-scale approach, and this requires the kind of close supervision the large communes could not provide. Historically speaking, as Bray observes for medieval Song China and Tokugawa Japan, when

> wet-rice cultivation systems become more productive and intensive there [is] a marked tendency for units of production to become smaller rather than larger, usually taking the form of family farms supplying the bulk of their own labour, but co-operating with other households at periods of peak demand or for the organization of such infrastructural work as maintenance of irrigation networks (Bray 1991: 201)

The demise of China's wet-rice-producing Communes occurred because the principle remains valid and ideologues ended up respecting it (Bray 1991: 212).

2   Indonesia's command-plus-subsidization strategy led to spectacular production results at the aggregate level. By the mid-1980s, Javanese peasants were producing twice as much as they had done in the late 1960s (Hüsken and White 1989: 253). For Indonesia as a whole, the increase in rice production meant that 'average rice consumption per person increased by about 30 per cent' (Ellis 1990: 44). Ellis concedes, however, that it is not clear how the aggregate increase had affected 'the command over food purchase of vulnerable groups like the urban poor or rural landless' (1990: 44). The outcome was also positive in political terms. As state patronage

through subsidies benefited smallholders as well as larger landholders, the problem of political unrest in rural areas eased off and the regime stepped up its law-and-order campaign by appointing civilian 'allies' at the village level (Hüsken and White 1989: 253). These allies were village heads brought in from outside the region and instructed to work closely with the police and army, two major beneficiaries of Suharto's Green Revolution programme.

3 Berry draws attention to the (now widely accepted) thesis that so-called customary law was created under colonial rule. She refers to Chanock who argued that 'colonial administrators not only "recognize[d] local custom" (Colson 1971: 193) but also codified it, imposing rigid rules and an individualistic ethos on formerly fluid, communal, and egalitarian societies (Chanock 1985: 46–7)' (Berry 1993: 103).

4 It was not the first time in Mandinka history that men 'fought back' against assisted attempts to erode their domestic powers. The notes of one colonial agricultural administrator show that also on an earlier occasion men had contested women's right to clear and claim virgin swamp land. Men had argued that 'if women mark the land and divide it, it will become "women's property", so that when the husband dies or when he divorces his wife, the wife will still retain the land, which is wrong. Women must not own land' (Carney 1988: 67).

5 Combining both rice field and house compound land, the details of the reform in Nadur village were as follows: '14 households lost land totalling 105.83 acres to their former tenants, while 145 households gained 102.14 acres, averaging 0.70 acres each. One household neither lost nor gained land, and 10 households in the 1987 sample derived their holdings from partitions of the households in the 1971 sample' (Franke 1992: 90).

6 The situation in Nadur is not unlike that in Arunpur, North India (Sharma 1985), where those who benefited from the abolition of landlordship, mostly by fraudulent means, are now having to make sure that they themselves are not ending up on the wrong side of the law. These 'nouveaux riches', like the many landowners who survived the reform (which was less thorough in Arunpur), are now granting

> part of their land to labourers as part of their wage. To prevent any legal tangles whereby the tiller may eventually claim the land he works as his own, the plot is often changed each year. The system of rotating the sub-let land is so flexible that it escapes the law and labourers are reluctant to complain for fear of losing their jobs and land (Sharma 1985: 68–70).

And so the cycle of indebtedness and bonded labour continues.

Chapter 4 Labour Organization on Smallholder Farms: Structure and Diversity

1 The GR package in the Philippines revolved around two innovations: first, the broadcasting of germinated seed directly on to the paddyfield and, second, controlling weeds with herbicides. Popular since the late 1970s, these innovations have enabled larger farmers 'to eliminate the labor cost of uprooting seedlings, hand transplanting, and weeding plus the problems of labor organization and discipline' (Banzon-Bautista 1989: 138).

2 In Java today, 'some 3 million rural households (one third of all farm operators, one fifth of all rural households) farm almost four-fifths of all irrigated riceland' (Hüsken and White 1989: 253). This skewed pattern of land ownership is visible, for instance in the village of Kali Loro, a relatively isolated area in south-central Java, where 6 per cent of the population owns more than half of all the irrigated rice land (*sawah*) and the rest of the population is split in roughly equal numbers between landless and small farmers (Stoler 1977). The latter, however, work farms that are too small to produce their own basic rice requirements. This implies that over 75 per cent of the villagers need to meet their subsistence needs through sources other than ownership and cultivation of rice land. Among these other sources are agricultural wage labour, various forms of market trade (which hardly pay) and garden cultivation for sale (Stoler 1977: 680).

3 Sharma argues that the devaluation of women's work is not confined to the high-caste/class women: 'By devaluing women's work and independence in production and imputing a higher status to those who are the most dependent and confined to reproduction activities, patriarchal ideology and relations within the household have reinforced the material subordination of rural women of all classes' (Sharma 1985: 83).

4 Research among poor hill women in Nepal has given similar results. Such women may be active in the market economy, as they belong to communities that are not too strictly orthodox, yet their living conditions are dire (Pradhan 1985: 263). Like their menfolk, poor hill women face exceedingly difficult times when working for a wage, not least because of the fast-declining production levels. Falling production depresses wage rates, both in the Tarai and in the high hills. It is estimated, writes Macfarlane,

> that the maize equivalent (the poor eat maize) of wage rates fell by roughly 30–60 per cent in the period 1968–9 to 1976–7 alone (Seddon 1987: 159). In the sample hill village, there has been an *approximate halving on the returns to labour during the last twenty years*, thus a halving in the standard of living. For instance, in 1970 it took just over a day's work to earn enough to buy a chicken. In 1990 it takes two or three days work to do so. (Macfarlane 1993: 108; emphasis added)

For the poor women and men who increasingly depend on income earned through casual seasonal wage labour, these deteriorating returns on their labour are bad news indeed. Unlike poor agricultural wage labourers in some parts of India, Nepal's rural poor do not have the benefit of more work overall.

In contrast to India, where production increases are regularly reported for 'advanced' agricultural zones, Nepal has seen a dramatic drop in food production. The past three decades have witnessed major transformations in the countryside. Most alarming has been the transformation of Nepal's middle hills from a grain surplus region to one known for its deficit. The future is not bright: in 1985 Nepal's food deficit was expected to increase tenfold by the year 2000 (Macfarlane 1993: 107). Despite heightened public investment in agriculture and infrastructure, the Tarai, Nepal's 'grain basket', also experienced rapid decline in rice production (Seddon 1993: 130), a slump caused by acute population pressure and environmental crisis. Nepal lost 50 per cent of its forest cover between 1961 and 1971 (Macfarlane 1993: 107).

For the central hill village where he collected data between 1970 and 1990, Macfarlane writes:

> there has been an almost 50 per cent drop in grain production as the land loses its fertility and goes out of production. In 1970 most families had enough rice for themselves and practically no rice was bought outside the village. By 1990 only a quarter of the villagers had enough rice for their needs; rice had become a luxury. (Macfarlane 1993: 108)

Livestock had also dropped by half, which meant less manure, poorer crops and the general worsening of a diet once rich in animal products (Macfarlane 1993: 108).

5   In the past, to be food-secure the landless would work not only for patrons, but also outside the village, since patrons gave an insufficient share.

6   Hüsken and White (1989) make the same point: it is poor women who suffered most from the introduction of cash in rice harvesting: 'Both men and women have been affected by these [technological] changes [introduced under the GR], but their impact on women in landless and near-landless households has perhaps been greater due to their greater reliance on wage incomes in transplanting, harvesting, and post-harvest work' (Hüsken and White 1989: 255).

7   Mencher notes better conditions for Kerala State, where women pull out the seedlings and control both harvesting and threshing (Mencher 1985: 360–1). Kerala men do not compete with women, Mencher suggests, because they get more casual non-agricultural work (1985: 361). Still, the situation for women workers in south India as a whole was inferior to West Bengal, where women got more work throughout the year and 'far more work in post-harvest activities' (Mencher 1985: 361).

8   While in this village the women harvesters could restore their position in harvesting the rice, the use of the sickle definitely reduced the number of harvesters to as little as one-third of the number of harvesters using the *ani-ani* (Wijaya 1985: 182).

Chapter 5 Playing the Food Market: Actual Markets, Moralities and Social Engineering

1 Fittingly, Vaughan recalls a tale by Samuel Johnson, the Christian Yoruba spokesman of the 1890s (cf. Barber 1995) in which a young woman bartered her mother to a trader for salt. The crime was so horrific that, on discovering it, the father/husband substituted the daughter for her mother. The moral of the story: people prepared to sell their mothers should not take part in the market; certain affective relations are by definition not to be commoditized.

2 The role of the anthropologist Audrey Richards in the making of this Bemba identity was considerable. Not only did Richards (1939) exaggerate the association between Bemba chiefly authority, Bemba ethnicity and the sexual division of labour, but she also presented the full picture as traditional and timeless (Moore and Vaughan 1994: 8, 20). There was also dilution, as 'much of the variability described by ecological and agricultural scientists was . . . lost as a result of the anxiety of officials to define and control what was, in fact, an enormously complex set of agricultural practices' (1994: 25).

3 Specifically, '*citemene* gardens provided some insurance against household food deficits and, importantly, supplied the central ingredient for beer-brewing, which, in turn, continued to constitute an important mechanism for gaining access to extrahousehold labor' (Moore and Vaughan 1994: 139).

4 About these non-contractual obligations, Harriss-White writes:

> . . . these mostly verbal contracts are laden with 'intangibles', with mutual, non-contractual obligations (e.g. for the lender and purchaser: to lend additional small quantities for urgent need, to distribute 'perks', to give advice and act as a social and political intermediary; for the borrower and seller: to sell the entire marketed surplus or raw materials to the lender, to deposit cash, to labour, to be loyal). These unsymmetrical mutual obligations can be construed as incentives, or as forms of oppression. Alternatively, they are relationships rooted in the uncertainties of future outcomes (Harriss-White 1996: 35).

Chapter 7 Famine Relief, Famine Prevention: Whose Analysis? Whose Solutions? Whose Patronage?

1 'At the peak of the crisis [in Maharashtra] nearly 5 million labourers were employed on public works throughout the state. During the twelve months preceding 1973 (the peak year of drought), relief workers generated nearly one billion person days of employment. In the more severely drought-affected districts, the contribution of wage income from employment on public works to total income was well above 50 per cent for most villages' (Drèze and Sen 1989: 129).

2 Precedents do exist, though, such as Oxfam's debate on its work during the 1979 famine in Cambodia (cf. Charny 1993).

Chapter 8 Attractive Simplicity? The Shape of Modern Agricultural Research and Policy

1 Among the clones released for on-farm trials in three regions of the Peruvian Andes (Mantaro, Cunas, Yanamarca), farmers have praised G-3 for its ability to meet market requirements, while S-24–73 was liked because of its uniform shape, which reduces labour input and cost at the time of harvest. S-24–73 can thus be praised as 'satisfying household needs' (Prain et al. 1992: 59–67).

2 In a revealing account of profits, Pat Mooney, executive director of the Rural Advancement Foundation International (RAFI), shows how absolutely vast the profits are that go to the North. Most official estimates, Mooney believes, are still conservative, yet all illustrate that the contribution of Third World farmers to the North is colossal (Mooney 1993: 175–8). Annual returns on investment in the North are staggering. IRRI's 1990 budget of $US30.6 million offered the North a twenty-two fold return on its annual investment. The North's returns for investment in CIAT in that same year were fourfold, while those for investment in CIMMYT were a hundredfold (Mooney 1993: 176, 178).

Bibliography

Adam, Michel (1980) 'Manioc, Rente Foncière et Situation des Femmes dans les Environs de Brazaville (République Populaire du Congo)', *Cahiers d'Etudes Africaines* 20 (1/2): 5–48.

Agarwal, Bina (1994a) *A Field of One's Own: Gender and Land Rights in South Asia*. Cambridge: Cambridge University Press.

Agarwal, Bina (1994b) 'Gender, Resistance and Land: Interlinked struggles over resources and meanings in South Asia', *Journal of Peasant Studies* 22 (1): 81–125.

Ahmed, Akbar S. and Cris N. Shore (1995) 'Is Anthropology Relevant to the Contemporary World?', in A. Akbar and C. Shore (eds) *The Future of Anthropology: Its Relevance to the Contemporary World*. London and Atlantic Highlands, NJ: Athlone, pp. 12–45.

Alexander, Jennifer (1987) *Trade, Traders, and Trading in Rural Java*. Singapore: Oxford University Press.

Amanor, Kojo, Kate Wellard, Walter de Boef and Anthony Bebbington (1993) 'Introduction', in W. de Boef, K. Amanor and K. Wellard, with A. Bebbington (eds) *Cultivating Knowledge: Genetic Diversity, Farmer Experimentation and Crop Research*. London: IT, pp. 1–13.

Amin, Samir (1976) *Unequal Development: An Essay on the Social Formations of Peripheral Capitalism*. New York: Monthly Review Press.

Anan Ganjanapan (1984) 'The Partial Commercialisation of Rice Production in Northern Thailand'. Ithaca: Cornell University, Ph.D. thesis.

Anan Ganjanapan (1989) 'Conflicts over the Deployment and Control of Labor in a Northern Thai Village', in Gillian Hart et al. (eds) *Agrarian Transformations: Local Processes and the State in Southeast Asia*. Berkeley: University of California Press, pp. 98–124.

Anderson, W. T. and D. Helm (1979) 'The Physician–Patient Encounter: A process of reality negotiation', in Gartly Jaco (ed.) *Patients, Physicians and Healers*. New York: The Free Press, pp. 259–71.

Appadurai, Arjun (1981) 'Gastro-politics in Hindu South Asia', *American Ethnologist* 8 (3): 494–511.

Appadurai, Arjun (1986) 'Introduction: Commodities and the politics of value', in A. Appadurai (ed.) *The Social Life of Things: Commodities in Cultural Perspective*. Cambridge: Cambridge University Press, pp. 3–63.

Apthorpe, Raymond (1984) 'Agricultures and Strategies', in E. J. Clay and B. B. Schaffer (eds) *Room for Manoeuvre: An Exploration of Public Policy for Rural Development*. London: Heinemann–Gower, pp. 127–41.

Arce, Alberto (1999) 'The Language of the Market and the Representation of Development', in Alberto Arce and Norman Long (eds) *Anthropology, Development and Modernities: Exploring Discourse, Counter-tendencies and Violence*. London: Routledge.

Arce, Alberto and Norman Long (1992) 'The Dynamics of Knowledge: Interfaces between bureaucrats and peasants', in Norman Long and Ann Long (eds) *Battlefields of Knowledge: The Interlocking of Theory and Practice in Social Research and Development*. London: Routledge, pp. 211–46.

Arce, Alberto and Norman Long (eds) (1999) *Anthropology, Development and Modernities: Exploring Discourse, Counter-tendencies and Violence*. London: Routledge.

Arnold, David (1988) *Famine: Social Crisis and Historical Change*. Oxford: Basil Blackwell.

Babb, Florence E. (1987) 'From the Field to the Cooking Pot: Economic crisis and the threat to marketers in Peru', *Ethnology* 26 (2): 137–49.

Bantebya-Kyomuhendo, G. (1994) *The Health Care Provider Woman Client Relationship: Health Workers' Perspectives*. Geneva: WHO/TDR.

Banzon-Bautista, Cynthia (1989) 'The Saudi Connection: Agrarian change in a Pampangan village', in Gillian Hart et al. (eds) *Agrarian Transformations: Local Processes and the State in Southeast Asia*. Berkeley: University of California Press, pp. 144–58.

Barber, Karen (1995) 'Money, Self-realization, and the Person in Yoruba Texts', in J. Guyer (ed.) *Money Matters*. Portsmouth, NH and London: Heinemann and James Currey, pp. 205–24.

Bardhan, K. (1993) 'Social Classes and Gender in India: The structure of the differences in the condition of women', in A. Clark (ed.) *Gender and Political Economy: Explorations of South Asian Systems*. Delhi: Oxford University Press, pp. 146–78.

Barker, Jonathan (1989) *African Communities Under Stress: Peasant Farmers and the State in Africa*. Cambridge: Cambridge University Press.

Barnes, Carolyn (1984) 'Differentiation by Sex among Small-scale Farming Households in Kenya', *Rural Africana* 15/16: 41–63.

Barth, Gerald A. (1984) 'Employment and Earnings in Food Marketing in a Philippine Regional Center', *Human Organization* 43 (1): 38–43.

Barthes, Roland (1992/1957) *Mythologies*. New York: Noonday Press.

Barton, T. and G. Wamai (1994) *Equity and Vulnerability: A Situation Analysis of Women, Adolescents and Children in Uganda*. Kampala: CHDC/UNICEF.

Bates, Robert (1981) *Markets and States in Tropical Africa*. Berkeley and Los Angeles: University of California Press.

Baudrillard, Jean (1975) *The Mirror of Production*. St Louis, Mo.: Telos Press.

Baudrillard, Jean (1981) *For a Critique of the Political Economy of the Sign*. St Louis, Mo.: Telos Press.

Beck, Tony (1989) 'Survival Strategies and Power amongst the Poorest in a

West Bengal Village', *IDS Bulletin* 20 (2): 23–32.

Belsky, Jill M. (1993) 'Household Food Security, Farms, Trees and Agroforestry', *Human Organization* 52 (2): 130–41.

Beneria, Lourdes and Gita Sen (1981) 'Accumulation, Reproduction and Women's Role in Economic Development: Boserup revisited', *Signs, Development and the Sexual Division of Labor* 7 (2): 279–98. Special issue.

Bennett, Jon (with Susan George) (1987) *The Hunger Machine: The Politics of Food*. Cambridge: Polity Press. (A Channel 4 book in association with Yorkshire Television.)

Berg, Trygve (1993) 'The Science of Plant Breeding: Support or alternative to traditional practice?', in Walter de Boef et al. (eds) *Cultivating Knowledge: Genetic Diversity, Farmer Experimentation and Crop Research*. London: Intermediate Technology Publications, pp. 72–7.

Berger, M. (1989) 'Giving Women Credit: The strengths and limitations of credit as a tool for alleviating poverty', *World Development* 17 (7): 1017–32.

Bernstein, Henry (1977) 'Notes on Capital and Peasantry', *Review of African Political Economy* 10: 60–73.

Bernstein, Henry (1990) 'Taking the Part of Peasants?', in H. Bernstein et al. (eds) *The Food Question*. London: Earthscan, pp. 69–79.

Bernstein, Henry (1994) '"And Now Who Plans Its Future?": Land in South Africa after Apartheid', in C. Hann (ed.) *When History Accelerates: Essays on Rapid Social Change, Complexity and Creativity*. London: Athlone Press, pp. 161–87.

Bernstein, Henry (1996a) 'South Africa's Agrarian Question: Extreme and exceptional?', *Journal of Peasant Studies* 23 (3): 1–52.

Bernstein, Henry (1996b) 'The Political Economy of the Maize Filière', *Journal of Peasant Studies* 23(3): 120–45.

Berry, Sara (1993) *No Condition is Permanent: The Social Dynamics of Agrarian Change in Sub-Saharan Africa*. Madison: The University of Wisconsin Press.

Berry, Sara (1995) 'Stable Prices, Unstable Values: Some thoughts on monetization and the meaning of transaction in West African economies', in J. Guyer (ed.) *Money Matters*. Portsmouth, NH and London: Heinemann and James Currey, pp. 299–313.

Bista, Dor Bahadur (1991) *Fatalism and Development: Nepal's Struggle for Modernization*. Calcutta: Orient Longman.

Bohannan, Paul (1953) *The Tiv of Central Nigeria*. London: International African Institute.

Bohannan, Paul and Laura Bohannan (1968) *Tiv Economy*. Evanston, Ill.: Northwestern University Press.

Boserup, Esther (1970) *Women's Role in Economic Development*. New York: St Martin's Press.

Box, Louk (1989) 'Virgilio's Theorem: A method for adaptive agricultural research', in R. Chambers et al. (eds) (1989) *Farmer First*. London: Intermediate Technology Publications, pp. 61–7.

Bramall, Chris (1995) 'Origins of the Agricultural "Miracle": Some evidence from Sichuan', *The China Quarterly* 143: 731–55.

Bratton, Michael (1980) *The Local Politics of Rural Development: Peasant and Party-State in Zambia*. Hanover, NH: University Press of New England.

Bray, Francesca (1983) 'Patterns of Evolution in Rice-Growing Societies', *Journal of Peasant Studies* 11: 3–33.

Bray, Francesca (1986) *The Rice Economies*. Oxford: Basil Blackwell.

Bray, Francesca (1991) 'Rice Economies: The rise and fall of China's communes in East Asian perspective', in Jan Breman and Sudipto Mundle (eds) *Rural Transformation in Asia*. Oxford: Oxford University Press, pp. 195–217.

Brown, Lynn R., Hilary Feldstein, Lawrence Haddad, Christine Pena, and Agnes Quisumbing (1995) 'Generating Food Security: Women as producers, gatekeepers and shock absorbers'. IFPRI Briefing Paper prepared for the Beijing Conference on Women.

Byres, Terry J. (1972) 'The Dialectic of India's Green Revolution', *South Asian Review* 5: 99–116.

Callear, Diana (1985) 'Who Wants To Be A Peasant? Food production in a labour-exporting area of Zimbabwe', in J. Pottier (ed.) *Food Systems in Central and Southern Africa*. London: School of Oriental and African Studies, pp. 217–30.

Cammann, L. (ed.) (1992) *Traditional Marketing Systems*. Munich: DSE.

Caplan, Pat (ed.) (1997) *Food, Health and Identity*. London: Routledge.

Carney, Judith (1988) 'Struggles over Land and Crops in an Irrigated Rice Scheme: The Gambia', in Jean Davison (ed.) *Agriculture, Women, and Land: The African Experience*. Boulder, Co.: Westview Press, pp. 59–78.

Chambers, Robert (1986) *Normal Professionalism, New Paradigms and Development*. Falmer, Sussex: IDS Discussion Paper 227.

Chambers, Robert et al. (eds) (1989) *Farmer First*. London: Intermediate Technology Publications.

Chanock, M (1985) *Law, Custom and Social Order: The Colonial Experience in Zambia and Malawi*. Cambridge: Cambridge University Press.

Charny, Joel (1993) 'Coping with Crisis: Oxfam America's Disaster Responses', in John Osgood Field (ed.) *The Challenge of Famine: Recent Experience, Lessons Learned*. West Hartford, Co.: Kumarian Press, pp. 147–71.

Chen, M. A. (1991) *Coping with Seasonality and Drought*. Delhi: Sage.

Chimwaza, B. M. (1982) 'Food and Nutrition in Malawi'. London: University of London, Ph.D. Thesis.

Clark, Gracia (1991) 'Food Traders and Food Security in Ghana', in R. E. Downs, Donna O. Kerner and Stephen P. Reyna (eds) *The Political Economy of African Famine*. Philadelphia: Gordon and Breach Science Publishers, pp. 227–56.

Clay, Edward (1985) 'The 1974 and 1984 Floods in Bangladesh: From famine to food crisis management', *Food Policy* 10 (3): 202–6.

Clay, Edward (1997) *Food Security: A Status Review of the Literature*. London, ODI: Research Report, March.

Cochrane, Glynn (1979) *The Cultural Appraisal of Development Projects*. New York: Praeger Special Studies.

Colletta, Nat J. (1990) 'Tradition for Change', in Mathur Hari Mohan (ed.) *The Human Dimension of Development: Perspectives from Anthropology*. New Delhi: Ashok Kumar Mittal Concept Publishing Company, pp. 85–118.

Colson, Elizabeth (1971) 'The Impact of the Colonial Period on the Definition of Land Rights', in Victor Turner (ed.) *Profiles of Change: African Society and Colonial Rule*. Vol. 3 of L. Gann and P. Duignan (eds) *Coloni-*

alism in Africa. Cambridge: Cambridge University Press, pp. 193–215.

Cooper, D., R. Vellve and H. Hobbelink (eds) (1992) *Growing Diversity: Genetic Resources and Local Food Security*. London: Intermediate Technology Publications.

Counihan, Carole and Penny van Esterik (eds) (1997) *Food and Culture: A Reader*. London: Routledge.

Cousins, Ben (1996) 'Livestock Production and Common Property Struggles in South Africa's Agrarian Reform', *Journal of Peasant Studies* 23 (3): 166–208.

Croll, Elisabeth (1981) 'Socialist Development Experiences: Women in rural production and reproduction in the Soviet Union, China, Cuba and Tanzania', *Signs (Journal of Women in Culture and Society)* 7(2): 361–99.

Croll, Elisabeth (1983a) *The Family Rice Bowl: Food and the Domestic Economy in China*. London: Zed Books.

Croll, Elisabeth (1983b) 'Production versus Reproduction: A threat to China's development strategy', *World Development* 11 (6): 467–81.

Croll, Elisabeth (1994) *From Heaven to Earth: Images and Experiences of Development in China*. London: Routledge.

Crow, Ben (1986) *US Policies in Bangladesh: The Making and the Breaking of Famine*. Milton Keynes: The Open University, Development Policy and Practice: Working Paper 4.

Da Corta, L. and S. Devereux (1991) *True Generosity or False Charity? A Note on the Ideological Foundations of Famine Relief Policies*, Centro Studi Luca d'Agliano, Turin and Queen Elizabeth House, Oxford, Development Studies Working Paper 40.

Davies, Susanna and Melissa Leach (1991) 'Globalism versus Villagism: Food security and environment at national and international levels', *IDS Bulletin* 22 (3): 43–50.

Davis, John (1996) 'An Anthropologist's View of Exchange', *Oxford Development Studies* 24 (1): 47–60.

Davison, Jean (1988) 'Land and Women's Agricultural Production: The context', in J. Davison (ed.) *Women, Land and Agriculture: The African Experience*. Boulder, Co.: Westview Press, pp. 1–32.

Davison, Jean (1993) 'Tenacious Women: Clinging to Banja household production in the face of changing gender relations in Malawi', *Journal of Southern African Studies* 19 (3): 405–21.

De Boeck, Filip (1994) 'When Hunger Goes Around The Land: Hunger, famine and the catalysing of societal and cultural order in Luunda land', *Man* 29 (2): 257–82.

de Garine, Igor (1971) 'Food Is Not Just Something To Eat', *Ceres* 4: 46–51.

Devereux, Stephen (1993) *Theories of Famine*. Hemel Hempstead: Harvester Wheatsheaf.

de Waal, Alex (1989) *Famine That Kills*. Oxford: Oxford University Press.

de Waal, Alex (1994) 'Dangerous Precedents? Famine relief in Somalia 1991–1993', in Joanna Macrae and Anthony Zwi (eds) *War and Hunger: Rethinking International Responses to Complex Emergencies*. London: Zed Books, with Save the Children (UK), pp. 139–59.

de Waal, Alex (1997) *Famine Crimes: Politics and the Disaster Industry in Africa*. London: African Rights and the International African Institute, in association with James Currey (Oxford).

de Waal, Alex and Rakiya Omaar (1994). *Humanitarianism Unbound*. London: African Rights, Discussion Paper 5.

DeWalt, Billie and David Barkin (1991) 'Mexico's Two Green Revolutions: Feed for food', in Della E. McMillan (ed.) *Anthropology and Food Policy: Human Dimensions of Food Policy in Africa and Latin America*. Athens and London: The University of Georgia Press for the Southern Anthropological Society, pp. 12–39.

DeWalt, Kathleen (1991) 'Integrating Nutritional Concerns into Adaptive Small Farm Research Programs', in Della E. McMillan (ed.) *Anthropology and Food Policy: Human Dimensions of Food Policy in Africa and Latin America*. Athens and London: The University of Georgia Press, pp. 126–44.

Dilley, R. (ed.) (1992) *Contesting Markets: Analyses of Ideology, Discourse and Practice*. Edinburgh: Edinburgh University Press.

Doughty, Paul L. (1986) 'Peace, Food and Equity in Peru', *Urban Anthropology* 15 (1/2): 45–59.

Doughty, Paul L. (1991) 'The Food Game in Latin America', in Della E. McMillan (ed.) *Anthropology and Food Policy: Human Dimensions of Food Policy in Africa and Latin America*. Athens and London: The University of Georgia Press for the Southern Anthropological Society, pp. 145–66.

Douglas, Mary and Baron Isherwood (1981) *The World of Goods*. New York: Basic Books.

Doyle, J. (1985) *Altered Harvest*. New York: Viking.

Drèze, Jean and Amartya Sen (1989) *Hunger and Public Action*. Oxford: Clarendon Press.

Drinkwater, Michael (1994) 'Knowledge, Consciousness and Prejudice: Adaptive agricultural research in Zambia', in Ian Scoones and John Thompson (eds) *Beyond Farmer First*. London: Intermediate Technology Publications, pp. 32–41.

D'Souza, Frances (1988) 'Famine: Social security and an analysis of vulnerability', in G. A. Harrison (ed.) *Famine*. Oxford: Clarendon Press, pp. 1–56.

Dzingirai, Vupenyu (1992) 'Accumulation and Response: A Study of Peasant Response to State Exploitation'. Harare: University of Zimbabwe, M.Phil. thesis.

Ellis, Frank (1988) *Peasant Economics: Farm Households and Agrarian Development*. Cambridge: Cambridge University Press.

Ellis, Frank (1990) 'The Rice Market and its Management in Indonesia', *IDS Bulletin* 21 (3): 44–51.

El Sammani (1990) 'Drought and Famine in Sudan: Implications for socioeconomic development', in ACARTSOD *Understanding Africa's Food Problems: Social Policy Perspectives*. London: Hans Zell Publishers, ACARTSOD Monograph Series, African Social Challenges 1, pp. 173–203.

Elson, Diane (1991) 'Male Bias in Macro-economics: The case of structural adjustment', in D. Elson (ed.) *Male Bias in the Development Process*. Manchester: Manchester University Press, pp. 1–28.

Englund, Harri (1999) 'The Self in Self-Interest: Land, labour and temporalities in Malawi's agrarian change', *Africa* 69 (1): 139–59.

Escobar, Arturo (1991) 'Anthropology and the Development Encounter: The making and marketing of development anthropology', *American Ethnologist* 18 (4): 658–81.

Escobar, Arturo (1995) *Encountering Development: The Making and Unmaking of the Third World.* Princeton: Princeton University Press.

Evers, Hans-Dieter (1994a) 'The Trader's Dilemma: A theory of the social transformation of markets and society', in H. D. Evers and H. Schrader (eds) *The Moral Economy of Trade: Ethnicity and Developing Markets.* London: Routledge, pp. 7–14.

Evers, Hans-Dieter (1994b) 'Javanese Petty Trade', in H. D. Evers and H. Schrader (eds) *The Moral Economy of Trade: Ethnicity and Developing Markets.* London: Routledge, pp. 68–75.

Evers, Hans-Dieter, Jayarani Pavadarayan and Heiko Schrader (1994) 'The Chettiar Moneylenders in Singapore', in H. D. Evers and H. Schrader (eds) *The Moral Economy of Trade: Ethnicity and Developing Markets.* London: Routledge, pp. 198–207.

Fairhead, James (1990) 'Fields of Struggle: Towards a Social History of Farming Knowledge and Practice in a Bwisha Community, Kivu, Zaire'. London: University of London, SOAS, Ph.D. thesis.

Fairhead, James (1991) 'Methodological Notes on Exploring Indigenous Technical Knowledge and Management of Crop Health', *RRA Notes* 14. London: IIED (International Institute for Environment and Development).

Fairhead, James (1992a) 'Paths of Authority: Roads, the state and the market in Eastern Zaire', *European Journal of Development* 4 (2): 17–35.

Fairhead, James (1992b) *Indigenous Technical Knowledge and Natural Resources Management in Sub-Saharan Africa: A Critical Overview.* Paper commissioned by the Social Science Council, New York.

Fairhead, James (1993) 'Representing Knowledge: The "new farmer" in research fashions', in J. Pottier (ed.) *Practising Development: Social Science Perspectives.* London: Routledge, pp. 187–204.

Fairhead, James (1994) 'Healthy Production and Reproduction: Agricultural, medical and linguistic pluralism in a Bwisha community, Eastern Zaire', in R. Fardon and G. Furniss (eds) *African Languages, Development and the State.* London: Routledge, pp. 122–41.

Fairhead, James and Melissa Leach (1996) *Misreading the African Landscape: Society and Ecology in a Forest-Savanna Mosaic.* Cambridge: Cambridge University Press.

FAO (Food and Agriculture Organization) (1983) *World Food Security: A Reappraisal of the Concepts and Approaches.* Director General's Report. Rome: FAO.

FAO (1996) *Synthesis of the Technical Background Documents.* Rome, World Food Summit, 13–17 November 1996. Rome: FAO.

Fegan, Brian (1989) 'The Philippines: Agrarian stagnation under a decaying regime', in Gillian Hart et al. (eds) (1989) *Agrarian Transformations: Local Processes and the State in Southeast Asia.* Berkeley: University of California Press, pp. 125–43.

Ferguson, James (1990) *The Anti-Politics Machine: Development, Depoliticisation and Bureaucratic Power in Lesotho.* Cambridge: Cambridge University Press.

Finan, Timothy J. (1988) 'Market Relationship and Market Performance in Northeast Brazil', *American Ethnologist* 15 (4): 694–709.

Firth, Raymond (1973) 'Food Symbolism in a Pre-industrial Society', in his *Symbols: Public and Private*. London: Routledge and Kegan Paul, pp. 249–75.

Firth, Raymond (1981) 'Engagement and Detachment: Reflections on applying social anthropology to human affairs', *Human Organization* 40 (3): 193–201.

Fleuret, Anne (1986) 'Indigenous Responses to Drought in Sub-Saharan Africa', *Disasters* 10 (3): 224–9.

Fogg, W. (1940) 'Villages, Tribal Markets and Towns: Some considerations concerning urban development in the Spanish and international zones of Morocco', *Sociological Review* 32: 85–107.

Fogg, W. (1941) 'Changes in the Lay-out, Characteristics, and Function of a Moroccan Tribal Market, Consequent on European Control', *Man* 41: 104–8.

Foucault, Michel (1986) 'Disciplinary Power and Subjection', in Steven Lukes (ed.) *Power*. Oxford: Basil Blackwell, pp. 229–42.

Foucault, Michel (1991) 'On Governmentality', in G. Burchell, C. Gordon and P. Miller (eds) *The Foucault Effect: Studies in Governmentality*. London: Harvester Wheatsheaf, pp. 87–104.

Fowler, Cary, Eva Lachkoviks, Pat Mooney and Hope Sand (1988) *The Laws of Life: Another Development and the New Biotechnologies. Development Dialogue* 1–2. Special issue.

Fowler, Cary and Pat Mooney (1990) *The Threatened Gene: Food, Politics and the Loss of Genetic Diversity*. Tucson: University of Arizona Press.

Franke, Richard (1992) 'Land Reform versus Inequality in Nadur Village Kerala', *Journal of Anthropological Research* 48 (2): 81–116.

Fujisaka, Sam (1992) 'Farmer Knowledge and Sustainability in Rice-Farming Systems: Blending science and indigenous innovation', in Joyce Lewinger Moock and Robert Rhoades (eds) *Diversity, Farmer Knowledge and Sustainability*. Ithaca and London: Cornell University Press, pp. 69–83.

Fujisaka, Sam (1994) 'Will Farmer Participatory Research Survive in the International Agricultural Research Centres?', in Ian Scoones and John Thompson (eds) *Beyond Farmer First: Rural People's Knowledge, Agricultural Research and Extension Practice*. London: Intermediate Technology Publications, pp. 227–35.

Gardner, Katy and David Lewis (1996) *Anthropology, Development and the Post-Modern Challenge*. London: Pluto.

Gatter, Philip (1993) 'Anthropology in Farming Systems Research: A participant observer in Zambia', in J. Pottier (ed.) *Practising Development: Social Science Perspectives*. London: Routledge, pp. 153–86.

Geertz, Clifford (1963) *Agricultural Involution: The Process of Ecological Change in Indonesia*. Berkeley: University of California Press.

Gell, Alfred (1986) 'Newcomers to the World of Goods', in A. Appadurai (ed.) *The Social Life of Things: Commodities in Cultural Perspective*. Cambridge: Cambridge University Press, pp. 110–38.

George, Susan (1976) *How the Other Half Dies: The Real Reasons for World Hunger*. Harmondsworth: Penguin.

Gerke, Solvay (1992) *Social Change and Life Planning of Rural Javanese Women*. Bielefeld, Germany: Bielefeld Studies on the Sociology of Development 51.

Gibson, James and Daniela Weinberg (1980) 'In Vino Communitas: Wine and identity in a Swiss Alpine village', *Anthropological Quarterly* 53 (2): 111–21.

Giddens, Anthony (1995) 'Epilogue: Notes on the future of anthropology', in Akbar S. Ahmed and Cris N. Shore (eds) (1995) *The Future of Anthropology: Its Relevance to the Contemporary World*. London and Atlantic Highlands, NJ: Athlone, pp. 272–7.

Goetz, A. M. and R. Sen Gupta (1996) 'Who Takes The Credit?: Gender, power and control over loan use in rural credit programmes in Bangladesh', *World Development* 24 (1): 45–63.

Goody, Jack (1958) *The Development Cycle in Domestic Groups*. Cambridge: Cambridge University Press.

Goody, Jack (1976) *Production and Reproduction: A Contemporary Study of the Domestic Domain*. Cambridge: Cambridge University Press.

Gould, Jeremy and Achim von Oppen (1994) 'Introduction: Representing "the market"', *Sociologia Ruralis* 23 (1): 3–12. Special issue: *Of Rhetoric and Market: The 'Liberalization' of Food Trade in East Africa*.

Greeley, Martin (1991) 'Environmental and Food Security Objectives in Rural Project Design', *IDS Bulletin* 22 (3): 35–42.

Guyer, Jane I. (1986) 'Intra-household Processes and Farming Systems Research: Perspectives from anthropology', in Joyce Moock (ed.) *Understanding Africa's Rural Households and Farming Systems: Perspectives from Anthropology*. Boulder, Co. and London: Westview Press, pp. 92–104.

Guyer, Jane I. (ed.) (1987) *Feeding African Cities: Studies in Regional Social History*. Manchester: Manchester University Press, for IAI.

Guyer, Jane (1996) 'Diversity at Different Levels: Farm and community in Western Nigeria', *Africa* 66 (1): 71–89.

Guyer, Jane and Pauline Peters (1987) 'Introduction', in 'Conceptualizing the Household: Issues of theory and policy in Africa', *Development and Change* 18 (2): 197–214.

Guyer, Jane and Paul Richards (1996) 'The Invention of Biodiversity: Social perspectives on the management of biological variety in Africa', *Africa* 66 (1): 1–13.

Haakonsson, N. T. (1985) 'Why Do Gusii Women Get Married? A study of cultural constraints and women's strategies in a rural community in Kenya', *Folk* 27: 89–114.

Hansen, Art (1991) 'Learning from Experience: Implementing farming systems research and extension in the Malawi agricultural research project', in Della E. McMillan (ed.) *Anthropology and Food Policy: Human Dimensions of Food Policy in Africa and Latin America*. Athens and London: The University of Georgia Press, pp. 40–65.

Hansen, Art (1994) 'The Illusion of Local Sustainability and Self-sufficiency: Famine in a border area of northwestern Zambia', *Human Organization* 53 (1): 11–20.

Harrell-Bond, Barbara (1986) *Imposing Aid: Emergency Assistance to Refugees*. Oxford: Oxford University Press.

Harriss, Barbara (1988) 'Limitations of the "Lessons from India"', in D. Curtis, M. Hubbard and A. Shepherd (eds) *Preventing Famine: Policies and Prospects for Africa*. London and New York: Routledge, pp. 157–70.

Harriss, Barbara (1990) 'The Intrafamily Distribution of Hunger in South Asia', in J. Drèze and A. K. Sen (eds) *The Political Economy of Hunger*. Oxford: Clarendon Press, pp. 351–424.

Harriss, Barbara (1992) 'Real Foodgrain Markets and State Intervention in India', *European Journal of Development* 4 (2): 61–81.

Harriss, John (1977) 'Implications of Changes in Agriculture for Social Relations at the Village Level: The case of Randam', in B. H. Farmer (ed.) *Green Revolution? Technology and Change in Rice-growing Areas of Tamil Nadu and Sri Lanka*. London: MacMillan, pp. 225–45.

Harriss-White, Barbara (1996) 'Free Market Romanticism in an Era of Deregulation', *Oxford Development Studies* 24 (1): 27–41.

Hart, Gillian, Andrew Turton and Benjamin White (eds) (1989) *Agrarian Transformations: Local Processes and the State in Southeast Asia*. Berkeley: University of California Press.

Hart, Gillian, Andrew Turton and Benjamin White (1989) 'Introduction', in G. Hart et al. (eds) *Agrarian Transformations: Local Processes and the State in Southeast Asia*. Berkeley: University of California Press, pp. 1–11.

Hartmann, Betsy (1987) *Reproductive Rights and Wrongs: The Global Politics of Population Control and Contraceptive Choice*. New York: Harper and Row.

Haswell, M. (1981) *Energy for Subsistence*. London: Macmillan.

Haugerud, Angélique (1988) 'Food Surplus Production, Wealth and Farmers' Strategies in Kenya', in R. Cohen (ed.) *Satisfying Africa's Food Needs*. Boulder, Co.: Lynne Rienner, pp. 153–89.

Hayami, Y. and M. Kikuchi (1982) *Asian Village Economy at the Crossroads*. Baltimore: Johns Hopkins Press.

Hendrie, Barbara (1994) 'Relief Behind the Lines: The cross-border operation in Tigray', in Joanna Macrae and Anthony Zwi (eds) *War and Hunger: Rethinking International Responses to Complex Emergencies*. London: Zed Books, in association with Save the Children (UK), pp. 125–38.

Hewitt de Alcántara, Cynthia (1992) 'Markets in Principle and Practice', *European Journal of Development* 4 (2): 1–16.

Hill, Polly (1982) *Dry Grain Farming Families: Hausaland (Nigeria) and Karnataka (India) Compared*. Cambridge: Cambridge University Press.

Hinton, W. (1972) *Fanshen: A Documentary of Revolution in a Chinese Village*. Harmondsworth: Penguin.

Hirsch, Philip (1990) *Development Dilemmas in Rural Thailand*. Singapore and Oxford: Oxford University Press.

Hirschmann, David and Megan Vaughan (1983) 'Food Production and Income Generation in a Matrilineal Society: Rural women in Zomba, Malawi', *Journal of Southern African Studies* 10 (1): 86–99.

Hobart, Mark (ed.) (1993) *The Growth of Ignorance: An Anthropological Critique of Development*. London: Routledge.

Hoben, Allan (1995) 'Paradigms and Politics: The cultural construction of environmental policy in Ethiopia', *World Development* 23 (6): 1007–22.

Hulme, David and Michael Edwards (eds) (1997) *NGOs, States and Donors:*

Too Close for Comfort? London: Macmillan, in association with Save the Children (UK).

Hüsken, Frans and Benjamin White (1989) 'Java: Social differentiation, food production and agrarian control', in Gillian Hart et al. (eds) *Agrarian Transformations: Local Processes and the State in Southeast Asia.* Berkeley: University of California Press, pp. 235–65.

IDRC (International Development Research Center) (1994) *People, Plants and Patents: The Impact of Intellectual Property on Trade, Plant Biodiversity, and Rural Society.* Ottawa: IDRC.

Ingold, Tim (1992) 'Culture and the Perception of the Environment', in Elisabeth Croll and David Parkin (eds) *Bush Base: Forest Farm. Culture, Environment and Development.* London: Routledge, pp. 3–56.

Ingold, Tim (ed.) (1996) *Key Debates in Anthropology.* London: Routledge.

Izzard, W. (1979) *Rural–Urban Migration of Women in Botswana.* Gaborone: Central Statistics Office.

Jefremovas, Villia (1993) *Riding the Green Tide: Strategies among the Sagada Vegetable Gardeners of Northern Luzon.* Baguio, the Philippines: Cordillera Studies Center Working Paper 22.

Jodha, N. S. (1975) 'Famine and Famine Policies: Some empirical evidence', *Economic and Political Weekly* (Bombay) 10 (41): 1609–24.

Jodha, N. S. (1988) 'Poverty in India: A minority view', *Economic and Political Weekly.* Special issue, November: 2421–8.

Johnson, Allen W. (1972) 'Individuality and Experimentation', *Human Ecology* 1 (2): 149–59.

Jones, Christine (1985) 'The Mobilization of Women's Labor for Cash Crop Production: A game-theoretic approach', in IRRI (ed.) *Women in Rice Farming.* Aldershot: Gower/IRRI, pp. 445–54.

Jones, Christine (1986) 'Intra-household Bargaining in Response to the Introduction of New Crops: A case study from North Cameroon', in Joyce Moock (ed.) *Understanding Africa's Rural Households and Farming Systems: Perspectives from Anthropology.* Boulder, Co. and London: Westview Press, pp. 105–23.

Juma, Calestous (1989) *The Gene Hunters: Biotechnology and the Scramble for Seeds.* London: Zed Books.

Kabeer, Naila (1990) 'Poverty, Purdah and Women's Survival Strategies in Rural Bangladesh', in H. Bernstein, B. Crow, M. Mackintosh and C. Martin (eds) *The Food Question: Profits versus People?* London: Earthscan Publications, pp. 134–48.

Kabeer, Naila (1994) *Reversed Realities: Gender Hierarchies in Development Thought.* London: Verso.

Kahn, Joel S. (1980) *Minangkabau Social Formations: Indonesian Peasants and the World Economy.* Cambridge: Cambridge University Press.

Kandiyoti, Deniz (1988) 'Bargaining with Patriarchy', *Gender and Society* 2 (3): 274–90.

Kandiyoti, Deniz (1990) 'Women and Household Production: The impact of rural transformation in Turkey', in K. Glavanis and P. Glavanis (eds) *The Rural Middle East.* London: Zed Books, pp. 183–94.

Kandiyoti, Deniz (1999) 'Modernization without the Market?: The case of the "Soviet East"', in Alberto Arce and Norman Long (eds) *Anthropology, Development and Modernities: Exploring Discourse, Counter-tendencies and Violence*. London: Routledge.

Keen, David (1991) 'Targeting Emergency Food Aid: The case of Darfur in 1985', in S. Maxwell (ed.) (1991) *To Cure All Hunger: Food Policy and Food Security in Sudan*. London: Intermediate Technology Publications, pp. 191–206.

Keesing, Roger M. (1990) 'Development Planning: An anthropological perspective', in Mathur Hari Mohan (ed.) *The Human Dimension of Development: Perspectives from Anthropology*. New Delhi: Ashok Kumar Mittal Concept Publishing Company, pp. 57–84.

Kervin, B. (1982) *La Dinamica de la Pequena Producción Campesina*. Cuzco, Peru: Proderm seminar paper.

Kiambi, Kihika and Monica Opole (1992) 'Promoting Traditional Trees and Food Crops in Kenya', in D. Cooper, R. Vellve and H. Hobbelink (eds) *Growing Diversity: Genetic Resources and Local Food Security*. London: Intermediate Technology Publications, pp. 53–68.

Koptiuch, Kristin (1997) 'Third-Worlding at Home', in Akhil Gupta and James Ferguson (eds) *Culture, Power, Place: Explorations in Critical Anthropology*. Durham, NC and London: Duke University Press, pp. 234–48.

Kyerematen, A. A. Y. (1971) *Inter-State Boundary Litigation in Ashanti*. African Social Research Documents 4. Cambridge: African Studies Centre, Cambridge University.

Lansing, Stephen (1987) 'Balinese "Water Temples" and the Management of Irrigation', *American Anthropologist* 89 (2): 326–41.

Lansing, Stephen (1991) *Priests and Programmes: Technologies of Power in the Engineered Landscape of Bali*. Princeton: Princeton University Press.

Last, M. and G. L. Chavunduka (eds) (1986) *The Professionalisation of African Medicine*. Manchester: Manchester University Press.

Leach, Melissa (1991) 'Locating Gendered Experience: An anthropologist's view from a Sierra Leonean Village', *IDS Bulletin* 22 (1): 44–50.

Leach, Melissa (1994) *Rainforest Relations: Gender and Resource Use among the Mende of Gola, Sierra Leone*. Edinburgh: Edinburgh University Press, for the International African Institute.

Leaf, M. J. (1983) 'The Green Revolution and Cultural Change in a Punjab Village', *Economic Development and Cultural Change* 31: 227–70.

Lerche, Jens (1995) 'Is Bonded Labour a Bound Category? Reconceptualising agrarian conflict in India', *The Journal of Peasant Studies* 22 (3): 484–515.

Le Thi Nham Tuyet (1985) 'Women and their Families in the Movement for Agricultural Collectivisation in Vietnam', in Haleh Afshar (ed.) *Women, Development and Survival in the Third World*. London and New York: Longman, pp. 211–19.

Levine, R. and Scrimshaw, S. (1983) 'Effects of Culture on Fertility: Anthropological contributions', in R. Bulatao and R. Lee (eds) *Determinants of Fertility in Developing Countries*. Vol. 2. New York: Academic Press, pp. 666–95.

Lévi-Strauss, Claude (1966) 'The Culinary Triangle', *New Society*, 22 December.

Lipton, Michael (1977) *Why Poor People Stay Poor: Urban Bias in World Development*. London: Temple Smith.

Lockwood, Matthew (1992) *Engendering Adjustment or Adjusting Gender? Some New Approaches to Women and Development in Africa*', Brighton,

Sussex: IDS Discussion Paper 315.

Long, Norman (1992) 'From Paradigm Lost to Paradigm Regained? The case for an actor-oriented sociology of development', in Norman Long and Ann Long (eds) *Battlefields of Knowledge: The Interweaving of Theory and Practice in Social Research and Development*. London: Routledge, pp. 16–43.

Long, Norman (1996) 'Globalization and Localization: New challenges to rural research', in H. Moore (ed.) *The Future of Anthropological Knowledge*. London: Routledge, pp. 37–59.

Long, Norman and Jan Douwe van der Ploeg (1989) 'Demythologizing Planned Intervention: An actor perspective', *Sociologia Ruralis* 29 (3/4): 226–49.

Long, Norman and Ann Long (eds) (1992) *Battlefields of Knowledge: The Interlocking of Theory and Practice in Social Research and Development*. London: Routledge.

Longhurst, Richard (1988) 'Cash Crops, Household Food Security and Nutrition', *IDS Bulletin* 19 (2): 28–36.

Longman, Timothy (1995) 'Genocide and Socio-Political Change: Massacres in two Rwandan villages', *Issue: A Journal of Opinion* 23 (2): 18–21.

McAlpin, Michelle (1987) 'Famine Relief Policy in India: Six lessons for Africa', in M. H. Glantz (ed.) *Drought and Hunger in Africa: Denying Famine a Future*. Cambridge: Cambridge University Press, pp. 393–413.

McCarthy, Florence (1984) 'The Target Group: Women in rural Bangladesh', in E. J. Clay and B. B. Schaffer (eds) *Room for Manoeuvre: An Exploration of Public Policy in Agricultural and Rural Development*. London: Gower, pp. 49–58

Macfarlane, Alan (1993) 'Fatalism and Development in Nepal', in M. Hutt (ed.) *Nepal in the Nineties*. Delhi: Oxford University Press, pp. 106–27.

MacGaffey, Janet (ed.) (1991) *The Real Economy of Zaire: The Contribution of Smuggling & Other Unofficial Activities to National Wealth*. London: James Currey; Philadelphia: University of Pennsylvania Press.

Mackenzie, Fiona (1986) 'Local Initiatives and National Policy: Gender and agricultural change in Murang'a district, Kenya', *Canadian Journal of African Studies* 20 (3): 377–401.

Mackenzie, Fiona (1989) 'Land and Territory: The interface between two systems of land tenure, Murang'a District, Kenya', *Africa* 59 (1): 91–109.

Mackenzie, Fiona (1992) 'Development from Within? The struggle to survive', in D. R. Fraser Taylor and Fiona Mackenzie (eds) *Development From Within: Survival in Rural Africa*. London: Routledge, pp. 1–32.

Mackintosh, Maureen (1990) 'Abstract Markets and Real Needs', in H. Bernstein et al. (eds) *The Food Question: Profits versus People?* London: Earthscan, pp. 43–53.

McMillan, Della (ed.) (1991) *Anthropology and Food Policy: Human Dimensions of Food Policy in Africa and Latin America*. Athens and London: The University of Georgia Press.

Mahmud, W. and S. Mahmud (1985) *Aspects of the Food and Nutritional Problem in Rural Bangladesh*. Geneva: ILO/WEP, Research Working Paper 10–6/WFP74.

Malinowski, Bronislaw (1922) *Argonauts of the Western Pacific: An Account of Native Enterprise and Adventures in the Archipelagoes of Melanesian*

New Guinea. London: Routledge and Kegan Paul.

Malkki, Liisa (1995) *Purity and Exile: Violence, Memory, and National Cosmology among Hutu Refugees in Tanzania.* Chicago: The University of Chicago Press.

Manning, Chris (1988a) *The Green Revolution, Employment, and Economic Change in Rural Java: A Reassesment of Trends under the New Order.* Singapore: ISEAS Occasional Paper 84.

Manning, Chris (1988b) 'Rural Employment Creation in Java: Lessons from the Green Revolution and oil boom', *Population and Development Review* 14 (1): 47–80.

Mararike Claude, Vupenyu Dzingirai and Johan Pottier (1995) 'Zimbabwe: Report of proceedings of an FSUS/PRA workshop held in Ward Six, Buhera District, 6–8 September 1993', in J. Pottier (ed.) *African Food Systems Under Stress: Proceedings of the Second International Conference, Gaborone, April 1994.* Brighton: Desktop Display, pp. 35–74.

Marcus, G. (1995) Ethnography in/of the World System: The emergence of multi-sited ethnography', *Annual Review of Anthropology* 24: 95–117.

Maurer, Jean-Luc (1989) 'Agricultural Modernization, Economic Diversification, Off-Farm Employment and Multiple Activities in Java'. Paper presented at the Workshop on Off-farm Employment in Rural Java, University of Tübingen, 9–12 April.

Maxwell, Simon (1990) 'Overview. Food Security in Developing Countries: Issues and options for the 1990s', *IDS Bulletin* 21 (3): 2–13.

Maxwell, Simon (1992) 'Food Security in Africa: Priorities for reducing hunger', Africa Recovery Briefing Paper 6, September, pp. 1–12. United Nations Department of Public Information, Communication and Project Management Division.

Maxwell, Simon (1996) 'Food Security: A post-modern perspective', *Food Policy* 21 (2): 155–70.

Maxwell, Simon and A. Fernando (1989) 'Cash Crops in Developing Countries: The issues, the facts, the policies', *World Development* 17 (11): 1677–708.

Mbilinyi, Marjorie (1990) '"Structural Adjustment", Agribusiness and Rural Women in Tanzania', in H. Bernstein et al. (eds) *The Food Question: Profits versus People?* London: Earthscan, pp. 111–24.

Meillassoux, Claude (1981) *Maidens, Meal and Money.* Cambridge: Cambridge University Press.

Mencher, Joan P. (1985) 'Landless Women Agricultural Laborers in India: Some observations from Tamil Nadu, Kerala and West Bengal', in IRRI (ed.) *Women in Rice Farming.* Aldershot: Gower/IRRI, pp. 351–71.

Mikell, Gwendolyn (1984) 'Filiation, Economic Crisis and the Status of Women in Rural Ghana', *Canadian Journal of African Studies* 18 (1): 195–218.

Mikell, Gwendolyn (1985) 'Expansion and Contraction in Economic Access for Rural Women in Ghana', *Rural Africana* 21: 13–30.

Miller, Daniel (1995) 'Consumption and Commodities', *Annual Review of Anthropology* 24: 141–61.

Mohanty, Chandra Talpade (1988) 'Under Western Eyes: Feminist scholarship and colonial discourses', *Feminist Review* 30: 61–88.

Montgomery, E. and J. W. Bennett (1979) 'Anthropological Studies of Food and Nutrition: The 1940s and the 1970s', in W. Goldschmidt (ed.) *The*

Uses of Anthropology. Washington, DC: American Anthropological Association, pp. 124–44.

Moock, Joyce Lewinger and Robert Rhoades (eds) (1992) *Diversity, Farmer Knowledge and Sustainability*. Ithaca and London: Cornell University Press.

Mooney, Pat (1993) 'Exploiting Local Knowledge: International policy implications', in W. de Boef, K. Amanor and K. Wellard, with A. Bebbington (eds) *Cultivating Knowledge: Genetic Diversity, Farmer Experimentation and Crop Research*. London: Intermediate Technology Publications, pp. 172–8.

Mooney, Pat (1998) *The Parts of Life: Agricultural Biodiversity, Indigenous Knowledge, and the Role of the Third System. Development Dialogue* 1–2). Special issue.

Moore, Henrietta (1988) *Feminism and Anthropology*. Cambridge: Polity Press.

Moore, Henrietta (1996) 'The Changing Nature of Anthropological Knowledge: An introduction', in H. Moore (ed.) *The Future of Anthropological Knowledge*. London: Routledge, pp. 1–15.

Moore, Henrietta and Megan Vaughan (1994) *Cutting Down Trees: Gender, Nutrition, and Agricultural Change in the Northern Province of Zambia, 1890–1990*. Cambridge: Cambridge University Press.

Morgan, Richard (1988) 'Drought-Relief Programmes in Botswana', in D. Curtis, M. Hubbard and A. Shepherd (eds) *Preventing Famine: Policies and Prospects for Africa*. London and New York: Routledge, pp. 112–20.

Moris, Jon (1991) *Extension Alternatives in Tropical Africa*. London: ODI, AAU Occasional Paper 7.

Morris, M. D. (1974) 'What is Famine?', *Economic and Political Weekly* 9 (45): 1855–64.

Morris, M. D. (1975) 'Needed – a New Famine Policy', *Economic and Political Weekly* 10 (5–7): 283–94.

Moser, Caroline (1980) 'Why the Poor Remain Poor: The experience of Bogotá traders in the 1970s', *Journal of Interamerican Studies and World Affairs* 22 (3): 365–87.

Muntemba, Maud Shimwaayi (1982) 'Women and Agricultural Change in the Railway Region of Zambia: Dispossession and counter-strategies', in Edna G. Bay (ed), *Women and Work in Africa*. Boulder, Co.: Westview Press, pp. 83–104.

Murray, Colin (1995) 'Structural Unemployment, Small Towns and Agrarian Change in South Africa', *African Affairs* 94: 5–22.

Mwape, D. and T. D. Russell (1992) 'Using an Analysis of Food Security Issues to Develop Research Priorities in the Copperbelt', in ARPT (ed.) *Nutrition and Household Food Security in Farming Systems Research*. Chilanga: ARPT, pp. 149–79.

Nabarro, David, Claudia Cassells and Mahesh Pant (1989) 'How Households Cope in the Hills of Nepal: Can development initiatives help?', *IDS Bulletin* 20 (2): 68–74.

Nagengast, C. (1994) 'Violence, Terror and the Crisis of the State', *Annual Review of Anthropology* 25: 109–36.

Neel, H. (1985) 'Aide Alimentaire Ambiguë', *Dialogue* 117: 68–71

Netting, Robert McC. (1968) *Hill Farmers of Nigeria: Cultural Ecology of the Kofyar of the Jos Plateau*. Seattle: University of Washington Press.

Netting, Robert McC. and Priscilla Stone (1996) 'Agro-diversity on a Farming Frontier: Kofyar smallholders on the Benue plains of central Nigeria', *Africa* 66 (1): 52–70.

Newbury, C. (1984) 'Ebutumwa bw'emihogo. The Tyranny of Cassava: A women's tax revolt in Eastern Zaire', *Canadian Journal of African Studies*, 18 (1): 35–54.

Nyangabyaki, Bazaara (1991) 'The Notion of "Food Self-sufficient Uganda": A critical examination', *Eastern Africa Social Science Research Review* 7 (2): 11–25.

ODI (Overseas Development Institute) (1993) *Patenting Plants: The Implications for Developing Countries*. London: ODI, Briefing Paper, November.

ODI (1994) *The CGIAR: What Future for International Agricultural Research?* London: ODI Briefing Paper, September.

ODI (1997) *Global Hunger and Food Security after the World Food Summit*. London: ODI, Briefing Paper 1, February.

Okali, Christine (1983) *Cocoa and Kinship: The Matrilineal Akan*. London: Kegan Paul.

Østergaard, Lise (1992) 'Health', in Lise Østergaard (ed.) *Gender and Development: A Practical Guide*. London: Routledge, pp. 110–34.

Pacey, Arnold and Philip Payne (eds) (1985) *Agricultural Development and Nutrition*. London: Hutchinson; Boulder, Co.: Westview Press.

Pærregaard, Karsten (1997) 'Imagining a Place in the Andes: In the borderland of lived, invented, and analyzed culture', in Karen Fog Olwig and Kirsten Hastrup (eds) *Siting Culture: The Shifting Anthropological Object*. London: Routledge, pp. 39–58.

Pagézy, Hélène (1985) 'The Food System of the Ntomba of Lake Tumba, Zaire', in J. Pottier (ed.) *Food Systems in Central and Southern Africa*. London: School of Oriental and African Studies, pp. 61–79.

Palmer, I. (1976) *Rural Poverty in Indonesia with Special Reference to Java*. Geneva: WEP Research Working Paper.

Parkin, David (1972) *Palms, Wine and Witnesses: Public Spirit and Private Gain in an African Farming Community*. London: Intertext Books.

Parpart, Jane L. (1993) 'Who is the Other? A postmodern feminist critique of women and development theory and practice', *Development and Change* 24: 439–64.

Parry, John and Maurice Bloch (eds) (1989) *Money and the Morality of Exchange*. Cambridge: Cambridge University Press.

Parsons, Talcott (1970) *Social Structure and Personality*. New York: Random House.

Payne, Robert (1990) 'Themes in Food Security: Measuring malnutrition', *IDS Bulletin* 21 (3): 14–30.

Payne, Robert and Michael Lipton (1994) *How Third World Rural Households Adapt to Dietary Energy Stress: The Evidence and the Issues*. Washington, DC: International Food Policy Research Institute, Food Policy Review 2.

Persoon, Gerard (1992) 'From Sago to Rice', in Elisabeth Croll and David Parkin (eds) *Bush Base: Forest Farm. Culture, Environment and Development*. London: Routledge, pp. 187–99.

Peters, Pauline (1986) 'Household Management in Botswana: Cattle, crops, and wage labor', in J. Moock (ed.) *Understanding Africa's Rural House-*

holds and Farming Systems. Boulder, Co. and London: Westview Press, pp. 133–54.

Pilger, J. (1989) *A Secret Country*. London: Zed Books.

Pinstrup-Andersen, Per (1986) 'Macroeconomic Adjustment Policies and Human Nutrition: Available evidence and research needs', *Food and Nutrition Bulletin* 9 (1): 69–86.

Plattner, Stuart (1985) 'Equilibrating Market Relations', in S. Plattner (ed.) *Markets and Marketing*. Lanhams Md.: University Press of America, Monographs in Economic Anthropology.

Poewe, Karla O. (1979) 'Regional and Village Economic Activities: Prosperity and stagnation in Luapula, Zambia', *African Studies Review* 22 (2): 77–93.

Popkin, Samuel L. (1979) *The Rational Peasant: The Political Economy of Rural Society in Vietnam*. Berkeley: University of California Press.

Pottier, Johan (1988) *Migrants No More: Settlement and Survival in Mambwe Villages, Zambia*. Manchester: Manchester University Press, for the International African Institute.

Pottier, Johan (1989a) '"Three is a Crowd": Knowledge, ignorance and power in the context of urban agriculture in Rwanda', *Africa* 54 (4): 461–77.

Pottier, Johan (1989b) 'Debating Styles in a Rwandan Cooperative: Reflections on language, policy and gender', in R. D. Grillo (ed.) *Social Anthropology and the Politics of Language*. London: Routledge, Sociological Review Monograph 34, pp. 41–60.

Pottier, Johan (1994a) 'Poor Men, Intra-household Bargaining and the Politics of Household Food Security', in Ingrid Yngström, Patricia Jeffery, Kenneth King and Camilla Toulmin (eds) *Gender and Environment in Africa: Perspectives on the Politics of Environmental Sustainability*. Edinburgh: Centre of African Studies, University of Edinburgh, pp. 156–74.

Pottier, Johan (1994b) *Food Security and Agricultural Rehabilitation in Post-War Rwanda*. London: Save the Children Fund Report, with John Wilding.

Pottier, Johan (1996) 'Agricultural Rehabilitation and Food Insecurity in Post-War Rwanda: Assessing needs, designing solutions', *IDS Bulletin* 27 (3): 56–75.

Pottier, Johan (1997) 'Land and Land Reform in Rwanda: Past, present and future'. Paper presented at the Conference on Understanding the Crisis in Central Africa's Great Lakes Region. Oxford: Refugee Studies Programme, Queen Elizabeth House. February.

Pottier, Johan (1998) 'The "Self" in Self-Repatriation: Closing down Mugunga camp, eastern Zaire', in Richard Black and Khalid Koser (eds) *The End of the Refugee Cycle? Refugee Repatriation and Reconstruction*. Oxford: Berghahn Books.

Pottier, Johan and James Fairhead (1991) 'Post-Famine Recovery in Highland Bwisha, Zaire: 1984 in its context', *Africa* 61 (4): 537–70.

Pottier, Johan and Augustin Nkundabashaka (1992) 'Intolerable Environments: Towards a Cultural Reading of Agrarian Policy in Rwanda', in J. Parkin and L. Croll (eds), *Bush Base: Forest Farm*. London: Routledge, pp. 146–68.

Pradhan, Bina (1985) 'The Role of Women in Household Production Systems and Rice Farming in Nepal', in IRRI (ed.) *Women in Rice Farming*. Aldershot: Gower/IRRI, pp. 257–86.

Prain, Gordon (1993) 'Mobilizing Local Expertise in Plant Genetic Resources Research', in Walter de Boef et al. (eds) *Cultivating Knowledge: Genetic Diversity, Farmer Experimentation and Crop Research*. London: Intermediate Technology Publications, pp. 102–10.

Prain, Gordon, Fulgencio Uribe and Urs Scheidegger (1992) '"The Friendly Potato": Farmer selection of potato varieties for multiple uses', in Joyce Lewinger Moock and Robert Rhoades (eds) *Diversity, Farmer Knowledge and Sustainability*. Ithaca and London: Cornell University Press pp. 52–68.

Pratt, Brian and Peter Loizos (1992) *Choosing Research Methods: Data Collection for Development Workers*. Oxford: Oxfam, Development Guidelines 7.

Prigogine, I. and I. Stengers (1985) *Order Out of Chaos: Man's New Dialogue with Nature*. London: Flamingo.

Prindle, P. (1979) 'Peasant Society and Famine: A Nepalese example', *Ethnology* 18: 49–60.

Rahman, A. (1992) 'The Informal Financial Sector in Bangladesh: An appraisal of its role in development', *Development and Change* 23: 147–67.

Raikes, Philip (1988) *Modernizing Hunger: Famine, Food Surplus and Farm Policy in the EEC and Africa*. London: James Currey / CIIR.

Raikes, Philip (1992) 'Changing Household Production in Kisii', in Preben Kaarsholm (ed.) *Institutions, Culture and Change at Local Community Level*. Roskilde: International Development Studies, Roskilde University, Occasional Paper 3, pp. 75–102.

Raikes, Philip (1994) 'Business as Usual: Some "real" food markets in Kenya', *Sociologia Ruralis* 23 (1): 26–44.

Rangan, Haripriya (1996) 'Development, Environment, and Social Protest in the Garhwal Himalayas, India', in Richard Peet and Michael Watts (eds) *Liberation Ecologies: Environment, Development and Social Movements*. London: Routledge, pp. 205–26.

Razavi, Shahrashoub (1994) 'Agrarian Change and Gender Relations in Southeast Iran', *Development and Change* 25: 591–634.

Reinwald, Brigitte (1997) '"Though the Earth does not Lie": Agricultural transition in Siin (Senegal) under colonial rule', *Paideuma* 43: 143–69.

Rhoades, Robert (1982) *The Art of the Informal Agricultural Survey*. Lima: International Potato Centre.

Rhoades, Robert (1984) *Breaking New Ground: Agricultural Anthropology*. Lima: International Potato Centre.

Rhoades, Robert (1986) 'Using Anthropology in Improving Food Production: Problems and prospects', *Agricultural Administration* 22: 57–78.

Richards, Audrey I. (1939) *Land, Labour and Diet in Northern Rhodesia*. London: Oxford University Press.

Richards, Audrey I. and E. M. Widdowson (1937) 'A Dietary Study in Northern Rhodesia', *Africa* 9 (2): 166–96.

Richards, Paul (1983) 'Ecological Change and the Politics of African Land Use', *African Studies Review* 26 (2): 1–72.

Richards, Paul (1986) *Coping With Hunger: Hazard and Experiment in an African Rice-Farming System*. London: Allen and Unwin, the London Research Series in Geography 11.

Richards, Paul (1989) 'Agriculture as a Performance', in R. Chambers, A. Pacey, and L. A. Thrupp (eds) *Farmer First*. London: Intermediate Technology Publications, pp. 39–43.

Richards, Paul (1990) 'Local Strategies for Coping with Hunger: central Sierra Leone and northern Nigeria compared', *African Affairs* 89 (335): 265–76.

Roberts, Pepe (1984) 'Feminism in Africa; Feminism and Africa', *Review of African Political Economy* 27/28: 175–84.

Robertson, A. F. (1983) '*Abusa*: The structural history of an economic contract', *Journal of Development Studies* 18: 447–78.

Robertson, A. F. (1984) *People and the State: An Anthropology of Planned Development*. Cambridge: Cambridge University Press.

Roe, Emery (1991) '"Development Narratives" or Making the Best of Blueprint Development', *World Development* 19 (4): 287–300.

Roe, Emery (1995) 'Except-Africa: Postscript to a special section on development narratives', *World Development* 23 (6): 1065–70.

Russell, Margo (1993) 'Are Households Universal? On misunderstanding domestic groups in Swaziland', *Development and Change* 24: 755–85.

Russell, Susan (1987) 'Middlemen and Moneylending: Relations of exchange in a highland Philippine economy', *Journal of Anthropological Research* 43 (1): 139–61.

Salas, Maria A. (1994) '"The Technicians Only Believe in Science and Cannot Read the Sky": The cultural dimension of the knowledge conflict in the Andes', in Ian Scoones and John Thompson (eds) *Beyond Farmer First: Rural People's Knowledge, Agricultural Research and Extension Practice*. London: Intermediate Technology Publications, pp. 57–69.

Salazar, Rene (1992) 'Community Plant Genetic Resources Management: Experiences in South-East Asia', in D. Cooper, R. Vellve and H. Hobbelink (eds) *Growing Diversity: Genetic Resources and Local Food Security*. London: Intermediate Technology Publications, pp. 17–29.

Salemink, Oscar (1998) Moral versus Political Economy and the Vietnam War'. London: School of Oriental and African Studies, Anthropology Department, EIDOS conference. Unpublished.

Saradamoni, K. (1983) 'Changing Land Relations and Women: A case study of Palghat District, Kerala', in V. Mazumdar (ed.) *Women and Rural Transformation*. Delhi: Concept Publications, pp. 35–171.

Schoepf, Brooke Grundfest and Claude Schoepf (1988) 'Land, Gender and Food Security in Eastern Kivu, Zaire', in J. Davison (ed.) *Agriculture, Women and Land: The African Experience*. Boulder, Co. and London: Westview Press, pp. 106–30.

Schoepf, Brooke Grundfest and Claude Schoepf (1990) 'Gender, Land, and Hunger in Eastern Zaire', in Rebecca Huss-Ashmore and Solomon H. Katz (eds) *African Food Systems in Crisis. Part Two: Contending with Change*. New York: Gordon and Breach, pp. 75–106.

Schoepf, Brooke Grundfest and Walu Engundu (1991) 'Women's Trade and Contributions to Household Budgets in Kinshasa', in Janet MacGaffey (ed.) *The Real Economy of Zaire: The Contribution of Smuggling & Other Unofficial Activities to National Wealth*. London: James Currey, pp. 124–51.

Schweizer, Thomas (1987) 'Agrarian Transformation? Rice production in a Javanese village', *BIES* 23 (2): 38–70.

Schweizer, Thomas (1989) 'Economic Individualism and the Community Spirit: Divergent orientation patterns of Javanese villagers in rice production and the ritual sphere', *Modern Asian Studies* 23 (2): 277–312.

Scoones, Ian and John Thompson (eds) (1994) *Beyond Farmer First*. London: Intermediate Technology Publications.

Scott, James C. (1976) *The Moral Economy of the Peasant: Rebellion and Subsistence in Southeast Asia*. New Haven, CT: Yale University Press.

Seddon, David (1987) *Nepal: A State of Poverty*. New Delhi: Vikas Publishing House.

Seddon, David (1993) 'Democracy and Development in Nepal', in M. Hutt (ed.) *Nepal in the Nineties*. Delhi: Oxford University Press, pp. 128–64.

Sen, Amartya (1981) *Poverty and Famines: An Essay on Entitlement and Deprivation*. Oxford: Clarendon Press.

Sen, Amartya (1990a) 'Gender and Cooperative Conflicts', in I. Tinker (ed.) *Persistent Inequalities: Women and World Development*. New York: Oxford University Press, pp. 123–49.

Sen, Amartya (1990b) 'More than 100 Million Women are Missing', *New York Review of Books*, 20 December, pp. 61–6.

Sen, Gita (1982) 'Women Workers and the Green Revolution', in L. Beneria (ed.) *Women and Development: The Sexual Division of Labor in Rural Societies*. New York: CBS Educational and Professional Publications, pp. 29–64.

Sharma, Hari P. (1973) 'The Green Revolution in India', in Kathleen Gough and Hari P. Sharma (eds) *Imperialism and Green Revolution in South Asia*. New York: Monthly Review Press.

Sharma, Miriam (1985) 'Caste, Class and Gender: Production and reproduction in North India', *The Journal of Peasant Studies* 12 (4): 57–88.

Sharma, Ursula (1980) *Women, Work and Property in North-West India*. London: Tavistock Publications.

Sharpe, Barrie (1990) 'Nutrition and the Commercialisation of Agriculture in Northern Province', in A. P. Wood, S. A. Kean, J. T. Milimo and D. M. Warren (eds) *The Dynamics of Agricultural Policy Reform in Zambia*. Ames: Iowa State University, pp. 583–602.

Shipton, Parker (1989) *Bitter Money: Cultural Economy and Some African Meanings of Forbidden Commodities*. Washington, DC: American Ethnological Society Monograph Series 1.

Shipton, Parker (1994) 'Land and Culture in Tropical Africa: Soils, symbols, and the metaphysics of the mundane', *Annual Review of Anthropology* 23: 347–77.

Shiva, Vandana (1992) 'The Seed and the Earth: Biotechnology and the colonisation of regeneration', *Development Dialogue* 1/2: 151–68.

Shiva, Vandana (1993a) *Monocultures of the Mind: Perspectives on Biodiversity and Biotechnology*. London: Zed Books.

Shiva, Vandana (1993b) 'The Greening of the Global Reach', in W. Sachs (ed.) *Global Ecology: A New Arena of Political Conflict*. London: Zed Books, pp. 149–56.

Sikana, Patrick and Eliab Simpungwe (1995) 'Zambia: Report of proceedings

224 *Bibliography*

of an FSUS/PRA workshop held in Kapatu, Northern Zambia, September 1993', in J. Pottier (ed.) *African Food Systems Under Stress: Proceedings of the Second International Conference, Gaborone, April 1994*. Brighton: Desktop Display, pp. 75–97.

Solway, Jacqueline (1994) 'Drought as a "Revelatory Crisis": An exploration of shifting entitlements and hierarchies in the Kalahari, Botswana', *Development and Change* 25: 471–95.

Sow, Abdoul (1988) 'Sociétés Indigènes de Prévoyance: Instruments de l'impérialisme colonial?', *Historiens-Géographes du Sénégal* 3: 8–16.

Sperling, Louise (1987) 'Food Acquisition during the African Drought of 1983–84: A study of Kenyan herders', *Disasters* 11 (4): 263–72.

Sperling, Louise (1992) 'Farmer Participation and the Development of Bean Varieties in Rwanda', in Joyce Lewinger Moock and Robert Rhoades (eds) *Diversity, Farmer Knowledge and Sustainability*. Ithaca and London: Cornell University Press, pp. 96–112.

Sperling, Louise and Urs Scheidegger (1995) *Participatory Selection of Beans in Rwanda: Results, Methods and Institutional Issues*. London: IIED, Gatekeeper Series 51.

Spitz, Pierre (1978) 'Silent Violence: Famine and inequality', *International Social Science Journal* 30 (4): 867–92.

Spivak, Gayatri (1996) *The Spivak Reader*. Edited by Donna Landry and Gerald MacLean. London: Routledge.

Statistical Publishing House (ed.) (1995) *Vietnam: Agriculture of Vietnam 1945–1995*. Hanoi, Vietnam: Statistical Publishing House.

Stoler, Anne (1976) 'Class Structure and Female Autonomy in Rural Java', in B. B. Hering (ed.) *Indonesian Women: Some Past and Current Perspectives*. Brussels: Université Libre de Bruxelles, pp. 124–50.

Stoler, Anne (1977) 'Rice Harvesting in Kali Loro: A study of class and labour relations in rural Java', *American Ethnologist* 4 (4): 678–98.

Sukkary-Stolba, Soheir (1989) 'Indigenous Institutions and Adaptation to Famine: The case of the Western Sudan', in Rebecca Huss-Ashmore and Solomon H. Katz (eds) *African Food Systems in Crisis. Part One: Microperspectives*. Vol. 7 of Food and Nutrition in History and Anthropology, New York / London: Gordon and Breach, pp. 281–94.

Svedberg, P. (1988) *Undernutrition in Sub-Saharan Africa: Is There a Sex Bias?* Stockholm: Institute for International Economic Studies, Seminar Paper 241.

Swetnam, John (1980) 'Disguised Employment and Development Policy in Peasant Economies', *Human Organization* 39: 32–9.

Swift, Jeremy (1989) 'Why are Rural People Vulnerable to Famine?', *IDS Bulletin* 20 (2): 8–15.

Swift, Jeremy (1993) 'Understanding and Preventing Famine and Famine Mortality', *IDS Bulletin* 24 (4): 1–16.

Tapper, Richard and Nancy (Lindisfarne) Tapper (1986) '"Eat this, it'll do you a power of good": Food and commensality among Durrani Pashtuns', *American Ethnologist* 13 (1): 62–79.

Tierney, Allison (1997) 'Local Concepts of Development: Women Food Sellers and Fishermen in an Oxfam Programme, Tabora Region, Western Tanzania'. London: LSE, Ph.D. thesis.

Tobert, Nathalie (1985) 'The Effect of Drought among the Zaghawa in Northern Darfur', *Disasters* 9 (3): 213–23.

Torry, William I. (1986) 'Drought and the Government–Village Emergency Food Distribution System in India', *Human Organization* 45 (1): 11–23.

Tuinenburg, Kees (1987) 'Experience with Food Strategies in Four African Countries', in J. Price Gittinger, Joanne Leslie and Caroline Hoisington (eds) *Food Policy: Integrating Supply, Distribution, and Consumption*. Baltimore and London: The Johns Hopkins Press, for the World Bank, pp. 497–508.

Turton, David and Pat Turton (1984) 'Spontaneous Resettlement after Drought: A Mursi case study', *Disasters* 8 (3): 178–89.

United Nations (1975) *Report of the World Food Conference, Rome 5–16 November 1974*. New York: UN.

van der Ploeg, Jan Douwe (1989) 'Knowledge Systems, Metaphor and Interface: The case of potatoes in the Peruvian Highlands', in Norman Long (ed.) *Encounters at the Interface: A Perspective on Social Discontinuities in Rural Development*. Wageningen: Landbouwuniversiteit, Wageningse Sociologische Studies 27, pp. 145–64.

van der Ploeg, Jan Douwe (1990) *Labor, Markets and Agricultural Production*. Boulder, Co.: Westview Press.

van der Ploeg, Jan Douwe (1993) 'Potatoes and Knowledge', in Mark Hobart (ed.) *The Growth of Ignorance: An Anthropological Critique of Development*. London: Routledge, pp. 209–27.

Vaughan, Megan (1983) 'Which Family?: Problems in the reconstruction of the history of the family as an economic and cultural unit', *Journal of African History* 24: 275–83.

Vaughan, Megan (1987) *The Story of an African Famine: Gender and Famine in Twentieth-century Malawi*. Cambridge: Cambridge University Press.

Vaughan, Megan (1996) 'The Character of the Market: Social identities in colonial economies', *Oxford Development Studies* 24 (1): 61–77.

von, Braun, J. et al. (1992) *Improving Food Security of the Poor: Concept, Policy and Programs*. Washington, DC: IFPRI.

Voss, Joachim (1987) 'The Politics of Pork and the Ritual of Rice: Redistributive feasting and commodity circulation in Northern Luzon, the Philippines', in J. Clammer (ed.) *Beyond the New Economic Anthropology*. London: MacMillan, pp. 121–41.

Voss, Joachim (1992) 'Conserving and Increasing On-Farm Genetic Diversity: Farmer management of varietal bean mixtures in Central Africa', in Joyce Lewinger Moock and Robert Rhoades (eds) *Diversity, Farmer Knowledge and Sustainability*. Ithaca and London: Cornell University Press, pp. 34–51.

Watson, William (1958) *Tribal Cohesion in a Money Economy: A Study of the Mambwe People of Zambia*. Manchester: Manchester University Press.

Watts, Michael (1983) *Silent Violence: Food, Famine and Peasantry in Northern Nigeria*. Berkeley: University of California Press.

Webber, Paul (1996) 'Agrarian Change in Kusasi, North-east Ghana', *Africa* 66 (3): 437–57.

Wheeler, Erica (1986) 'To Feed or to Educate?: Labelling in targeted nutrition interventions', in G. Wood (ed.) *Labelling in Development Policy: Essays in Honour of Bernard Schaffer*. London: Sage Publications, pp. 133–41.

Wheeler, Erica and M. Abdullah (1988) 'Food Allocations within the Family: Response to fluctuating food supply and food needs', in Igor de Garine and G. A. Harrison (eds) *Coping with Uncertainty in Food Supply*. Oxford: Clarendon Press (Oxford Science Publications), pp. 437–51.

White, Benjamin (1985) 'Women and the Modernization of Rice Agriculture: Some general issues and a Javanese case study', in IRRI (ed.) *Women in Rice Farming*. Aldershot: Gower/IRRI, pp. 119–48.

White, Benjamin (1989) 'Problems in the Empirical Analysis of Agrarian Differentiation', in Gillian Hart et al. (eds) *Agrarian Transformations: Local Processes and the State in Southeast Asia*. Berkeley: University of California Press, pp. 15–30.

White, Sarah (1992) *Arguing with the Crocodile: Class and Gender in Rural Bangladesh*. London: Zed Books.

Whitehead, Ann (1981) '"I'm hungry, mum": The politics of domestic budgeting', in Kate Young et al. (eds) *Of Marriage and the Market*. London: CSE Books, pp. 88–111.

Whitehead, Ann (1990a) 'Food Crisis and Gender Conflict in the African Countryside', in H. Bernstein, B. Crow, M. Mackintosh and C. Martin (eds) *The Food Question: Profits versus People?* London: Earthscan Publications, pp. 54–68.

Whitehead, Ann (1990b) 'Rural Women and Food Production in Sub-Saharan Africa', in Jean Drèze and Armatya Sen (eds) *The Political Economy of Hunger*, Vol. 1. Oxford: Clarendon Press, pp. 425–73.

Wijaya, Hesti R. (1985) 'Women's Access to Land Resources: Some Observations from East Javanese Agriculture', in IRRI (ed.) *Women in Rice Farming*. Aldershot: Gower/IRRI, pp. 171–85.

Wilson, C. Anne (1976) *Food and Drink in Britain: From the Stone Age to Recent Times*. Harmondsworth: Penguin.

Witt, S. C. (1985) *BriefBook: Biotechnology and Genetic Resources*. San Francisco: California Agricultural Lands Project.

Wolde Mariam, Mesfin (1986) *Rural Vulnerability to Famine in Ethiopia: 1958–1977*. London: Intermediate Technology Publications.

Wolde Mariam, Mesfin (1990) 'Drought and Famine in Ethiopia: Social impact and socio-economic development', in ACARTSOD (ed.) *Understanding Africa's Food Problems: Social Policy Perspectives*. London: Hans Zell Publishers, ACARTSOD Monograph Series, African Social Challenges 1, pp. 204–44.

Wood, Adrian (1985) 'Food Production and the Changing Structure of Zambian Agriculture', in J. Pottier (ed.) *Food Systems in Central and Southern Africa*. London: School of Oriental and African Studies, pp. 138–68.

Worede, M. (1992) 'Ethiopia: A Genebank working with Farmers', in D. Cooper, R. Vellve and H. Hobbelink (eds) *Growing Diversity: Genetic Resources and Local Food Security*. London: Intermediate Technology Publications, pp. 78–96.

World Bank (1981) *Accelerated Development in Sub-Saharan Africa: An Agenda for Action*. Washington: World Bank.

World Bank (1986) *Poverty and Hunger: Issues and Options for Food Security in Developing Countries*. Washington: World Bank Policy Study.

World Bank (1993) *Uganda Social Sector Strategy. Vols. I and II*. Washington, DC: World Bank.

Index

LaVergne, TN USA
10 January 2010
169494LV00003B/1/P